Implementing a Digital Asset Management System

Acquisitions Editor: Angelina Ward
Associate Editor: Becky Golden-Harrell
Assistant Editor: Rachel Epstein
Marketing Manager: Christine Degon
Cover Design: Eric DeCicco

Implementing a Digital Asset Management System

For animation, computer games, and web development

Jens Jacobsen, Tilman Schlenker, and Lisa Edwards

ELSEVIER

AMSTERDAM • BOSTON • HEIDELBERG • LONDON • NEW YORK • OXFORD
PARIS • SAN DIEGO • SAN FRANCISCO • SINGAPORE • SYDNEY • TOKYO
Focal Press is an imprint of Elsevier

Focal Press

Focal Press is an imprint of Elsevier
30 Corporate Drive, Suite 400, Burlington, MA 01803, USA
Linacre House, Jordan Hill, Oxford, OX2 8DP, UK

First published 2005

 Recognizing the importance of preserving what has been written, Elsevier prints
its books on acid-free paper whenever possible.

Library of Congress Cataloguing in Publication Data
A catalog record for this book is available from the Library of Congress

British Library Cataloguing in Publication Data
A catalog record for this book is available from the British Library

ISBN 13: 978-0-240-80665-5
ISBN 10: 0-240-80665-4

05 06 07 08 09 10   10 9 8 7 6 5 4 3 2 1

For information on all Focal Press publications visit our website at:
www.focalpress.com

Typeset by Charon Tec Pvt. Ltd, Chennai, India
www.charontec.com
Printed in the United States of America

Cover images:
Robota © 2004 Doug Chiang. All rights reserved
CGI picture created by Attitude Studio for Doug Chiang

Contents

Preface   ix

1 Introduction   **1**

   1.1 What is it all about?   1
   1.2 What does this book cover?   1
   1.3 What's an asset anyway?   2
   1.4 What is Digital Asset Management?   3
   1.5 How is this book structured?   6

2 What can asset management do for you?   **7**

   2.1 What can happen …   7
      Example: A typical project without DAM—Case study of
         ProperPictures   7
      Example: Case Study of project management in computer games   15
   2.2 … And how it can be avoided   16
   2.3 Who needs DAM?   17
   2.4 What companies expect from Digital Asset Management (DAM)   19
   2.5 What DAM is (and what it is not)   20
   2.6 General benefits of DAM systems   25
   2.7 Benefits for different departments   28
   2.8 The case for Return On Investment (ROI)   29
      Example: Money saved by working faster   30
   2.9 Industries benefitting from DAM   33

3 Assess your individual situation   **43**

   3.1 Analyze the business—find out where you are   43
      Example: Business processes in web development—Case study of
         ProperProduction   46

Example: Team and platforms in computer game development—
Case study of GreatGames, Inc. 54

3.2 Define desired improvements—find out where to go 55
Example: Desired improvements of asset management in web
development—Case study of ProperProduction 56

3.3 Analyze value of desired result—find out what you gain 57
Example: Value of desired result of asset management in computer
game development—Case study of GreatGames, Inc. 57

4 Plan what you need 60

4.1 What is your business objective? 60
4.2 What do your assets want? 64
Example: Projected number of files and volume for website
production—Case study of ProperProduction 67
4.3 What do your users want? 70
4.4 What your new workflow should look like 71
Example: The new workflow for animation film production—
Case study of ProperPictures 76
4.5 Compile a list of features needed 78
Example: The features needed for animation film production—
Case study of ProperPictures 84
4.6 Other important features of asset management systems 85
4.7 The most important consideration: focus 86

5 Find the right solution 87

5.1 Types of DAM solutions 87
5.2 Complexity and capabilities of the solutions 90
5.3 Which size fits for you? 102
5.4 What if there is no suitable system? 103
5.5 Rent a DAM solution 105
5.6 Don't over-engineer 105
5.7 Questions to ask potential vendors 107
5.8 Sample scenarios for the application of DAM 107
Example: Advertising agency introducing an image library 108
Example: Web agency introducing image library and SCM 110
Example: Animation studio introducing ProdAM 113

6 Implement the solution 116

6.1 Planning 116
6.2 Testing 121
6.3 Team preparation 123

6.4 Workflow integration 126
Example: Implementation plan in game production—Case study of GreatGames 131

7 Success stories **134**

7.1 Lionhead Studios 134
7.2 Sony Pictures Imageworks 140
7.3 Scholz & Volkmer 145
7.4 Framfab 153
7.5 Attitude Studio 161
7.6 Pixelspell Animation Studios 165

Appendix 1: Product overview 171

Appendix 2: Glossary 234

Appendix 3: References 241

Index 245

Preface

Who should read this book?

This book is for anyone who ever cursed at the computer after searching for a specific file that you know exists but received the message, "The search is complete. There are no results to display". It is for everyone who has had to recreate an entire day's work because an overzealous colleague overwrote their recent changes. And it is for anyone who wants to make the production process in his or her firm more reliable, more streamlined, and more productive. Even if you are just dealing with a large amount of files, but don't necessarily want to implement a full Digital Asset Management system, you will benefit from this book.

Since the focus is on the production process, this book is for you if you are a:

- Project manager
- Graphical designer
- 3D designer
- Programmer
- Sound designer, audio artist, or director
- Student preparing for such a job.

You will get the most out of this book if your field is:

- Animation film
- Computer games
- Web design
- A similar industry with big, complex projects involving a large team.

What do you get out of this book?

This book will explain how Digital Asset Management can make your working life easier—how it can help you stay organized, have fewer team conflicts due to misunderstandings, find files faster, and work more productively overall.

You will learn by example how to implement a Digital Asset Management system step by step and avoid the common pitfalls. When you finish reading, you will have a clear picture of what to expect from the solutions, how to select the one that fits your specific needs, and how to get it running in the shortest time possible.

Why is Digital Asset Management important?

Life and project deadlines pass too quickly to waste your time. To stay competitive, you need to consider the quality boost the introduction of Digital Asset Management can offer.

Why we wrote this book

We have experienced for ourselves how frustrating it can be working in a company with the traditional just-drop-your-files-anywhere-and-hope-for-the-best-later attitude:

- No way to trace changes in decisions and garbled communication lines
- Random workflow patterns and haphazard "signoffs"
- Crossing your fingers that the right version of the file ended up in the final product.

Because there is no comprehensive guide to finding solutions to these problems and implementing Digital Asset Management—not on the Web, nor on the book market—we decided to fill this gap and share the knowledge we gained over the years through trial and error, observation, and some formal testing. To broaden our perspective, we conducted interviews with people in the trenches at both industry-leading and smaller, but powerful, new companies.

We hope you will find all the information we compiled useful in your endeavors. Please let us know if you feel something is missing, if you want to share your experience, or if you disagree with a particular point by dropping us an e-mail: dam@jensjacobsen.net

About the authors

Jens Jacobsen works as a consultant and information architect for website, museum, and edutainment projects. He received a Diploma in Biology from the Technical University in Munich, Germany, and started as a technology writer. Soon he became fascinated by multimedia and began working in this field, first as programmer, then as a project manager. He led the creation of several large websites, interactive exhibits for science centers, and web-based training applications. He has written or co-written several books, among them the *Director Compendium* for Macromedia Director MX 2004. This is the sixth edition of the 1000-page book, which has been the standard reference in Germany since its first edition in 1997. Jens has also written a book on information architecture and workflow for creating successful websites.

Tilman Schlenker has been working as an Application Engineer and Product Specialist for the Alienbrain product line at Avid/NXN Software for the last four years. He received a Diploma in Media Technology from the University of Applied Sciences in Mittweida. Having worked on several different media projects, including CGI, real-time architectural visualizations, multimedia, and web-based VR, he is currently putting his experience to good use in a variety of customer projects.

Lisa Edwards is an experienced technical writer/editor with a background in digital media production and business intelligence software. She received a B.A. in English from Davidson College in North Carolina. An employee of NXN Software, she has worked in the asset management industry for several years and is intimately familiar with the tools, technologies, and processes used in a variety of vertical markets. She continues to write manuals on using and administering the Alienbrain software package, and various other technical publications in the digital asset and production management fields.

Acknowledgements

We would like to thank the following people:

Gregor vom Scheidt from Avid/NXN Software for pushing this project forward, for contribution and analytic examination of both subject matter and project direction, for volunteering his vast industry knowledge, and for general support during the long and tremendous process of writing this book.

Paul McLaughlin from Lionhead Studios for sharing his extensive wisdom of game development with us.

Steve Lucas and Hamish Young from Criterion for telling us about the "Evil Hack File" and how to squelch game programmers' bad habits.

Ralf Zender from Pixelspell Animation Studios for divulging many details of his work and providing fantastic pictures to illustrate this book.

Laurent Guilleminot and Nathalie Etchepare for spending some of their valuable time, and everyone at Attitude who shared their knowledge.

Xilam Animations for contributing some stunning illustrations.

Bill Villarreal, Sam Richards, and Manson Jones at Sony Pictures Imageworks for sharing valuable insights on how to create award-winning productions.

Jasjyot Singh, Bernie Segal, Kirsty Weston, Eliel Johnson, and Rachel Switzky from Framfab United Kingdom for readily revealing their approach when implementing DAM.

Sabine Schmidt and Thorsten Kraus from Scholz & Volkmer for explaining how they create their impressive projects.

Andreas Zitzelsberger for contributing some of the product descriptions in the book's appendix.

Katrin Röder for suggesting excellent sources of information and for making many valuable contacts.

Nicolas Johns and Achim Stremplat for sharing information on best practices in game development and introducing us to some important people in gaming.

Hakan Çakar for coming up with pictures and illustrations and always sending them faster than we could look at them.

Inga von Staden for making contact with several important and helpful people—as she always does like no one else.

Jens would like to specially thank his wife Cornelia for steady encouragement and many helpful discussions on countless topics addressed in the book.

Tilman would like to thank Jana and Lea-Sophie for accepting his spending even more time in front of the monitor.

Lisa would like to thank the people who didn't let "the never-ending story" end before its time, and the third-floor crew at NXN for finding the saga oh-so-amusing.

Last but not least, we would like to thank Joanne Tracy and Becky Golden-Harrell, our great editors, for being always helpful and swift, and the entire Focal Press team for remaining patient with us and giving us the chance to produce this book.

We hope you have as much fun reading this book as we had writing it!

1 Introduction

1.1 What is it all about?

In the modern workplace, we all create assets with any task we perform—regardless of our profession. We write e-mails, letters, and faxes. We create diagrams, flowcharts, and reports. We take pictures with our cameras and create videos. We write text messages and leave messages on voicemail systems. We write memos summing up meetings and phone conferences. As a consequence, finding things on a computer or even on a mobile phone—which today are more like PDAs—is more difficult than finding things on our desks!

Everyone knows how difficult it can be to keep things in order—be these tangible things we have to get our hands on, or digital things we can only get a hold of with the use of a technical device. In our private lives we can usually cope with this problem on our own (and if not, there are home organization consultants and entire stores filled with shelving and containers to help!). And sometimes we don't mind searching—looking through the shoebox of all the pictures you took last year hunting for Tim's wedding photos can be a lot of fun.

But at work, managing your assets poorly can waste valuable time and cause excessive frustration. On the organizational side, this burns too much money due to low productivity and lost assets. These problems prompted the evolution of Digital Asset Management as people tried to find ways to reduce search times, improve reliability, and increase productivity in the process of creating and handling assets.

1.2 What does this book cover?

This book contains all the information you need to make use of the best practices in Digital Asset Management that have been developed steadily over the last two decades. You will learn which techniques for workflow design, project management, and teamwork can be used to get better results and take the pain out of the process. You'll have a checklist of what to look for if you plan to buy or build a software system that helps you with asset management. Step by step, you will compile your own specific requirements catalog. Then you can compare it with the features the systems available on the market have to offer and find out which of these is a good match.

The focus of this book is on the production process, so we will look at companies where the production is complex and product cycles are long. We show how you can benefit most from Digital Asset Management if you work in an industry—mainly game production, animation film, web design, and similar industries—that create complex digital products. But if you work in a design agency, a photographer's studio, or manage a complex website, you will also benefit from this book. Since it is not industry specific, anyone interested in improving the way they work with digital assets will gain lots of new ideas.

Several case studies point out common problems and open your eyes to similar situations in your own company—often, we are so used to our own habits that even glaring problems are overlooked. Success stories from well-known companies reveal how some of the most powerful global players in game production, animation film, and web design are working. These examples provide models for your own firm—even if your projects are smaller or less complicated.

1.3   What's an asset anyway?

Defining an asset is not an easy task. The word stems from the financial world, where an asset is something of a certain value like cash, real estate, stocks and shares, or a piece of art.

In the IT and media world there are two widely accepted definitions for assets, both of which aren't completely satisfactory. Both agree that a digital asset includes a digital file, but one definition says an asset is a digital file plus the rights to use it, and the other definition states that an asset is a digital file plus a description of it—the so-called metadata.

The first definition (asset = file + rights) is more widely used in the context of assets that have a certain value on their own. For example, think of an MP3 file of a song from your favorite band. From a business perspective, it is useless as long as you don't have the right to do something with it—i.e., use it in a movie you make, sample it in your own song, or

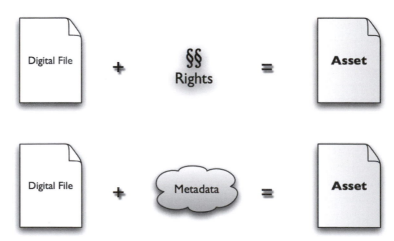

Figure 1.1   *The two most common definitions of a digital asset*

broadcast or sell it to your customers. That means that only the file *together with* the rights to do something with it build an asset.

The second definition (asset = file + metadata) comes from the usage in large companies. A file containing information is only useful if you know what is in it. This might sound trivial if you only have a collection of files you created yourself. In this case, the metadata is either stored in your own brain (you know what is inside), or it is easy to generate the metadata on the fly (you can just open the file and see what is inside). But this approach becomes impractical if you have hundreds or even hundreds of thousands of files which are created by many different people. Then it becomes essential to tag the files with the relevant information about their contents to make it possible to retrieve them. Otherwise, they will be lost in the sheer amount of information. That is why only a file *together* with metadata is considered an asset.

These two concepts are complementary. Of course, a file you can find easily but you don't have the right to use is not an asset to you. On the other hand, a file you have the right to use but which you can't find due to missing metadata is not much of an asset either.

For this book it is not necessary to nit-pick—we won't deal much with theory here. We will simply consider an asset to be a digital file you just need. That's the reason why you want to manage it, and to do so you need metadata. Metadata can be as simple as the filename itself, the time the file was created and modified, and to which program it belongs.

1.4   What is Digital Asset Management?

Digital Asset Management is a way of keeping an overview of your digital files and making sure they don't get lost or altered unintentionally. You can do this simply by using sensible directory structures and consistent names, and by tracking carefully what happens with your files and what is in them.

But usually you will want to use an application to help with this because as the number of files and team size increase, the greater the difficulty in dealing with the assets. Managing digital assets without a Digital Asset Management system soon becomes quite a headache for all.

The first pioneers who used DAM systems were media producers, the publishing industry and large corporations. In media and publishing, the main challenge was to collect images, audio and video assets, to publish/broadcast them, and to archive them. In large corporations, millions of documents had to be stored and retrieved. With the advent of the Web, everyone publishing there faced similar problems. With the growing number of files created every day and their increasing size and complexity, asset management became necessary in virtually every industry. Now, Digital Asset Management is a widely used practice and has proven its return on investment within a short time in countless cases.

Today, DAM systems come in many different flavors—from simple to set up and use Open Source solutions available for free, to complex commercial packages that take months to implement and cost several million dollars.

In this book we will concentrate on systems that provide great benefits to productions, but that are still reasonable in terms of price and effort to implement at small to mid-sized companies in the web design, game production, and animation film fields.

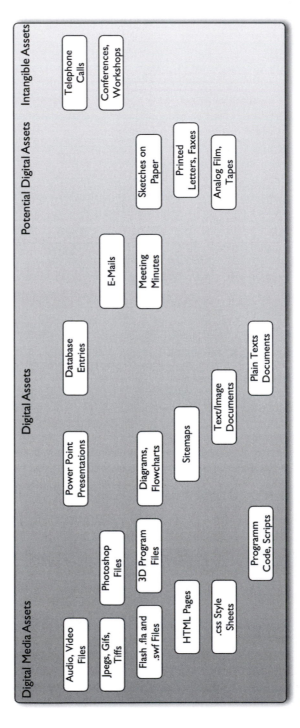

Figure 1.2 *Some common types of digital asset files*

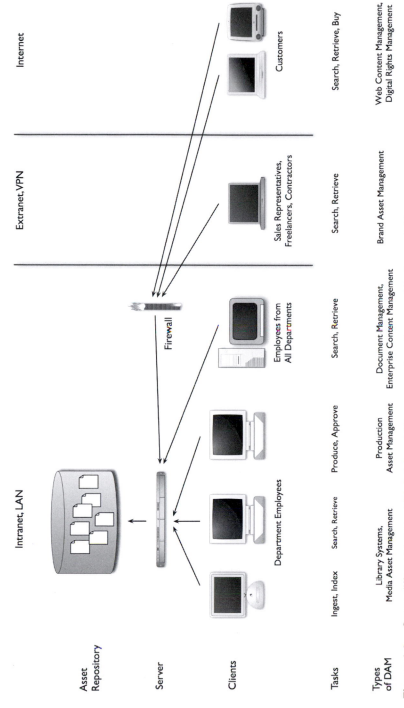

Figure 1.3 Some different types of Digital Asset Management systems and their specialties

Note that hardware like tape libraries, special networks, or disk arrays is sometimes labeled with the tag DAM, but these topics are beyond the scope of this book.

1.5 How is this book structured?

The structure of this book follows the steps you should take when implementing a Digital Asset Management system in your own firm:

Chapter 1, which you are currently reading, gets you ready to kick off your quest for a DAM solution.

Chapter 2 will reveal what can happen without DAM, and how it can be avoided. It describes numerous problems, some of which will seem familiar and some you might not even know you have. You'll also discover where Digital Asset Management can help.

Chapter 3 helps you to assess your current situation. First find out where you are, and then where you want to go.

In Chapter 4, you'll learn how to plan for your needs by compiling a list of all the essential and nice-to-have functions a DAM solution should provide for your team. Evaluating this list should help you determine what can realistically and successfully be implemented given your individual situation.

Chapter 5 is your guide to the right solution. You'll explore the many different types of Digital Asset Management systems available to help you find your way through the feature lists posted on websites and in brochures. And you'll learn how to ask the sales representatives the right questions to make sure you get everything you need, but don't pay for unnecessary features.

Chapter 6 will take you through implementing the system you have chosen. It points out common problems and explains how to avoid them, or work with them if they do arise. It covers technical aspects as well as how to prepare the team for your new way of working.

Chapter 7 presents the approach to asset management taken by several renowned companies. You will see how famous computer game producers like Lionhead Studios tame their enormous projects, like the development of their acclaimed game *Black & White*. You'll read about Sony Pictures' best practices to keep the development of feature-length animation films with terabytes of data under control. And you can find out how Scholz & Volkmer keeps pace with the production of a large and complex website while making sure quality and timeline targets are met.

Finally, the Appendices offer a wealth of additional information: an extensive overview on the most relevant DAM solutions on the market today, with an assessment of their strengths and weaknesses; a glossary with important keywords, buzzwords, and phrases; and references for other sources of information, like books and websites, if you want to explore a topic further.

Now, let's dive into the next chapter and find out what Digital Asset Management can do for you!

2 What can asset management do for you?

2.1 What can happen...

In this chapter we'll look at all the problems that can arise during production, and you'll see how Digital Asset Management can help you avoid these obstacles in future productions.

Most of us know this story all too well. With fresh energy, the team starts a new project. Everyone is eager to push things forward, and every day more and more content is produced. The creative folks write conceptual documents, draw mind maps, and spin out idea after idea. Graphical artists scribble on any surface available. Project managers hold numerous meetings and produce piles of memos, protocols, and memorandums. Countless e-mails are written and received.

But sooner or later, the project manager gets this odd feeling. Is everything really under control? Does he have an accurate assessment of the project's progress? Maybe the creative people are starting to experience trouble. Some files have been overwritten by other versions, a few latest versions couldn't be found, and more than a bit of double work was done because someone used an old version of another person's file. The more files created, the more often these problems occur.

If the team is small or the project manager does a great job of reining things in, even if the project becomes more and more chaotic, it will be finished just a bit late and just a bit over budget. But more often than not, things don't work out so well.

Example: A typical project without DAM—Case study of ProperPictures

Imagine ProperPictures, a mid-sized animation studio that creates computer-generated films for advertising, TV sequels, and occasionally short films to be submitted to film festivals. There are 15 animation artists, two programmers and occasionally three project managers working at ProperPictures.

The current project is a 30-second commercial for a manufacturer of HiFi equipment, in which a human cartoon character commands three metal robots to bring him the best sound experience possible. The duration of this project is fixed as three months. At the beginning of the project, Sven, the art director, talks to the customer and starts scribbling down his ideas right away. He does this while commuting on the train, during lunch doodling on paper napkins, and around the office using every scrap of paper he can get hold of. He collects all these artifacts on his desk. For brainstorming, he shows them to his colleagues, which results in more scribbles from all the artists involved. Finally, a proper storyboard is made. Some of the scribbles are scanned, and Sven creates other images from scratch with a tablet in Adobe Illustrator.

Richard, one of the project managers, is responsible for keeping all the files in order. He provides directories on the server where all the sketches and documents, and later the models, textures, and completed films, should go.

For this project, eight of the graphical artists are involved. Two construct the 3D models, two create all the textures and bitmaps needed, and four animate the characters and do the lighting and entire composition of the scenes. Sven also serves as director and is therefore always walking from desk to desk to see what the graphical artists are up to. An external contractor who is briefed by Sven and Richard provides sound for the clip.

The project starts smoothly; model after model is ready in a draft version. In parallel, the textures are created and are applied to the models for a first test. Sven often wants reworks of the models and sometimes he asks for a different texture. More and more files are stored on the server. Artists create subfolders to maintain a transparent structure, but file names meant to track content and status ("Texture_Mod1_new.bmp", "Char31_old_old.ma", and "Copy of Character 193.ma", for example) become confusing. The shouting across the room becomes bothersome to other employees not staffed to this project. ("Hey, Bill, which version of your brushed steel texture should I use for Righteous Robot?" "Liz, where do you want me to save the finished Commander Tom to?") Richard tries to sort the files and repeatedly asks his teammates to use consistent names. Slowly he loses his overview of how many characters, shots, and scenes are completed, and how much work there is still left to do.

Every night, all the workstations and the small render farm of ProperPictures produce some clips for review. After the midpoint of the project, at least once a week an entire render job has to be redone because one of the characters has the wrong texture or uses an outdated model. Tension in the team grows because it happens too frequently that someone overwrites the file a teammate spent hours or even days improving.

But the real trouble begins when the client wants to see a preview. This was not part of the project plan; the client was supposed to approve only stills of the models and the background used. So five days (and nights) of frantic work ensue. The entire team tries to make the sample as polished and impressive as possible. Finally, they are only able to present two-thirds of what they had planned, but the client is happy nevertheless.

After a short rest, the team returns to their normal work schedule. They discover that some of the files that were nearly finished but were not included in the preview are definitely lost and must have been overwritten. A search on the backup tapes doesn't produce any results. The files have to be recreated from scratch. And every now and then, Sven finds one of the old elements they used in the preview mixed in with the current work. They just seem to creep back into the project.

At some point in the project Richard, the project manager, gives up on keeping the directories and files in order. From time to time, he just asks the team members how much work they have left and when they will be finished. When the deadline is one week ahead, he learns that three of the graphical artists can't continue working because they are waiting for files to be created by the texture team, who underestimated the time needed for details—"the dull work", they called it. It took them three additional days to finish.

Richard informed the customer that the delivery would be a week late, which caused major problems. They were quite upset because they wanted to present the animation clip at an event taking place one week later, but Richard was able to calm them down.

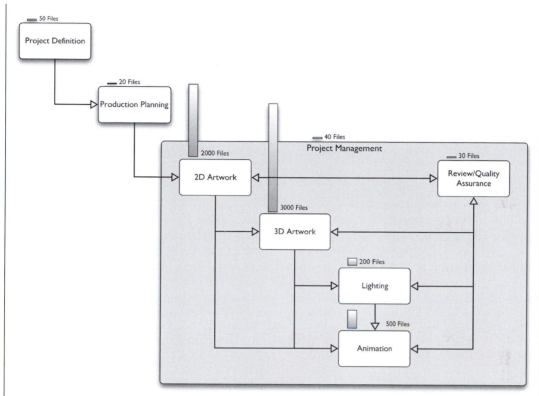

Figure 2.1   *Production steps and number of files created*

When the original deadline passed, the graphical artists told Richard that there were some problems with the integration of the characters into the scene and that they would need one more week, minimum. Richard decided to hire Claudia, a top-notch 3D artist he worked with at his former employer. She helped finish the remaining scenes, but after a few days it became apparent that they would miss the new deadline also.

Richard had no choice. He had to talk to the customer again and tell them that they would need two more weeks. Surprisingly, they accepted the news without much discussion (they may have anticipated this delay already). They simply said that they would never work with ProperPictures again.

Finally, three weeks after the first promised deadline, Richard presented the finished clip to the customer. They were satisfied, but not thrilled, as the team had hoped at the beginning. Everyone on the team was exhausted from the long hours of overtime and weekends spent in the office. They felt disappointed because they were not able to achieve the standards they defined when the project started.

Of course, the project was a financial loss. The costs of extra manpower and the 25 percent extension of the project duration ate up all expected profit. And, even worse, they lost a customer.

Although there are no official statistics, most game developers, web agencies, animation studios, and design firms agree that there are more projects that are cancelled, slip or do not reach the desired quality than projects which are completed on schedule, on budget, and with the desired quality.

The many reasons for this can be roughly divided into two areas: project management issues and technology- or process-related issues. With bad project management, it does not matter how good your tools are, your project will be in trouble anyway. But even with adequate project management in place, it is very difficult to complete a project on time with good quality if you don't have the right tools.

There are dozens of great books on project management (see Appendix 3 for some recommendations), and every project manager has read some of them. Implementing solid project management practices is a prerequisite for successful development, but doing so is highly dependent on experience, personal skills, and the circumstances of the project at hand.

However, using appropriate tools and a sensible project setup can solve many problems that potentially could occur in almost every project. Typical problem areas are described and analyzed in the following section, and after reading this you will see how asset management can resolve them.

The typical problems

Most of the problems in electronic media projects do not become apparent until full production mode starts. After pre-production, the team size doubles or triples. Graphical artists design textures, interface elements, product details, and so on. 3D modelers build characters and objects. Programmers create tools, scripts or program code. Sound experts compose effects and the score.

As all these people start their work packages, they begin to generate media assets at an average rate of between 50 and 10,000 files a week, with lower numbers at the beginning and higher numbers towards the end of the project.

Directory structure/permissions

These files are generally stored in a large directory structure on a central server, and everyone, including inexperienced team members, adds, removes, and modifies files. As the project progresses, it becomes increasingly difficult to say who created a file, where that file is used, and what its latest version is.

Some project users create and initially maintain their data locally, and a single person in the team is responsible for integrating the local copies into the master file tree to maintain consistency. This practice introduces a bottleneck into the production process, and as the project grows, integrating new data and keeping the master copy consistent often becomes a tedious full-time job.

When many people have access to the server and certain files need to be worked on by several people, collisions start to occur.

- In a game project, the script that one level designer changed today will be overwritten when his colleague copies local files back to the server tomorrow. Two artists work on the

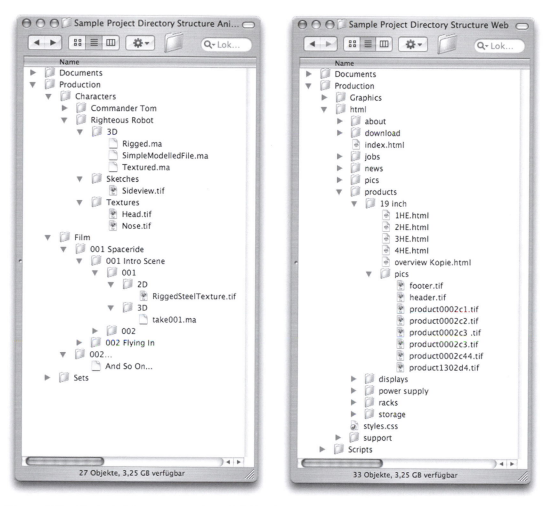

Figure 2.2 *Typical data structures for a CG film (left) and a website project (right)*

same file without knowing it, and whoever saves last wins. A programmer makes changes to some central configuration files while a level designer is doing a game build on his machine, and the subtle errors this introduces cost half a day to track down.

- In a web development effort, a designer updates some interface elements but accidentally also copies his local test changes back to the server, breaking the design for everybody else.
- In 3D design, one designer changes the size of a small component locally on his computer, but not on the server. Weeks later he recognizes that all his teammates used the old version of his component as part of their models—resulting in a fix session of several days, because this very component is used in so many models and the sizes of their other parts have to be corrected manually.

Increasing team size during project

During pre-production, or in projects with three to five people, which are very small by today's standards, it is feasible to synchronize with others by shouting across the room. However, in a team of 20 people or more, it becomes much harder to find out who is doing what, to communicate that a file is about to be worked on, or to track down the change that broke your setup. The number of communication paths is tremendous. It is obvious that real-time, verbal communication can be very expensive in larger teams because it is disruptive and impractical.

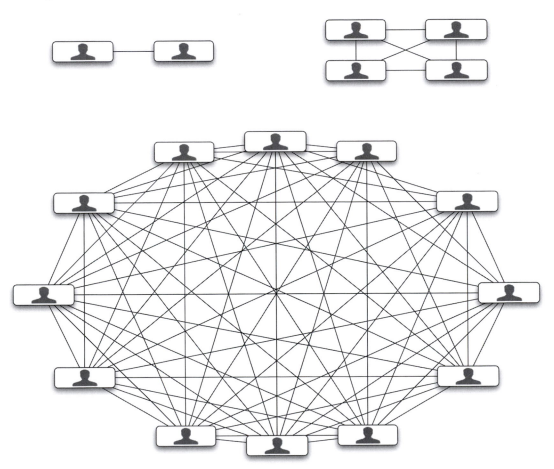

Figure 2.3   *Communication paths in projects with 2, 4, and 12 people*

Because many people can access the master file tree, it is not uncommon that someone accidentally wipes out a day's work by deleting a network directory that they thought was not used any more. However, more commonly, individual files are lost because they are misplaced rather than deleted: inexperienced team members get lost in the directory structure and store their files where they will never be found again.

No backup strategy

When the worst happens and vital files are actually deleted, people need to refer to backups to restore them. In most projects, a structured backup system exists. But the backups are usually incremental, which means that someone has to trace back through dozens of tapes to restore a two-month-old file. It is virtually impossible to go back to specific older versions of files from most backups, since they do not contain information about the history of your files.

Most projects have no additional safety measures that check a file update's consistency against other files. Therefore, some files on the server may reference files on someone's local machine that will not be present when the final product is compiled. Many file formats reference other files by paths, and when any of these files are moved to a new location, the fragile link between the files breaks. As the number of assets grows, rearranging the directory structures to make their nesting deeper or introducing new categories and substructures to make navigating the file tree easier just doesn't work.

In electronic media projects, virtually all of the money allocated to production is spent on the files that are generated, but very little is done to protect and document these assets.

Old versions

Most artists like to keep older versions of their files around in case they need to go back to them later. As artists begin to perform a kind of manual version control, files start to appear in variations such as "texture.bmp", "texture_rough.bmp", and "texture_rough_rougher.bmp". Because one artist does not always know what the others are working on, very similar graphics are created.

When the art director reviews and approves the final look, all previous file versions become obsolete. But because of the complexity of the project, people forget or are afraid to delete these files, and so they remain in the central tree and possibly even the final product, taking up valuable resources. For example:

- In a computer game, the PlayStation version includes assets that were meant for Gamecube, and the PC version still includes 8-bit textures in some parts, although the engine has long ago moved on to 16-bit.
- In web design, old versions of pictures remain in the HTML directories, eventually being duplicated several times if a design serves as a template for other sections. This takes up storage capacity and makes finding the right file for correction unduly harder.

In a typical project, between 10 and 30 percent of the assets on the final data carrier or server are not actually used. Because the production format is only rarely the target format, artists have to cope with multiple instances of the same file in different formats (e.g. Photoshop, BMP, TIM, GIF, JPEG). This applies to images, 3D models, sound effects, animations, and scripts. Constantly performing the required conversions and keeping these formats in sync consumes valuable artist resources.

Because many projects use many custom-built tools that are specific for just that endeavor, building parts of the project may, for example, require running four batch files in the right order with the right parameters. Two more batch files are required to preview the final product. Artists need to learn how to use these tools, and need to be notified and trained on each new tool or substantial change. When a tool or format is updated, team members may forget to change their local copies or run the required conversions, and then spend hours locating the cause of the resulting problems.

Communication about changes

When the number of people and the number of files in a project grows, the complexity increases very quickly. In addition to the increasing number of communication paths mentioned before, the relationships between files generate an intricate web of dependencies that are difficult to track manually.

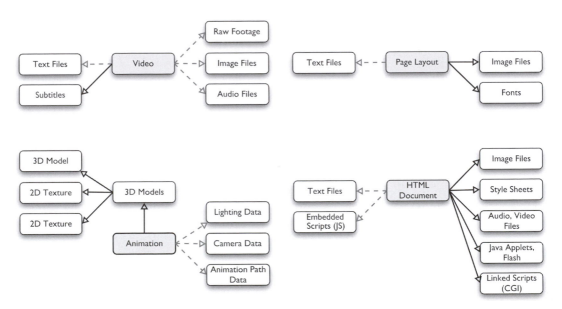

Figure 2.4   *Examples of common file types with dependencies*

When changes in files, formats, and the project structure are not tracked, keeping the file tree up to date is virtually impossible. The complexity of the tool set and the project structure requires artists to develop an intimate knowledge of large parts of the project, which wastes their time and makes it more difficult to train newcomers.

Preliminary versions (demos, etc.)

Creating preliminary versions is necessary in most projects. For example:

- During the production of a computer game, there are generally between one and five demo versions that have to be produced to meet milestones, for the press, for trade shows, cover-mount CDs, and for in-store display.
- In computer-generated film productions, there are usually daily and weekly screenings of models, shots or scenes to approve them and discuss changes.
- In web design, preliminary versions are needed for approval and for usability testing.

- In 3D design, there are sketches, storyboards, prototypes, and models to be presented to decision makers or customers.

Producing these demos or prototypes often stalls the main development effort, since it is difficult to work on two parallel versions of the project without risking interference. In large teams, man-weeks or even months are lost to this kind of production stall. Similar problems arise in cross-platform development and in localization efforts.

Project management

From a project management perspective, lack of transparency in a project makes it very difficult to track its status.

Towards the end of the project, it may suddenly be discovered that the models in levels 12–15 of a game are not yet optimized, that 25 percent of the textures have not been touched up for the target platform's low-bit-depth format, and the behavior scripts for the monsters in the last third of the game have not been tested at all. Or in another project, some part of a large website under development still uses a navigation pattern that was abandoned weeks before.

If this had been known in advance, additional people could have been brought on to the team, or more time could have been allocated for completing these tasks. Planning uncertainties and a certain amount of scheduling inaccuracies are always to be expected. But generally, such problems are detected much later than is optimal and, by that time, the options for addressing the problems are already substantially reduced.

Some skeptics say that all projects will be late. But most people in the know will agree that computer game projects have the reputation of being worst in terms of slipped schedules, so we'll have a closer look at their project management issues to figure out the problem. Though computer games may not be your field, you'll recognize some similarities in your own projects.

Example: Case study of project management in computer games

The history of computer game development is littered with late and overdue projects. These games are late for many reasons, and delays vary from weeks to years. Explanations also vary widely, but they basically boil down to a few basic patterns: loss of focus on shipping a product, inadequate project and asset management techniques, and miscellaneous mishaps and false estimations.

Some famous game projects have shipped years after their initial announcements, generally after churning through several generations of artists and programmers. These games—*Duke Nuke'm Forever* is a recent example—were mostly delayed because the management in charge got lost in an endless pattern of adding or changing aspects of the game and lost their focus on the goal of a finished product. As can happen in entertainment, however, some of these bets have paid off in the end. Studios and individuals like John Carmack at id Software (*Doom*, *Quake*), Peter Molyneux at Lionhead (*Black & White*), and Shigeru Miyamoto at Nintendo (*Zelda*) have made it their philosophy to ship their games only when they feel they are ready—whenever that may be. Unfortunately, very few projects have that liberty.

Game projects that are delayed by mere weeks, however, are almost worthy of respect. Planning a project that requires dozens of people to complete tens of thousands of assets over the period of a year or more with technology that is partly still developed as the project progresses is fiendishly difficult. Slips of the order of weeks generally stem from minor false estimations and small technical bets that went wrong. If the crew did not have to work night shifts for several months, the processes these teams were using were probably adequate.

Many, if not most, projects are delayed by several months, though. This is too short to reflect a complete loss of focus and too long to attribute to minor false estimations. You can generally assume that the project and asset management processes used by these teams were inadequate for the scope of the project. When asked about the causes, these teams report a combination of causes: data was lost, time was lost because the wrong versions of assets were used, and progress was tracked on too many or too few tasks and with insufficient accuracy.

2.2   ...And how it can be avoided

So, the typical digital content production project involves a lot of hassle. If you look at it from a distance, nearly all of it has to do with the assets. That's no wonder, as at the end of all these projects stands a collection of assets: a computer game, a computer-generated movie, a website, or a detailed construction plan for an item to be manufactured.

It follows that if you manage your assets better, the entire process will run more smoothly. Don't be misguided by the fact that you hear only of asset management when talking about technology. Some aspects of asset management can be achieved by discipline alone; technology is just a helper. Let's have a look at the possibilities of asset management in more detail.

How can digital asset management help?

The preceding pages outlined and analyzed the causes of the majority of non-project management problems in digital content production projects. The majority of the problems are related to the lack of a central entity that keeps track of files, attributes, and transactions to coordinate the production process and make it more transparent and controllable. While this is not the complete answer, it highlights the most important aspect that a solution (or an individual, or the whole team) must provide: central control over what is going on in the project. This may sound simple at first, but there are myriad requirements that make the solution difficult: this entity should be unobtrusive, scalable, secure, allow the use of existing tools, and it must be sufficiently customizable to fit into all of the various development styles of your projects.

With well-defined processes, you can implement a non-digital (well, at least a low-digital) asset management solution. If you have the right processes you can succeed with the standard tools like a calendar, paper, e-mail, spreadsheets, and text documents alone. For small projects this is definitely possible. It just requires a great project manager with much experience and, most importantly, a team of people that all have great discipline.

But your main goal is to have a great product. So you select the team members by their talent, and maybe also by their ability to cooperate with the rest of the team. Discipline in naming files is surely not a part of any job description. People want to, and should, concentrate on their work, not on the organization of their work.

This is where technology comes in. The right software solution takes the burden of organizing the production away from the team. Of course, you still need a good project manager, but there are so many tasks a Digital Asset Management (DAM) system can make run smoothly that it is undoubtedly worth the effort of finding a solution for this.

2.3 Who needs DAM?

If you have a team of more than three people working on a project for more than three months, a Digital Asset Management solution is highly advisable. It can reduce the time spent searching for files, mistakes like using old versions, and catastrophes like accidentally overwriting other people's work. Additionally, DAM helps you keep old versions through backup and file archiving.

Electronic media companies trying to step up professionalism in their projects often recognize the importance of employing a DAM system. It not only saves each single team member time, it also makes work more enjoyable. Frustration because of lost files vanishes. DAM has enormous impact on morale: if you work with a professional system, you work more professionally. That means DAM also has an impact on quality.

Four types of digital content production

Table 2.1 explains the four major types of digital content production. We'll have a closer look at each to see which aspects of Digital Asset Management they offer.

Table 2.1   *Types of digital content production*

	(A) Creation of digital products	(B) Creation of digital ingredients	(C) Creation of digital designs	(D) Creation of digital chunks
Output	Self-contained, complex digital products	Multiple digital ingredients	Design contribution (e.g. for physical product development)	Digital chunks for continuous content feeds
Examples	Computer games CG films Computer-Based Training (CBT) applications Visualization/ simulation systems Software applications	Web design Graphic design Advertising Video post-production Film visual effects Software localization Technical documentation	3D design Automotive design Fashion design Illustrators	Broadcast editing TV news illustration Web news News photographers
Typical production profile	Large teams (5–300) with long cycles (6–36 months)	Smaller teams (2–6) with shorter cycles (3–12 weeks)	Groups of interconnected small teams with short cycles	Individual artists with very short cycle times (one day or less)

Of course, there are hybrid forms of development and some companies won't fit in perfectly to one category, but it helps to point out the different production workflows and their characteristics to find out where DAM can assist.

Type A: Creation of digital products

A computer game or a CG film is a hefty endeavor. It usually takes years from start to finish, and can involve up to 300 people. Creating large Computer-Based Training (CBT) applications or software applications can be equally challenging.

What these projects all have in common is that teamwork is key. Everyone is working on assets that are the foundation for the creation of a teammate's assets, and often the result is another asset that another teammate uses for his work. These dependencies make such productions difficult to manage: if one person is not able to deliver on time, the production of all other assets based on its work will also be late. Changing one seemingly small thing will usually affect several assets that are owned by different people.

Digital Asset Management can help prevent these problems by enabling reliable communication, secure transfer of assets, and tracking of schedules.

Type B: Creation of digital ingredients

Graphical design and advertising agencies served as the role model for many of today's media firms. They usually have teams of two to six people, and a typical production seldom takes more than 12 weeks. Many web design agencies evolved from graphical design agencies and therefore similar processes are found in both: A senior person talks to the customer and gives creative direction to designers, writers, and other members of the production team. They produce drafts that are approved by the customer. Then the final product is created—be it a brochure layout or a completed website.

Although the techniques and end products for video post-production, film visual effects, software localization, and technical documentation are disparate, they still share the same general process and workflow characteristics. Therefore, they all can benefit from file management and change tracking. The bigger the team and the longer the project lasts, the more they also profit from teamwork collaboration features found in DAM systems.

Type C: Creation of digital designs

Digital designs are needed for industries like fashion design, industrial design such as automotive design, and other fields. In these cases the teams are usually quite small and can work independently for a short time on their projects and hand the work over when it is complete. The same is true for 3D design agencies that specialize in still images (not animation) or in firms that produce elaborate and complex illustrations.

All these firms can benefit from Digital Asset Management solutions that help them archive and retrieve their work, but teamwork and workflow features are usually not critical here.

Type D: Creation of digital chunks

News production and broadcasting is a tough business, be it on the Web or on air. Speed is paramount and quality should always match or even outperform the standards of the competitors.

The teams here are small; more often than not, a single person works on an asset like a story, a video clip, or an illustration. The package usually has to be finished within a few hours.

Finding the required information and assets quickly is vital here and, as a consequence, archiving the assets produced is equally important. The workflow is simple but has to run smoothly without any glitches or delays. DAM systems for this kind of asset creation must guarantee this above all.

2.4   What companies expect from Digital Asset Management (DAM)

We'll now concentrate on the options DAM systems have to offer you. These are the reasons why companies start investigating whether it makes sense to implement DAM.

Provide consistency

A Digital Asset Management system keeps your files in order. It always knows which version is the most recent and where to find it. So if you send out files to the customer, make a game build, render a shot, launch a website, or hand over files for production, a DAM solution makes sure you will always include the newest files—and just the newest files.

Prevent the disaster

Disaster can have many faces when you don't have a DAM system. The hard disk of the server crashes. An inexperienced team member accidentally overwrites a week's work. The customer changes his mind and wants to go back to an older version.

A good DAM system keeps all versions of all files and provides a robust backup solution.

Shorten processing time

When you introduce Digital Asset Management, it's the right time to think about your production processes. You can easily streamline them because most solutions provide tools for optimization. DAM handles review and approval, and continually gives the project manager a clear picture of the project's status.

Reduce time for searching

One of the most valuable benefits is the reduced time spent on searching for files. Due to the central storage and management of files, you have everything at your fingertips. Flexible search mechanisms also allow you to mine your data and retrieve files based on tailored sets of search criteria.

Enable multiple versions

Quite often you have to provide multiple versions of the final product, be it for different languages, for different platforms, or for short and extended versions. With DAM systems you can tag every file with which version it belongs to and don't have to maintain this information manually.

Track versions

Going back to a previous version is no problem if you have a DAM solution with versioning features. This means, for example, you can reproduce bugs someone finds in an early beta version even if you are several versions ahead now. You always know exactly which files in which versions were part of every release you made.

Control access

User rights can be controlled by operating systems, but this control is always limited. DAM systems can set any rule for the access of any file. Some users might be able to view BMP files, but may not edit them. Others can edit them, but only if another person approved them before. Good DAM software controls access in a way that fits your processes.

Enable re-use

Because the DAM system has full control over all the files, it is easy to re-use any file from any project. This can save a lot of work.

But re-use in development seldom works as promised by software manufacturers. Programmers and artists alike want to make assets from scratch each time, because they always want to improve their previous work. Nevertheless, it is a good idea to encourage re-use and make it as simple as possible. "Boring" assets are more likely to be re-used if it is easier to find them than to remake them. For example, usually the model of a tree will be reused if it can be found quickly, but maybe not the complete tree. It is always possible to polish the final look a bit.

What does work is to re-use to publish the content in different ways and formats. Multiple use of the assets, such as in multi-channel publishing (wireless, PDA, web, print, etc.), is made easy with DAM. They can even be used in ways not foreseen when the asset was created.

2.5   What DAM is (and what it is not)

Over the past few years, the term "Digital Asset Management" (DAM) has been used to describe almost any process or technology that deals with the storage, management, or delivery of digital assets. It is difficult to separate out the asset management processes and technologies that make sense for digital content production from the dozens of other, often unrelated, concepts. The term "Production Asset Management" (ProdAM) is more specific, but it didn't really catch on.

This book focuses on how asset management applies to digital content production. More specifically, we will look at systems designed for workgroups and multi-user facilities where digital content is created.

Other areas of asset management that are not covered in this book include Brand Asset Management, video libraries, and Document Management systems. We will have a brief look at these, however, to point out differences and similarities and to show where these categories will converge in the future.

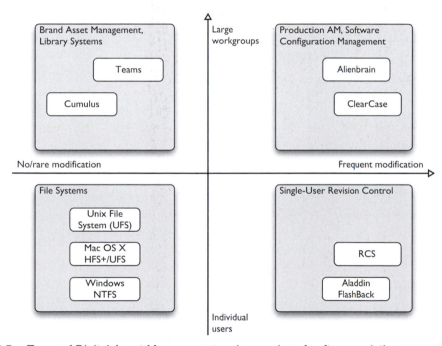

Figure 2.5 *Types of Digital Asset Management and examples of software solutions*

The three characteristics that differentiate the systems we will look at from library systems and other asset management solutions are:

1 They are project based
2 They provide a direct mapping into the file system
3 They are designed for frequent content modification.

Such systems and library systems can peacefully coexist. One environment that needs both support for content production and for traditional library systems is the broadcast industry.

While it may be desirable to have a unified system that handles both, the needs of each application are so different that today this is not possible.

Generally, five use cases for asset management can be distinguished:

1 Manage completed assets
2 Index content
3 Support content creation
4 Manage source code
5 Manage web content.

We will have a closer look at these in the next section.

Table 2.2   *Use cases for asset management and some supporting products*

Use case	Corresponding categories	Product examples
Manage completed assets	(Brand) Digital Asset Management Enterprise Content Management	Cumulus Artesia Teams
Index content	Asset Tracking	Avid MediaManager
Support content creation	Production DAM Document Management (DM)	Avid Alienbrain (ProdAM) Documentum (DM)
Manage source code	Software Configuration Management (SCM)	Perforce IBM Rational ClearCase
Manage web content	Web Content Management (WCM)	Vignette Interwoven TeamSite

Types of asset management

Manage completed assets

If you only manage completed assets, you don't care about how the content is created. You're just saving files to specific places, providing metadata for it (like a content description, artists, date, and so on) and eventually retrieving it later.

"Brand Asset Management" is a term commonly used for this kind of asset management because it is often used for all the data necessary for a major brand. Companies use such systems to keep track of their company and brand logos, provide material for external contributors, and make sure that each employee in every corporate branch all over the world works with the correct versions of these assets.

A subcategory of this type of asset management is Document Management. It is mainly focused on text data like legal notes, contracts, memos, letters, faxes, e-mails, documentation, and so on. The focus here is to make sure nothing is lost and everything is well recorded for the integrity of internal processes and for legal reasons. File formats usually are text documents, presentations, spreadsheets, and some bitmaps (with photos, charts, and sometimes scanned documents like faxes or letters). But the Document Management systems of today also help you during the creation of all these assets; that is why they can be better filed under "support content creation".

Index content

Indexing content can be a tough job. Especially for film footage of news or documentaries, it can take longer than the playback time to index the footage properly. Because of the tremendous amount of data, usually an asset management system is used to help index the scenes. Optical recognition systems scan the different scenes. More elaborate systems can even detect faces or categorize scenes.

For still images, there are also automatic indexing systems, but usually there is still the need for a human operator who checks the metadata (descriptions and so on) and edits it so it is accurate and appropriate for what you can see on the screen.

Here, Document Management comes into play again: in big companies, often faxes and letters are ingested into the system to automate further processing. For text, there is optical character recognition (OCR), which translates the visual information into text. It is also possible to automatically index the content then, but this functionality still has quite severe limitations.

Support content creation

If you want to utilize a DAM system that also supports you while you create your content, it has to support your workflow. It should track which file is created by whom, who modified it, what its status is, and so on. This category of systems is the focus of this book.

Such a system has to control access to the files and maintain old versions. Also, the existing tools must be integrated to ensure a smooth workflow and not complicate matters.

Manage source code

Software Configuration Management (SCM) deals with the management of source code. It enables simultaneous work on a larger programming endeavor by a big team and provides tools to test changes locally. When work is complete or in a useful state, SCM software integrates the small chunks of code into one version and helps to solve problems when there are versioning conflicts.

Manage web content

Web Content Management (WCM) is probably the most well-known category of DAM. Such systems offer solutions for developing and maintaining large websites by a team of many people with different roles. In addition, most of the WCM systems support some form of collaboration (workflow) features so that assets only hit the public web server after proper approval.

Differentiation

To help you get a better understanding of the many aspects of DAM, the following section compares Production Asset Management (Production AM), which we focus on in this book, with other related categories with which it is often mixed up.

Production AM vs. databases

The most basic type of asset management system in the broader sense is a database. A database can be used in any of the use cases described previously.

Databases are quite flexible in structure and it is possible to implement features that support the production workflow with them. One main drawback, however, is that databases are made for handling information, not assets as such. This means they can easily handle textual information, but most of them have difficulties handling files, especially if they are as large as Photoshop or video files. They are limited in the file formats they support, the software they integrate with, and in the processing of the assets they can provide. On top of that, it is a lot of work to set a database up properly, especially since databases usually don't have a real user interface. Providing a user interface means developing one, which involves a lot of work from several programmers.

Often, a database is a first attempt a company makes to organize their asset management. After a short time though, the limitations become clear and a more elaborate solution is needed.

Production AM vs. catalogs

Digital catalogs are used in most companies that produce a lot of assets but are not technology oriented (for example, advertising agencies or photographer's studios).

The principle of such software is simple and familiar: physically sorting assets in folders and files into the operating system (using Finder, Explorer, etc.). Most catalogs don't maintain working versions of the images, and they usually don't support production workflow. You don't need much training to use a media catalog.

Production AM vs. Web Content Management (WCM)

What distinguishes Production Asset Management from traditional (Web) Content Management is that it goes beyond housing existing content for processing and retrieval by the end-user while the project/product is on the market. Production AM focuses on the entire production cycle from concept to completion. It includes both the tools and the processes that are required to share information, manage the content, and keep a production on track. When a media project or product hits the market, Production Asset Management has already contributed to its success.

Another difference is that Web Content Management (WCM) manages mainly content, not files. It saves textual content and puts it into pre-defined templates that are published. Of course, WCM also publishes pictures that are part of the HTML pages, but it is also treated as content, not as a file that undergoes the whole cycle of production.

Production AM vs. Software Configuration Management (SCM)

Software Configuration Management is common in companies that are technology driven, like game producers. It deals primarily with source code and provides more or less elaborate ways to control the development of complex software.

Production Asset Management provides more ways of integrating tools, namely visual tools for graphical art. The possibilities for automatic conversion of file formats, preview, and manipulation are usually much greater than in SCM systems.

So tell me again, what is it?
Production Asset Management is more than technology: it is also a method of improving workflow and communication within a company that improves the success rates of projects and increases overall profitability. Work becomes more streamlined for the employees and external contributors. Project managers can easily assign tasks and control their completion, and are always up to date on the progress of each project.

2.6 General benefits of DAM systems

Now we will look at the most important general benefits Digital Asset Management systems have to offer.

Benefits for the organization

There are five primary, general benefits that implementers of asset management systems look for:

1 Higher productivity
2 Organizational scalability
3 Increased reliability
4 Better quality
5 Greater flexibility.

Let's examine these in detail in the following sections.

Higher productivity
Introducing a Digital Asset Management system leads to higher productivity in content production and also to higher overall productivity in the organization.

Usually there are two methods and measures for realizing such productivity gains:

1 Achieve given production value at lower cost
2 Achieve higher production value for given cost.

Decide whether you want to lower your costs, or increase quality or volume of your output—or you can even decide to shorten production schedules. In most cases the productivity gain is invested in polishing artwork or increasing the quality of the product in comparable ways.

The introduction of DAM makes this possible because time spent finding, filing, sharing, losing and replacing, overwriting and recreating files can take up 25–40 percent of a creative person's working day, according to independent research firms like Gistics, which specialize in the area of Digital Asset Management. There are DAM systems that are specifically designed to reduce this overhead to negligible amounts. Just cutting the time spent on these clerical activities in half can provide productivity gains of 12.5–20 percent, Gistics determined.

For companies whose primary business is the creation of digital content, any increase in productivity has immediate and significant impact on the bottom line. That means DAM can save money by shortening production cycles, or it can help strengthen a company's market position by delivering higher quality.

Organizational scalability

Introducing Digital Asset Management means an investment in software and of time for implementation and training the users. But the return on investment pays back rapidly because you can expand the organization without compromising quality, profitability, and/or employee motivation.

For example, a design firm that takes on many new contracts can provide the same high quality as when they had fewer projects, because after they implement a DAM solution they can produce 15–35 percent more in a given time. Simultaneously, employee motivation stays high because the environment is more professional when working with an asset management solution. It takes common frustrations out of the picture because no one has to recreate lost files.

Companies often introduce DAM when they grow beyond a certain size—be it in number of employees, in project size, or in the number of projects worked on in parallel. It is invaluable if you recognize that you surpassed the stage of business development where an unstructured workflow and a just-do-it attitude towards asset management worked without major risk to the whole endeavor. The earlier DAM is introduced, the easier it is to keep up with the development of your business without halting all production, running extra training sessions, and spending large sums of money all at once.

Increased reliability

With DAM in place, it becomes easier to reliably meet deadlines, budgets and quality targets—the main reason being that DAM makes the end-to-end production process more efficient and transparent. Everyone on the team knows what to do when, and where to find the files needed for it, and is aware of what is missing and who is responsible for it. Digital Asset Management systems with integrated workflow features can also help streamline the production. Automated notification and approval functionality makes sure only these artifacts that are final and that passed quality control go to the next level of production.

For the project managers, tracking status is a breeze. Since all assets are in one central place, it is possible to get a clear picture of the production progress within a short time. Reporting tools can even reduce this to the push of a button for pre-defined statistics like how many assets are final, how many are in progress, and how many are not yet started.

Every project manager knows how important it is to have precise information about the project's status at all times to detect problems as early as possible, and to take measures to solve the problems at once. Slipped deadlines can cost a fortune due to penalties for breach of contract, lost customer loyalty, bad press, and additional payroll to hire more people to put out fires.

Better quality

There are two distinct measures of quality:

1 Tangible/quantitative (reducing the defect rate)
2 Intangible/qualitative (better artistic/visual quality).

With a Digital Asset Management system you can improve both. The defect rate is reduced because the system tracks all the assets. It makes sure that only the most recent versions are used and that only these versions are integrated into the final product or sent to the customer. No old or interim versions can creep in, and no unresolved problems can be overlooked.

The overall artistic quality increases due to more working time. And since working with different versions is easy, artists are encouraged to go the extra mile with fine polishing.

Greater flexibility

Companies with DAM implemented are able to respond faster to change or problems and to leverage opportunities.

Digital Asset Management systems increase the flexibility to react to adjustments in product specifications, budget, or schedule, and to changes in personnel or organizational structure. Especially if production cycles are long, this is an important advantage. For example, if the customer changes some of the requirements in the middle of production, many assets can be affected. In this case, it is crucial to know their dependencies and their current status, and to track which assets are already modified to meet the new requirements and which are not.

Another recurring issue is that a member leaves the team or new members are recruited. Often, it is close to impossible to find items on another person's computer because everyone has their own method of structuring. With a DAM system, all important files, bearing sensible file names, are stored in a central place with a well-thought-out and defined structure. Additionally, search features are there to help new team members who may only have a vague idea about file contents.

The flexibility to react quickly to changing circumstances allows you to stay on top of today's market demands.

Individual benefits

What will an individual team member get out of using a DAM system? The following benefits:

Work faster
Less time is spent on clerical tasks because you find content faster and need less time to file the content or to communicate with other team members about it.

Work in parallel
Thanks to a good DAM system, it is possible to work in parallel. It stores all the data on a central server and enables things to be tested out locally without touching the files on the server. Later, if you decide that you want to incorporate your changes into the project, the system automatically puts the files in the right places or else assists you in doing so.

Quick rollback
A DAM system with the focus on production keeps all the versions of all files so you can go back to an earlier version quickly. You don't have to try to remember which files were included in the earlier version of the product, and don't have to sort through piles of backup tapes to find the old files.

Easy versioning
Developing different versions is no longer a hassle. A Digital Asset Management system ensures, for example, that only English texts appear in the English version of a website—no more surprise foreign versions which pop up if all changes are made by hand.

Secure access control
Systems can be set up so that every team member just sees the assets that he or she needs to. And everyone can edit, delete or move only the files they should. This makes finding files fast and, most of all, it dramatically minimizes the risk of damage.

Transparent project status
A Production Asset Management system helps the project manager keep the project's progress under complete control. He or she can always see which assets are complete, which are under construction, and which are still missing. This is much faster and more reliable than checking everything manually or wandering from desk to desk asking everybody how it's going.

Control workflow
The system can also help enforce workflow rules; each asset type can follow a defined pattern. For example, a piece of art is labeled as "work in progress" when it is created. When the artist tells the system he is done with it, it is tagged as "draft". The team leader responsible is notified and asked for approval by the system. If there are any comments, they can be noted directly in the system. The file, together with the leader's comments, is presented to the artist again. Only when the leader accepts the file is it marked as "final". This automatically leads to an accurate picture of the project's progress for the project manager.

2.7   Benefits for different departments

Asset management brings general improvements to nearly every department in an organization. All the departments are better integrated, communicate more easily with each other, and have access to the most recent versions of all the assets they need. But some DAM benefits particularly benefit certain departments.

Production departments (visual art, sound, CAD, programming)

The most important improvement brought about by DAM is the time saved by finding files more quickly. Additionally, re-use is simple, and assets developed but not used in the actual project can be stored (and later, in fact, be found) for incorporation in a future project.

Intellectual property rights/sales department

If your company sells the right to use your assets to other organizations, DAM can boost their activities. This group can see all the assets the whole company produces and can easily find other assets that are similar or interesting as add-ons for their customers.

With a good DAM system they can convert the asset into any format the customer asks for, without the help of the person that created the asset.

Sales and marketing department

People from marketing and sales have access to all assets created by the design department, production, etc., so they don't have to send countless follow-up e-mails to get hold of files or accidentally use out-of-date versions. With everything at your fingertips and organized to boot, publishing separate catalogs for different countries or customer groups is much less complicated.

Also, assets for which publishing rights have been purchased can be located. You'll never pay twice for the same asset because you didn't know it was already bought for an earlier project.

2.8 The case for Return On Investment (ROI)

Since the implementation of a DAM system will not go unnoticed in the budget, it is often necessary to make a strong case to those in charge. Listing the benefits previously given is often enough, since virtually everyone who is familiar with real-life productions will realize the associated business value.

But, especially in large corporations, it is usually required to prove the dollar value benefit before a decision concerning the introduction of a big system is made. For this purpose, Return On Investment (ROI) is a widely accepted tool, but it has its limitations for Digital Asset Management; DAM is often used to aid the work of creative teams, and they are not only reluctant to let their work be measured in dollar values out of principle, but often it is impossible to even do so. How much value is created exactly when a digital artist polishes his 3D model a bit more so that everyone says "Wow, this is a great improvement, it looks really cool now!", and the praise makes the artist actually look forward to coming to work tomorrow morning?

Therefore, it might make more sense to identify the strongest overall arguments for why the implementation of a DAM system is worth it. Ideas are listed in the previous section, "Benefits for different departments".

If you nevertheless have to create an ROI calculation, take the five benefits mentioned there as a basis to assess the financial potential and use the examples that follow to get you started. In addition, reports from market research firms like Gistics (see Appendix 3) can be a great help.

Some additional points you might consider including in your calculation are also found in the following section.

Examples of calculating tangible improvements

If you want to make a realistic calculation, you need the exact dollar values of one man-hour of each staff position involved. Salaries in different countries and regions differ widely, as well as the overhead costs you have to calculate for each company.

We will look at three common benefits, the return on which can be calculated relatively easily.

Working faster

The most important benefit that the introduction of DAM brings, from an accountant's viewpoint, is higher productivity. This can be used to shorten project time, but usually it is used to increase quality instead.

If you want to calculate how much money working faster could save, here is an example:

Example: Money saved by working faster

Even if the fully-loaded personnel cost associated with content creation makes up only 50 percent of overall company spending, a 20 percent productivity increase reduces expenditure by 10 percent and increases profitability by 10 percentage points. For example, a web design agency with $5 million in annual revenues and a 7 percent profit margin would more than double their profit before taxes, from $350,000 to $850,000. A simple formula to calculate the return for a given period could be:

Number of assets handled $\times$ Time saved finding/managing it = Saved time

Now to translate that into a dollar value:

Saved time $\times$ Cost of employee = Return

So let's assume the employees in the marketing department usually handle 30 assets per day. Ten of them they find within 30 seconds, 10 they find within 3 minutes, nine within 5 minutes, and for one they have to search 20 minutes. Some files are on the server, some are on different workstations, and some are on CD-ROM. Comparing versions and making sure they have the most recent one comprises this time.

When you are working, you usually don't realize how much time you actually spend each day on such activities. The best way to find out about the actual times in your company is to watch people doing their daily work, and not just look at the time spans they need for their activities.

For our example, we calculate that finding an asset takes about 3 minutes on average. This totals 100 minutes each day for one single person (see Table 2.3).

Table 2.3   *Sample calculation for time spent finding assets on one single day*

	Number of assets	Time searching for an asset	Time total for all assets	Average time
	10	30 seconds	300 seconds	
	10	180 seconds	1800 seconds	
	9	300 seconds	2700 seconds	
	1	1200 seconds	1200 seconds	
Sum	**30**		**6000 seconds**	**200 seconds**
Sum (minutes)			**100 minutes**	**3.33 minutes**

Let's assume, by introducing DAM, the search time can be reduced so that of the day's 30 assets, 20 are found within half a minute, nine within 1 minute, and one within 2 minutes. With this assumption we certainly are on the safe side. Experience shows it is actually quite a conservative estimate. These values compute to an average of 42 seconds to find an asset. That means you spend only 21 minutes in total searching instead of 100 each day (see Table 2.4).

Table 2.4 *Sample calculation for time spent finding assets on one single day with a DAM system implemented*

	Number of assets	Time searching for an asset	Time total for all assets	Average time
	10	30 seconds	300 seconds	
	10	30 seconds	300 seconds	
	9	60 seconds	540 seconds	
	1	120 seconds	120 seconds	
Sum	**30**		**1260 seconds**	**42 seconds**
Sum (minutes)			**21 minutes**	**0.7 minutes**

In total, you have a time saving of 79 minutes (1.3 hours), which equals 13–16 percent each day, depending on the working hours of the employee (8–10 hours assumed).

If you know that an employee in this department costs the company $80 an hour, and there are 15 such employees, you would end up saving $80 \times 1.3 \times 15 \times 5 = $7800 every week.

What you can also add to this return is the money saved by not having to recreate assets that are lost or overwritten. To do so, you have to find out how often this happens in the specified department and how much it costs to recreate such assets, using the formula:

$$\text{Number of assets recreated} \times \text{Time used for it} = \text{Saved time}$$

Let's assume that this happens once a week to every person in our department we look at. They need 6 hours on average to recreate the asset, so DAM could save an additional $6 \times 20 \times $80 = $9600 per week.

As already stated, such calculations should be done carefully, since it must always be considered whether the increase in productivity will lead to working faster or to working better. It could also happen that it just leads to the employees socializing more often in the kitchen (which is not necessarily a bad thing, as breaks lead to refreshed work, and kitchen talk often brings to light interesting perceptions of the current project and future work ideas).

Since you can see the savings in man-hours, it may be tempting to imagine reducing staff to save additional costs, but planning to cut jobs by implementing DAM is not a good bet. First, you need one or even several people to implement the system. The workflow has to be set up, the installation has to be done, and the users need to be trained. The system administrators have to maintain the system and, depending on the number of users, it can take a great deal of time at the beginning. Once the system is running properly and the users know what they are doing, however, maintenance costs should be quite low. In this phase the benefits of DAM become real. But to get so much benefit out of it that you can actually reduce your workforce, you would need quite a lot of employees doing the same job in the first place. Usually the implementation of DAM is seen as a chance to increase quality or productivity, not to cut jobs.

Reduced costs for storage

The larger a project without DAM is, the larger the wasted amount of disk space. There are two reasons for this:

1 Multiple copies of the same files
2 Multiple versions of files.

If the assets are not stored in a central place, people tend to keep copies of their files and of all files they need from teammates on their machines. Sometimes they are even copied several times to different places on the server. Usually such copies are not deleted because it is so difficult to track which are still important and which are just additional copies.

On top of this, most people not used to working with a Digital Asset Management system tend to save multiple versions of each file to have the ability to compare changes later.

In these days of hard disks of several hundreds of gigabytes, this might seem a minor problem, but in larger scale it adds up. This is especially true if the assets are images or even video files, which tend to grow rapidly in size.

Saving mailing and conversion costs

In particular, if you work with many external contributors and freelancers or have to send things physically to customers, a reduction in costs for CD/DVD-ROMs, packaging, couriers, parcel services, and mail is an important factor to consider. Costs of mailing things again because the wrong items were sent can be fully eliminated by introducing DAM.

Converting files manually from one format to another can be a lot of work. For example, an artist has to retrieve a certain Photoshop file, open it, remove the layers not needed on this particular occasion, and export it as JPEG. Especially if the document has a large file size or has a complex layer structure, this can easily take a quarter of an hour or more. If a DAM system is tailored to your workflow, such manual conversions no longer have to be done. In the best case, the person needing a specific asset can retrieve it from the system him or herself and have it created automatically in the required format.

Examples of incalculable improvements

Apart from the tangible improvements mentioned, there are even more intangible improvements, which are nearly impossible to calculate in an ROI.

A Digital Asset Management system is reliable and reduces sources of frustration and team conflicts substantially. Working "feels" more professional, which leads to an increased morale in the team. Higher morale leads to higher job satisfaction, which results in increased productivity, less frequent turnover, and a better image of the company as an employer.

If the increase in productivity is used to improve product quality, the public's image of the company and their products grows stronger—together with customer loyalty. All this will bolster the market position of the company and lead to higher profits in the long run.

2.9 Industries benefitting from DAM

Every industry can benefit from asset management, but since we're focusing on Production Asset Management, we'll have a closer look at the production of computer-generated films and computer games, web development, and 3D design, where the production process is complex. We describe how these industries work to give all readers a clear picture of how projects are realized in the sectors with which they are not familiar. In anticipation of their later growth, smaller firms can see how the big players in their industries do things.

The processes described in the following section represent the accumulated best practices of several firms that are considered top-notch in their respective fields.

Computer-generated (CG) films

A brief history of CG films

Computer animation films, or CG (computer-generated) films, are a new creative medium that did not exist before 1995, when Pixar Animation Studios released *Toy Story*, the first ever feature-length movie completed entirely with computer-generated imagery. It was a blockbuster and won an Academy Award (Oscar). This new kind of film offered unprecedented creative freedom to filmmakers, but also brought with it unprecedented complexity and technical challenges that take decades to resolve.

Figure 2.6 *Today, CGI is not only used to tell amusing stories.* Kaena, *an 85-minute film by Xilam, France, features a multifaceted story, complex characters, and a dark look that fascinates with an incredible wealth of details (© Xilam Animation. All rights reserved)*

How images get on the screen

At the heart of all computer animation films is a digital three-dimensional representation of the world that will later appear on cinema screens. This digital representation is created with sophisticated tools over a long period of time by production teams that can consist of up to 300 people. Once all aspects of the 3D representation of a shot have been modeled, specialized rendering algorithms transform the 3D world into two-dimensional digital images. These images can then be transferred to celluloid and shown in any cinema.

A world of 3D data

The most important items that make up the 3D representation of each shot are the basic geometry and surface patterns of all the various on-screen elements (sets, characters and props), the animation curves that modify this geometry from frame to frame, camera positions for each frame, and information about the position, color and intensity of light sources in the scene. A feature-length film may contain thousands or even tens of thousands of digital models.

Roles on a CG production team

The digital 3D world required for a computer animation movie is generally created by artists who perform specialized roles. Modelers create the 3D geometry for sets, characters, and props. Animators are the actors that make characters move. Lighting artists position and tune the digital light sources. Set dressers make sure each scene looks complete. Layout artists position characters and props on the set, and define how the camera moves around and where it looks. Compositors combine multiple layers of rendered images and effects to create more realistic imagery.

Editors splice the composited shots together and fine-tune the timing of the film. The director makes sure everything fits together and that the final film provides the intended experience to the viewer.

Each sequence and maybe each shot is assigned to a lead artist (sequence lead/shot lead). Each specialty may also have a lead artist assigned to each shot or sequence (lighting lead, lead set dresser, etc.). Primary characters and groups of secondary characters will also have lead animators that stay with the character for the entire duration of the movie.

Some key metrics of digital films

Films are played at the standard rate of 24 frames per second. A 90-minute feature film therefore requires roughly 130,000 frames or images. Changes of camera position or location separate the film into shots; a typical movie will have anything from 1100 to 1500 shots. To make this volume manageable during production and to allocate work to sub-teams, shots are generally grouped into larger units called sequences; a typical movie may have 30–50 sequences.

The production process

Organizing any project with more than 100 staff members is a challenge. For computer animation movies, the challenge is particularly daunting because its digital data is intangible, highly interconnected, and subject to a creative decision-making process.

To organize content production in this complex environment, computer animation film studios have defined elaborate pipelines that describe how and by whom each piece is created, how it is handed off to others that need to work on it, and how everything fits together in the end to produce the movie.

Key challenges

When interviewed about the major challenges they are facing, computer animation studios generally mention:

- *Communication.* Because productions teams are large and schedules are tight, good communication is key. Results of reviews, art packets, change requests, and any other form of communication must be efficient, documented, and accessible. A simple misunderstanding can result in weeks of rework, so clear and referenceable communication accelerates production and saves money.
- *Creative context.* The effort required to model and shade a 3D object can vary considerably; it depends on the required level of detail. An object that appears in a close-up and that interacts with an animated character needs tremendous detail, but the same object appearing somewhere off in the distance could be represented by a simple colored sphere or box. The difference in cost is enormous, so providing context about an object—information on where and how it is used—generates significant savings.
- *Abstraction.* The primary technical challenge for studios is realism, while the primary process challenge is higher productivity. Both must be addressed by allowing artists to work with more powerful tools on a higher level of abstraction. Instead of dealing with thousands of files, they should deal with logical elements like characters, shots, and props. Instead of having to know where each piece of content is, they should be able to jump into their work directly from the logical element they want to work on—everything else must be automatic.

Because computer animation films are highly complex digital projects, there are of course also hundreds of technical challenges with various levels of difficulty to be overcome.

Game development

The state of game development

A few years ago, a small group of friends could make a successful game within a few months. Today, however, game development is an industrial-sized effort, more and more often involving over 100 people working on a single title for years.

The number of assets produced during development has grown exponentially, and that number is still growing fast. Getting an overview of all these assets is hard enough, but communicating about them in a large team setting so that everyone is on the same page seems nearly impossible. In addition, too much time is wasted searching for files, finding out which version is the latest, and determining which files are obsolete.

Most importantly, the traditional unstructured approach to file management is prone to errors, but no one can afford errors, at least not the big ones. Losing a single art file because

Figure 2.7 *Today's games are complex worlds the players can immerse themselves in for weeks. Creating such a product—like* The Movies *from Lionhead Studios seen here—is a colossal effort (© Lionhead Studios. All rights reserved)*

it is overwritten is unfortunate, but losing a week's work of programming can lead to severe and unacceptable delays. In times of tight schedules and demanding publishers, production must be quick and accurate. The results have to be perfect—today's game buyers are not a forgiving audience.

Overview

Numerous disparate roles and an extremely fast pace often lead to chaos in the game development environment. Programmers are pushing the limits of the hardware, and artists are always trying to squeeze more detail into every character or level. Level designers push for more levels, and managers try to bring it all in on time and under budget.

To navigate through this chaos, artists, programmers, designers, and managers need to be able to work as cohesively as possible, using the tools they're familiar with, or with a minimal change in the way they work.

Game design document

Like all art, games start with an idea that must turn into a design and then into reality. A game designer does this by putting together a design document. It describes the basic premise of

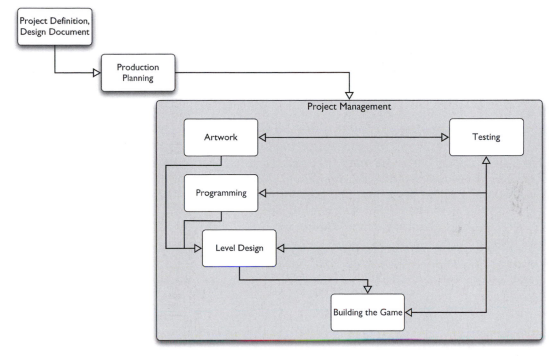

Figure 2.8 *Workflow for producing a computer game*

the game, the characters, the gameplay, the levels or environments through which the character will pass, and anything else that makes the game unique or marketable.

The design document is the first asset of any game. It is important to have it available to every member of the team for reference. It is a good idea to start asset management right away with this first asset. DAM helps maintain the different versions of the texts, sketches, and other conceptual documents in a location accessible to all team members.

Production planning/management
The steps of the production have to be planned carefully in advance. The main challenge is to provide enough time for things not foreseen. In every project there are delays due to illness of team members, loss of data, misunderstandings, change of plans, etc. The better you allow for the unexpected, the more likely it is that the project will finish on budget, in time, at the desired quality.

Communication
Team members are always looking for files. "Where's that lamp?", "Which level are we using?", and so on are questions sent back and forth through e-mail all the time. Providing

an easy method for communication is important. It should not be too formal or complicated on the one hand; ambiguity or lack of documentation should be avoided on the other.

Artwork
Artists create the visual components of the game. Generally it starts with some scribbles by the lead artist and results in visual guidelines that usually become part of the design document.

2D artists create bitmaps that become textures for 3D models or that are mapped as a backdrop or a simple object.

3D artists make models of characters and items in a program like 3D Studio Max or Maya. Often, the work of one artist relies on assets produced by another artist. A character, for example, is first modeled then this model is handed over to rigging, and then might go on to animation. Another artist might prepare the textures.

Game programming
The job of the programmers is to translate the ideas of the game design document into a playable game. They provide all the components like the render/display engine, the physics model, effects, artificial intelligence, network code (game engine), etc., and all the tools necessary.

Level design
The level designers bring all the assets together with the vision described in the game design document and finally build the game. Using the tools game programming provided, they take the finished models, animations and bitmaps, put them into virtual spaces, add sound, and finally script the actions that should take place here.

Review
Reviews are required often during production. For example, a modeler might have to make several versions of a character before finally getting approval to send it on to the next stage in the pipeline. Before the physics library is approved, the developer may want his programming lead to review his code.

Building the game
To check the progress of the game, the lead programmer will do an incremental build. A build lets the team see the exact project status. It might be sent to the publisher or it can be used as a demo.

Testing
The testing department seems to have the fun work: playing the game. But they have a tough job too. They have to find every bug or inconsistency, and they have to report it thoroughly. They provide feedback on whether the game is playable at all and whether it is fun.

All their results go into a database with a concise description of the bugs found, explanations on how to reproduce them, and assessments on how important it is to fix each bug.

Web development

Websites can consist of anything from some simple HTML pages with a few pictures to conglomerations of hundreds of thousands of pages, PDFs, animations, games, videos, or binary files for download. To make them manageable, huge website projects are usually broken down into smaller sub-projects that last from three to six months.

With the tools available today, everyone can create a website. We'll just look at professional companies that have high-quality standards and teams with experienced project managers, information architects, designers, and HTML and script coders.

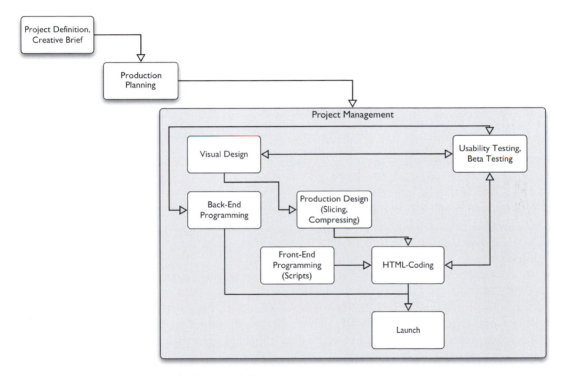

Figure 2.9 *Workflow for producing a website*

Project definition

At the beginning of every professional website development there is an extensive definition phase. Here it is clarified what the goals of the project are, who the target audience is, and what the users should use the site for. Usually there is also some research on competing sites or on sites that can serve as inspiration—or as bad examples.

All the information collected in this phase is usually written down in one or more project definition documents (e.g. the creative brief).

Information architecture

When all the information that should appear on the site is collected, it is structured in a way that is assumed to be understood without problems by the target audience. The structure developed is called the information architecture of the site and is usually laid down in a preliminary site map.

Navigation architecture

The next step is to define the way the user will navigate through the site. For this wire frames, or very simple sketches of the prospective HTML pages, are created. They show only the functional elements of the most important pages. They neither define the design nor the contents of the pages. Usually they are created in a tool like Microsoft Visio, OmniGraffle, or in Illustrator.

Content creation

Now that the overall structure is clear, content can be created. Writers populate the prospective pages with text; they make existing text web-ready by shortening it, writing summaries, sub-headings, and breaking it into screen-readable chunks.

If the site features animations, video, audio, games, or other more elaborate functions, these are also created now.

Visual design

When all content and functions are ready, visual design starts. In some cases this has to be done previously in parallel with the earlier steps because many customers insist on "seeing" how their site will look as early as possible.

It is still common for designers to create their designs in Photoshop. It then has to be recreated in HTML later, usually by an HTML expert. It is more efficient when the designer has enough knowledge of HTML and CSS to create the page designs already as functional prototypes in an HTML editor.

Usability testing

Starting with the development of the information architecture, several techniques of usability engineering are applied. Some future users of the site (or people with similar background, professional roles, etc.) are invited to review different structure proposals, wire frames, layouts, or functional prototypes.

This gives the designers a clue as to how real users will interact with the site. The results are discussed in the team and usually also with the customer. Then modifications are made to better meet the expectations of the users and to improve usability.

Usability tests are conducted again later in the process to test how the pages work in a browser and in a more realistic environment. These results lead to changes that can have an impact on information architecture, navigation architecture, and design, as well as on content.

Production/programming

The final step—which outsiders (and, more often than not, also customers) think is the only step—is producing the final HTML pages by creating/slicing the graphics and coding the HTML.

In this phase programming also takes place, perhaps for shop integration, visitor feedback, forums, personalization, and so on.

Beta testing

Beta testing (also called functional testing) can be brief if the site is small and has only simple, static HTML pages. The more dynamic pages and special features it has to offer though, the more time is needed for testing—and for fixing the bugs found.

This is also the time for a check whether all content is in its correct place and is complete.

Launch and maintenance

When all problems found are (hopefully) fixed, the site is launched. All the final files—HTML pages, images, scripts, files for download—are transferred to the server. Immediately another test is run—you can never be sure that the site works exactly the same way on the final server as on the testing machines.

In professional projects, this is not the end. The site is submitted to search engines and catalogs, and is promoted on- and offline. User feedback from the site is collected and log files of the user's activities are analyzed. Then the site is improved based on this information. Existing content is updated; new content is added. Sooner or later the next relaunch is scheduled, and the entire process starts anew.

3D design

3D design is used today for many different purposes: from architecture and interior design, to industrial design, scientific visualization, advertisements, and art. The workflows in use for 3D design are as diverse as these fields.

A single artist working for a few hours on a 3D model may not benefit much from Digital Asset Management. But if working on this model for a longer time, a DAM system could be a valuable tool, especially if he/she needs to cooperate with another artist. We will look now at a typical workflow in 3D design that can benefit from DAM.

A typical workflow

Since 3D programs are quite complex and it takes a while to construct exactly what you have in mind, most designers start with a sketch on paper or use a digitizing tablet and "paint" into an application like Illustrator or Freehand.

When the designer, the customer, or the art director is happy with the ideas, the designer starts modeling. Each part of the object has to be precisely defined in the 3D program by using base forms like spheres, cubes, cylinders, and so on. These are cut, combined, distorted, or modified coordinate by coordinate. The more complex the object is, the longer this process lasts. That is why most artists use packages of pre-defined models. They choose the basic form from this library as a start and modify it to fit their ideas for the look of the actual object they are shooting for. Often, models from previous projects are used. Another technique is to scan a real object or a model made of clay. This data builds the base for the 3D model constructed and fine-tuned in the application. A 2D image can also be used as a first step, to which the third dimension is "added".

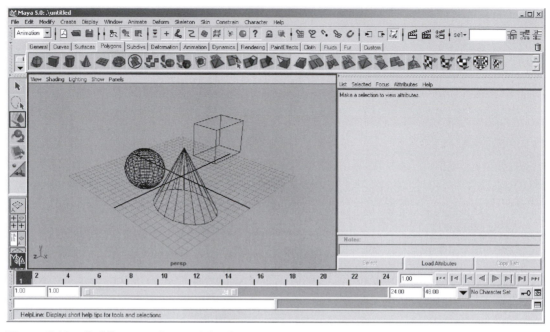

Figure 2.10   *Building complex models often starts with creating the most basic shapes in a 3D program like Alias Maya*

When the model is done, its outer appearance is defined and textures are applied to it. 2D patterns are "wrapped" around different parts of the 3D model to define its surface. Here, artists can also create their own textures or use some from a library.

This process has to be repeated for every object that should appear in the picture. When all of this is ready, a background has to be defined. Then the artist polishes the final look by choosing the "camera angle"—the position from which the virtual scene is seen. More often than not, he or she also defines some light sources that lead to a more realistic looking picture or that can emphasize special parts of some objects.

Finally, the picture is exported as a standard image file like TIFF or BMP. In traditional 3D design, these files are the final product that is handed over to the customer.

Other industries benefitting from DAM

Virtually everyone can benefit from DAM. Even if you work alone and produce just a few text files a week, a simple Digital Asset Management system can help you. This book was written using DAM to keep track of the different versions of the supporting text, chapters and images, and share the files between the authors.

So, it's not a question of whether you are in a industry where DAM can help, but of how to find a solution that is right for you. To do so, take the next step and continue to the next chapter!

3 Assess your individual situation

3.1 Analyze the business—find out where you are

To find out how Digital Asset Management can help your company solve both common and unique problems, you should first examine and take inventory of your current situation.

This section will take you through finding all the information necessary to plan the implementation of a Digital Asset Management system and teach you how to analyze all your business processes that involve assets. This analysis will indicate potential benefits from the introduction of Digital Asset Management and how the resulting success of the system should be measured.

Ask the right questions

Do you know exactly how you manage your assets right now? You may have written guidelines and set up pipelines for handling assets in your teams, but with the hectic pace of today's productions, are these procedures being followed and, more importantly, do they even help significantly? Review your current method of managing assets. Step back and take an honest look at your business from the viewpoint of an outsider. What does this person see?

Still don't have a clear picture? Then try to look at your business from the viewpoint of an asset. How does it come to life? Which people does it see and when, and what do they do with it? Does it see some people several times? Does it eventually get lost, or does it perish in the middle of the process and have to be brought to life again as a consequence? How does it make its way to the client? Does it find its final rest in an archive? Will it stay there forever or can it be found and see daylight again?

TO DO

To get the most out of the following pages, take a moment to write down a brief description of the current asset management situation in your company. Add to it anything else that comes to mind while reading this chapter. Then you'll have the basis for your analysis of the situation—a good starting point.

Existing business processes

Virtually all projects in all industries start with a document written in a word processing application. It defines how the products—and therefore the assets of which it consists—should look, what they are used for, and who should use them. In many ways, a design document for a computer game or a feature film is no different from a document defining a corporate website or the design of a new refrigerator. Sketches, technical drawings, or even prototypes such as physical models or sample code eventually accompany this document.

The roads all these assets travel can vary widely. They might just be stored on the computer of the project manager, and then printed out for the team members and eventually delivered to the client. They can live on a central server where the internal team and outside clients have access to view them. They could even be classified and locked in a secret place. The same is true for all assets in a project.

Usually a project management plan and a schedule are also drafted. Each team member gets his or her assignments. These items are also important assets, so it is important to track and handle them appropriately.

How are your assets created and stored? During the life of the project, assets are produced at different paces. Depending on the nature of the project, just one asset per month or one asset every few minutes could be the norm. What is important is to get reliable figures of the number of assets created by each team member within a given period of time and over the course of the project.

Also be sure to *think about the way the assets find their way into the digital world.* Are they created from scratch digitally, directly? Or are they drawn on paper and scanned later? Transferring data from the analog world into the digital one is often a labor- and cost-intensive process. It is not only the scanning but also the correct cataloging that takes so much time. You have to file the assets in such a way that they can be retrieved later. This can be easy for a simple sketch on paper, but it can take hours for one single videotape because you have to look through all the scenes and provide metadata describing the contents.

Which existing assets should be included in the system? Is it necessary to incorporate assets from projects already finished for reference and/or re-use? This can be quite an expensive undertaking, especially if your assets are not organized in a well-structured manner.

Another crucial question is how communication about the assets occurs. *How do the people in the team know about the assets produced by others, and how is handover organized?* In a very small team, a team member just sticks his head into the next cubicle and says, "Hey, it's done." In larger teams, maybe they use paper-based lists, or the project manager traces the progress of each person's work with a spreadsheet or project management software.

How are your assets published? At the end of the project, the assets may have to be handed over to the client (internal or external) or published in one form or another. This can happen via a network (e-mail, ftp, direct connection, broadcast), on a CD/DVD-ROM, on DVD-video, on a video cassette, or even physically on film or on paper.

How are change requests handled at your company? After the client reviews the results, he or she usually has change requests. These can be communicated over the phone, via e-mail, or in a more automated way, such as by entering all change requests in a database.

How are your finished assets and resources archived? Finally, all finished assets have to be stored. Sometimes they just stay on the computers of each team member or on the server until the end of days. In other cases, they are burned on CD/DVD-ROMs as they are. Seldom are the assets sorted in a way supporting later retrieval and re-use with proper documentation.

Critical success factors for your business

Each business has its own measure of success. A news agency is challenged to be the first to cover a story, while an airplane manufacturer has to focus on quality because no mistakes are tolerable.

In addition, the market niche and the philosophy of the company play an important role. When a company focuses on high-profile products and premier customers, the need for quality is certainly higher than at a company in the low-priced segment of the market, where staying within budget may be the most important factor.

It is crucial to define the so-called showstoppers. Which problems would prevent the delivery or the success of your product?

Value creation

All of the factors that have an influence on the success of the production should be identified. They should be sorted from most to least influential to determine the priorities.

Support for your product after delivery can be an important factor that adds value to your product. For example, if you are a web design agency, being able to react to customer requests for changing things or preparing an asset for publishing in another medium quickly is a competitive advantage and therefore creates value.

Value destruction

All the problems that can destroy value in your business should also be noted. Not managing change requests or not documenting approvals from clients can destroy significant value in your business, for example. It can lead to extra work your company doesn't get paid for in the last phase of a project, which is usually too busy already.

Additionally, the delivery of an application that is not stable can destroy the confidence a customer has in your company.

Cost of processes

The amount of money spent on the various stages of a project can vary widely in different industries, and even from project to project in the same company. The bulk of the budget could be spent on the concept stage, though often development is most expensive. Sometimes even quality assurance, defect correction, and support are the biggest items in the calculation.

Determine where your money goes to find out where trying to reduce costs could create the biggest value.

Example: Business processes in web development—Case study of ProperProduction

Imagine ProperProduction, a small web design agency with two information architects, a project manager, five graphical artists, and three web programmers.

Project definition

When a new project begins, one of the information architects talks to the customer and constructs documents defining the scope of the project. These include a description of the purpose of the website, personas to give the team a picture of the intended audience, and a creative brief. All these are created as Microsoft Word documents and are stored on the computer of the information architect. They are sent to the customer via e-mail and discussed with them mainly on the phone, but partly via e-mail.

Often, one of the graphical artists already starts experimenting with different designs. He does some sketches on paper that he piles on his desk until his desk is too messy and then he puts them all on a shelf in the copier room for storage.

The information architect creates a new file for every revision of each document. He includes the current date in each file name to identify the latest version.

Production planning

Carla, the project manager, sets the budget, creates the schedule, and assigns the team members. All this is done in Word, Excel, and MS Project. Carla stores the files locally on her computer.

When production starts, Louis, the information architect, creates the sitemap in a diagramming tool, usually OmniGraffle. These files stay on his computer. He writes the text or edits existing text for all the pages and decides which graphics and animations should be created. All this is in a Word document, stored on the company server in a folder the project manager, Carla, created. The information architect calls Carla when the document is ready.

Carla then sends these documents to the customer for approval. E-mails are sent back and forth, and phone calls, faxes and letters are exchanged daily during this phase. The paper documents are sorted into a folder sitting on the floor next to Carla's table during production.

Production

The senior graphical artist, Peggy, creates a design in Adobe Photoshop for the layout of the homepage and a few succeeding pages. She stores the files on a Zip disk because she often continues the work she could not finish in the office later at home. She produces color printouts for the presentation to the customer. After a few changes that the customer wanted, Peggy produces the style guide in Illustrator, also saved to her Zip disk. She makes a PDF of this and copies it to the server.

Then, one of ProperProduction's artists creates animations in Macromedia Flash. She saves all the intermediate files locally on her Mac. Just the finished ".swf" files for incorporation in the website are transferred to the server.

Her colleague creates the static graphics in Adobe Photoshop. He also saves only the exported Gif and Jpeg files to the server, and the rest stays on his local disk.

Then, one of the coders assembles the HTML pages in Macromedia Dreamweaver. External style sheets (.css) are used to define the visual properties of the pages. He walks over to the graphical artist every time he starts a new page to ask which files are the newest versions and where they are located on the server. All the HTML pages are saved into a special folder on the server, as well as copies of the picture and animation files.

Finally, the scripting is done for forms processing user input on the HTML pages. The PHP scripts are developed and stored locally. The programmer who has done this loads all the files from the server along with his scripts to the staging area of the HTTP server.

Quality assurance

During production, a contractor conducts usability tests. He sends his findings in the form of a Word document to Carla, the project manager, who summarizes them and discusses the issues with the whole team. She then assigns the necessary changes to the team members. From time to time, she checks the files on the server to see if the changes are complete.

In the meantime, Carla also tests if all the functions planned are included and whether the pages load quickly enough.

Launch

Immediately after the launch, Carla prepares the required accompanying documentation for the customer. She asks Peggy, the senior graphical artist, to complete the style guide so that the client can use it later to extend the site. She has to ask Peggy to copy the text to Word so that she can work with the style guide, since she doesn't have Illustrator on her computer, and doesn't know how to use the program either.

The information architect, Louis, provides a few sentences explaining how new HTML pages should be incorporated in the site structure, how the text should be written, and so on. Finally, Carla compiles a comprehensive document out of these bits and pieces and delivers this as a Word file to the customer via e-mail.

She saves it to the server and copies all the files in the working folders on the server to several CD-ROMs to free hard disk space for an upcoming project. She brings the CD-ROMs to the copier room and places them on the same shelf that has the paper sketches.

Maintenance

After a few weeks, the customer wants to assess the success of the website. He mails the log files to Carla, who feeds them into analysis software. She produces some graphics from this and places them in a Word document. Here she adds her comments and recommendations. The file is saved on her hard disk and sent to the customer via e-mail.

After a few e-mails and some telephone calls, the site is fine-tuned a bit and the team produces more texts, graphics, and HTML pages in the usual manner.

At the end, Carla burns another CD-ROM for the shelf in the copier room with the additional data. She visited the room frequently in the last few days because she had to look for a specific file that one of the teammates needed for her work again and again.

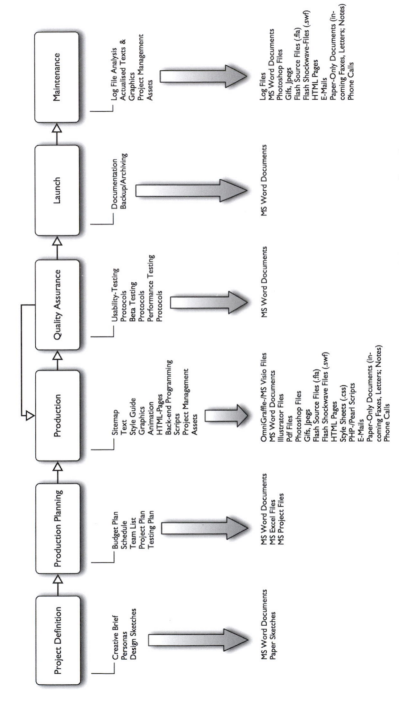

Figure 3.1 *Overview of the stages of a typical project at ProperProduction and the assets produced*

Identification of assets

When Carla steps back and takes a look at the current workflow at ProperProduction, she identifies these assets:

- Project management assets
- MS Project files
- MS Word documents
- MS Excel files
- E-mails
- Paper-only documents (incoming faxes, letters, notes)
- Phone calls
- Information architecture assets
- OmniGraffle/MS Visio files
- Graphical assets
- Paper sketches
- Illustrator files
- PDF files
- Photoshop files
- Gifs, Jpegs
- Flash Source files (.fla)
- Flash Shockwave files (.swf)
- Programming assets/source code files
- HTML pages
- Style Sheets (.css)
- PHP/Pearl scripts
- Log files.

Carla compiles a list of the digital assets produced by her team (see Table 3.1). For analysis purposes, she examines a typical smaller website project that is completed in three months, with 100 HTML pages, 10 Flash animations and some light scripting for forms processing.

Carla finds some surprises: the number of assets is quite high. More than 1200 files are created for a website that consists of only 100 pages. Yet the amount of data is far less that she imagined—roughly 320 MB. That fills only half of a CD-ROM. The main problem is that these 320 MB are spread over so many different locations.

Location of assets

Carla finds that there are at least 13 places where an asset can be located:

- Her hard disk
- Information architect's (Louis) hard disk
- Senior artist's (Peggy) hard disk
- Flash artist's hard disk
- Producing artist's hard disk
- Programmer's hard disk
- LAN server
- Senior artist's (Peggy) Zip disk (*continued on page 53*)

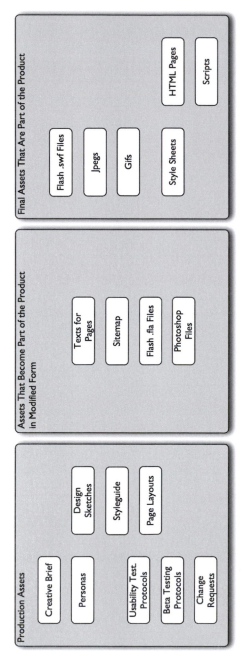

Figure 3.2 *The assets sorted by type (without the mainly project management-related assets)*

Table 3.1 Format, number and size of digital assets produced during a typical project at ProperProduction (numbers and total size include all versions of the documents that are eventually saved; that's why there are 300 HTML pages though the final site has only 100, for example)

	Production assets			Assets that become part of the product in a modified form			Final assets that are part of the product			Total assets	
	Format	Number	Total size (MB)	Format	Number	Total size (MB)	Format	Number	Total size (MB)	Number	Size (MB)
Production manager	Word, Excel, Project, Outlook	500	20							500	20
Information architect	Word	10	10	Word, OmniGraffle/ Visio	15	20				25	30
Senior graphical artist	Illustrator, PDF	15	10							15	10
Animation artist				Flash .fla	50	5	Flash .swf	12	1	62	6
Producing artist				Photoshop	50	250	Gif, Jpeg	250	3	300	253
HTML programmer							HTML, Style Sheets, Scripts	300	4	300	4
Tester	Word	2	0.5							2	0.5
Total										**1204**	**323.5**

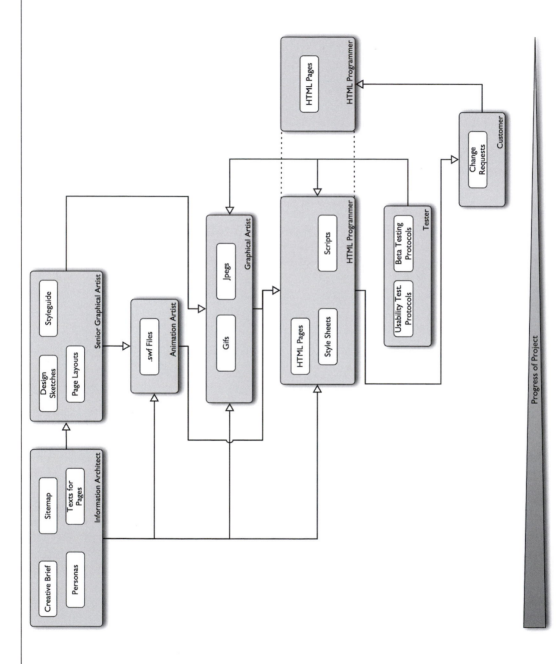

Figure 3.3 *Simplified asset-centric workflow diagram. The focus is on the product (the web pages), so all mainly project management-related assets are omitted*

- Desk of graphical artist
- Bundle of papers on the shelf in copier room
- E-mail system
- Her production folder on the floor
- CD-ROM (several)
- Non-tangible (e.g. phone calls).

Carla spends a lot of her time searching for files, as do all of her co-workers. Now she realizes why this is the case.

Workflow and communication

To get a clearer picture of the workflow, Carla draws a diagram of the workflow at ProperProduction.

To keep it simple, she leaves out all project management-related assets and focuses solely on the assets that are directly connected with the final products, i.e. the web pages (see Figure 3.3).

Carla knows that the communication within the team is quite casual. People mostly talk face to face; sometimes they use e-mail. There is no formal way of labeling the version of which file is most recent. To track the project status she has to gather all the information from the different people all over the office. From time to time, a project finishes late because one of her co-workers had over-estimated the amount of work he already finished.

Success factors

Carla is aware that one of the most critical success factors of ProperProduction is the high visual quality of the websites delivered. The company has won various awards for sites they produced and are therefore hired by customers who demand impressive design.

Carla also identifies reliable planning of production time as important because only two information architects are available to do all the conceptual work. Overlapping of projects should be avoided to prevent overtime and sloppy work. Reliable support after delivery is another one of the competitive advantages of ProperProduction. Because of this, they often get repeat business.

Failing to fix problems with customer websites within hours would destroy trust in the professionalism of ProperProduction. It is also crucial that all websites that are launched run flawlessly on all computers regardless of operating system or browser.

Carla determines that usually the planning stages comprise a quarter of the budget, development half of it, and quality assurance (testing, bug fixing) the remaining quarter.

This example shows that even a comparatively small project like a website with 100 HTML pages produces assets of many different types at many different locations. Here the number of files is not overwhelming, but if you have a closer look you can recognize why work becomes so difficult towards the end of the project, when the number of assets increases exponentially. The bigger the project, the more difficult communication about the assets and asset location becomes.

TO DO

Draw a diagram with the typical project stages in your own firm. Don't include too much detail; it should just give you an overview of your current workflow (take Figure 3.3 as an example). Then compile a table with the formats and numbers of assets created during a typical project at your firm (see Table 3.1).

Who are your users?

So you know what processes you use and which assets are involved. But the final success of every Digital Asset Management system implementation depends mainly on one factor: the people. If your team has the feeling DAM hinders their work or it is too much hassle for too few benefits, they just won't use it. They might even try to work around it.

So get to know your potential users. What is their professional background? How seasoned are they in working with computers? A computer game programmer uses the computer differently than a musician composing the score for a computer-generated movie. If you don't know how all the groups work, go to their offices and (unobtrusively) watch them doing their daily tasks. This exercise can be quite enlightening. Don't judge, just watch.

Keep in mind that the better the DAM system fits their habits, the faster the time to get up to speed and the greater the acceptance by the team.

At this stage, you should also count how many people are working on a project at each stage and in which teams to see what phases of the production could use the most help and which roles you might search out targeted features for.

Which platforms do you work on?

Compile a list of all the platforms your team works on. Don't forget freelancers, external contractors, or clients that should have access to your system too. Count how many machines you have running each platform. Then project how many there will be in five years. You should plan assuming the success and growth rate you'd like to attain!

Example: Team and platforms in computer game development— Case study of GreatGames, Inc.

GreatGames, Inc. is a mid-size game developer that produces a game every two years. They usually work on only one or two titles at a time. They have a basic production staff of project managers, graphical artists, and programmers. For other roles, they hire freelancers or outsource tasks completely.

Gil, the CEO of GreatGames, compiles a list of all the people on his payroll. He adds all the other people that had access to the firm's LAN in the last two years (see Table 3.2).

Table 3.2 *People and platforms involved in a typical project at GreatGames*

Position/role	People	Processor/platform
Project manager	2	1.7 GHz, Win XP
Graphical leader	1	2.8 GHz, Win XP
2D graphical artists	12	1.8 GHz Dual, Macintosh OS X 2 GHz Dual, Macintosh OS X
3D graphical artists	13	2 GHz Dual, Macintosh OS X 2.8 GHz Dual, Win XP 3 GHz, Win XP 3.2 GHz Dual, Win XP
Programmer	15	2.8 GHz, Win XP 2.8 GHz Dual, Win XP 3 GHz, Win XP
Level designer	5	2.8 GHz, Win XP
Sound designer	2 (freelancer)	1.8 GHz Dual, Macintosh OS X
Tester	5 (freelancer)	2.8 GHz, Win XP 2.8 GHz Dual, Win XP (and others)
Administrator	1	3.4 GHz Dual, Linux
Customer (publisher)	6	1.2 GHz, Win 2000 2 GHz Dual, Win XP (and others)

Gil notes that there are 49 computers permanently in the LAN, excluding his own and the computers of the administrative staff. Additionally, there were up to seven more machines in the LAN for a certain time—the computers of the freelancers. Furthermore, some of the publisher's computers are online sporadically via a dial-up connection for downloading press material and review packages.

The platform is mainly Windows XP, but some Mac OS X computers are also in use. Only the central server runs on Linux. The customer still uses Windows 2000 on some machines that are used rarely to access data on GreatGames' LAN.

For his company, Gil projects a 25 percent increase in turnover in the next three years. That means he has to plan for twice as many computers for the next five years to be on the safe side. Additionally, he has to take into account that the volume of data will increase drastically from year to year as the computing power of the average gamer will make more detail possible, and the gamers will demand it.

3.2 Define desired improvements—find out where to go

Now that you've closely analyzed the way you've been working up till now, you can identify the sour spots. Where are the most glaring problems in terms of asset management? What would you get out of fixing these?

Another good source of this information is to talk to the project leads of the different departments—for example, the lead programmer, the lead artist, and the project manager. They usually have a clear picture of what goes wrong and therefore what is most important to improve. They also need this experience to feel involved in the process of selecting a DAM system; this feeling is essential so that they back the DAM system's introduction in your company later.

Post-mortem meetings are also great opportunities to gain insight. When projects end, teams often discuss what they did and didn't do well during the specific project. Everyone is invited to criticize, but also point out positive things (it's usually the job of the moderator to keep a balance). It's good to get this feedback when thoughts are still fresh, and it makes a strong case for aspects of the DAM you propose when you have recent evidence as justification.

Think of saving money, increasing output, improving quality, and reducing error rates. Have a look back at Section 2.3 to get further ideas. Don't forget the intangible results like productivity boosts, more fun at work, and fewer conflicts in the team due to misunderstandings. Define targets that the implementation of the DAM system should achieve, both tangible (financial/quantitative) and intangible (qualitative). Ideally, focus on measurable targets.

Example: Desired improvements of asset management in web development—Case study of ProperProduction

Carla, the project manager at ProperProduction, compiled all the required information on how she and her colleagues currently work. She knows which assets are produced, where they are stored, and how communication about them occurs. She also listed the typical problems that occur in virtually every project.

Now she's able to make a list of the desired improvements Digital Asset Management should bring to ProperProduction:

- Better documentation of communication with customers
- Easy access to all conceptual documents for the whole team
- Simplified sharing of assets
- No more rework due to overwritten or lost files
- Better overview of project status
- Easy creation of prototypes for review and testing
- Documentation of change requests
- Reliable backups
- No more going to the copier room on the hunt for previous versions.

Carla imagines that working would be so much easier if all these wishes came true. This could result in:

- Fewer misunderstandings
- Less overtime because of recreating items that were lost
- No more team conflicts over overwritten files

- Better morale due to the feeling of working with a well-functioning system and workflow
- Fewer battles with customers about change requests
- Less work for her because of instant retrieval of assets.

With the help of DAM, Carla thinks she can regain the nearly-forgotten feeling she had on her first project long ago: that she is on top of things!

3.3 Analyze value of desired result—find out what you gain

To know whether it is worth it, find out what you will gain from the effort of introducing Digital Asset Management in your company. This is for your own benefit (before you jump into implementation), and also helps you secure support for your project—both from the decision makers and from the production team.

As a first step, look at the problems you found out in your analysis of a typical production. You've already got your list with all the ideas for improving existing processes or introducing new processes through Digital Asset Management in your company. Together with the project leads, sort these desired improvements into descending order, with the improvements that seem most valuable to you on top.

Describe what consequences are possible for each problem that is not solved. On the flip side, describe what you could gain if each desired improvement could be realized. For quantitative/tangible targets, include also an assessment of how much time or money could be saved, if possible. You can even calculate dollar values (for a discussion of the drawbacks and limits of such calculations, see Chapter 2, Section 2.8). Don't spend too much time on the details though—an educated guess is probably enough. For qualitative targets, define the importance to your business (proposed categories: critical, very beneficial, useful, somewhat relevant).

With this list in hand, you are immune to becoming overwhelmed by the many promises made by DAM system manufacturers. It is easy to get impressed by all the features they have to offer and start thinking, "Wouldn't it be nice if we had that?" But you can check your list to make sure you buy only features that can bring you a real value. Quite often, a smaller solution is enough—and it usually costs less to purchase, is easier to set up and maintain, and is faster to learn to use.

Example: Value of desired result of asset management in computer game development—Case study of GreatGames, Inc.

Gil, CEO of GreatGames, is sure he needs to introduce DAM in his company to stay competitive. In general, he is happy with the quality of the games they produce, but he feels there is still much room for improvement. In the last few weeks of every project, everything's too hectic and some cool features always get dropped because time is running out. Also, the teams are exhausted after two or three months of long evenings and weekends spent in the office.

Gil calls David (the lead artist), Charles (the lead programmer), and Elisa (one of the project managers) up to his office. Gil talks to them about what went right and what went wrong in their latest game production. Then they compile this list of desired improvements together:

- Easy access to all conceptual documents for the whole team
- Finding files faster
- Simplified sharing of assets
- Simplified communication in the team
- Unified system for e-mail and internal communication
- No more rework due to overwritten or lost files
- Better overview of project status
- Easy creation of beta versions for approval and testing
- Documentation of change requests/bug report and fixes
- Reliable backups.

As a next step, Gil, David, Charles, and Elisa sort these possible improvements, listing the most valuable things first. They write down what would be the consequence if these problems remain. Finally, they assess what value each of the desired improvements would bring. You can see their result in Table 3.3.

Table 3.3　*Prioritized list of possible improvements and consequences of realizing or not realizing these for GreatGames*

Desired improvement	Consequence of not having it	Value of having it
No more rework due to overwritten or lost files	Wasted time; frustration	Critical (around 6 h time saved per person and month)
Documentation of change requests/bug report and fixes	Bugs in end product	Critical
Reliable backups	Several days of lost work	Critical
Finding files faster	Wasted time; frustration	Very beneficial (around 1 h time saving per person and week)
Easy creation of beta versions for approval and testing	Wasted time; difficulties of tracking what was in prototypes later	Very beneficial (around 5 person-days saved per version)
Easy access to all conceptual documents for the whole team	Misunderstandings, possibly rework due to this	Useful
Simplified sharing of assets	Recreation of things already there	Useful
Simplified communication in the team	Misunderstandings; team conflicts	Useful
Better overview of project status	Discovering late that deadline can't be met	Useful
Unified system for e-mail and internal communication	Having to maintain two systems	Somewhat relevant

With this list, Gil now has a solid reason to believe that Digital Asset Management will in fact bring many valuable benefits for GreatGames. He feels confident that he will convince the board to make an investment in a DAM system soon.

In the previous example, the list of benefits is purposefully short enough to be applicable to as many companies as possible. It makes sense to include more details relevant to your specific situation.

Also think of possibilities for improving cooperation with your customers, integrating the work of external contributors/freelancers, integrating data input, adding publishing solutions to the workflow, and so on.

TO DO

List your desired improvements. Then try to assess what it will cost you not to implement them, and conversely the value that implementing them provides, just like in the example above.

Now you know exactly why it is worth continuing with your search for the best DAM solution for your company. Now, read on and plan what you need.

4 Plan what you need

4.1 What is your business objective?

In the last chapter you determined which areas of your production could improve with the introduction of Digital Asset Management. In this chapter, we'll compile a comprehensive list of all the features you need to make it happen!

The features you truly need depend highly on your business and on the way you work. From a business objective standpoint, there are four basic methods of working with assets:

1 Archiving and retrieval
2 Collaboration
3 Publication
4 E-commerce.

Table 4.1 *Basic types of working with assets*

	Workflow	Number of people typically involved in creation	Number of people typically accessing an asset at the same time	Examples
Archiving and retrieval	Linear	1–3	1	Photographers, illustrators
Collaboration	Parallel	5–50	2–20	Game development, 3D design, animation
Publication	Sequential	10–100	10–100,000	Websites, papers, magazines
E-commerce	Linear	1–20	100–100,000	Web stores (shops, picture catalogs)

Archiving and retrieval

In a photographer's or illustrator's studio, the workflow is linear: the asset is created and then fed into a library or an archive. The image might need a bit of color correction after that, or maybe the drawing ought to be cropped to remove the coffee stains it got during the last meeting, but typically there is not much additional work, and what there is usually can be done in one quick step. One important thing to do, though, is to provide relevant metadata—like keywords about what you can see in the image, the date, the artist's name, etc. This metadata has to be entered when the asset is ingested into the archive. Skipping this step is like throwing a single straw into a barn filled with piles of straw—the asset will never be found again.

If you have this type of workflow, usually only one person accesses one asset at a time.

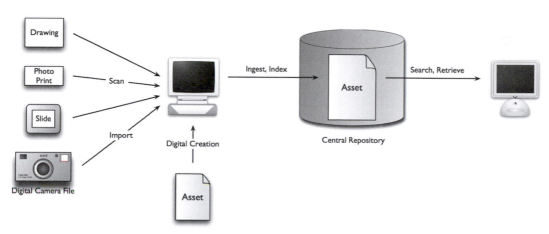

Figure 4.1 *Asset-centric workflow diagram for archiving and retrieval*

Collaboration

When working, for example, with complex animated 3D models, collaboration is very important. Usually many people use the assets at the same time, and teams are big. The assets are often handed back and forth. For example, if a character cannot be animated in a natural way, it has to be modified by the artist responsible for rigging (defining the joints of the model's skeleton). Maybe he or she even has to hand the asset back to the modeler who created the basic shapes that make up the model. Then the corrected model passes back through the production pipeline to be approved. In the process, maybe even the person responsible for the outer appearance of the model (skin and textures) has to modify his work also.

But once the project is complete, the assets are seldom accessed—asset re-use is still rare in most companies that do 3D design and animation, as well as in computer game development.

Publication

In the publication business there are many people working on one paper, magazine or website, but usually they can work quite independently. A copywriter writes an article and

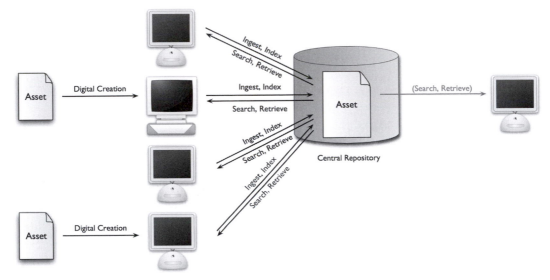

Figure 4.2 *Asset-centric workflow diagram for collaboration*

sends it to the editor. The editor makes his corrections and sends it to the editor-in-chief. The editor-in-chief approves the article and sets the publication date.

In parallel, a photographer or an illustrator works on the graphical part of the article. Once they are done, an editor approves their work.

If the publication is to be printed or if no content management system is used, usually a designer does the layout of the article.

Once the publication is online, the number of people accessing the assets at the same time can be tremendous. But the potential for conflict is low because they only view, and don't change, the assets.

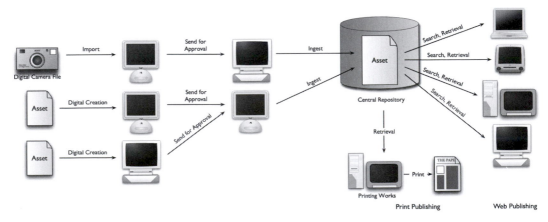

Figure 4.3 *Asset-centric workflow diagram for publication*

E-commerce

For the implementation of an e-commerce site, typically only a few people are needed. The workflow is linear, although for bigger sites it can be similar to the sequential publication workflow.

The number of people accessing the items on e-commerce sites at the same time can vary—from one to hundreds of thousands.

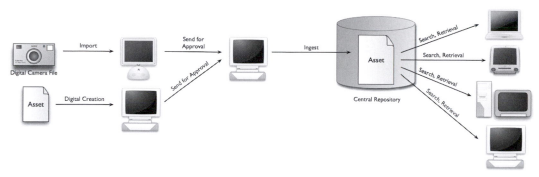

Figure 4.4   *Asset-centric workflow diagram for e-commerce*

Summary of workflow types

It is not unusual if you find more than one workflow in your company. If you work in a blue-chip firm, it is even the norm. There you need archiving and retrieval of product shots and marketing collateral. You need collaboration features for working out product specifications and other document management features. More often than not, you will also need to publish in the form of websites, brochures, advertisements, catalogs, and so on. In some cases you will even set up e-commerce as well.

Every firm and every project is different. If you think none of the above workflows accurately describes the way you work, no problem. They can just prompt you to think about how Digital Asset Management can improve your own workflow and at what exact points you want DAM to assist you.

In any case, no matter whether you are a one-person firm or an international corporation, the two most important questions you have to ask yourself are:

1 Do you want the system to just archive your assets and make it easy to find them?

   or

2 Do you want the system to help you during production?

If you want DAM for archiving and retrieval only, implementing it will be fairly easy and fast—at least if you know the common pitfalls (which you will discover in the following chapters). But most people researching what DAM has to offer also want to at least explore the options available for improving the production workflow by implementing a DAM system.

To determine what makes sense for your company, let's look first at the two most important things: your assets and your users.

4.2   What do your assets want?

As a start, look at what your assets need:

File formats

Which formats do you use? Most common are:

- JPEG, GIF, PNG, RAW, TIFF (which color models? RGB, CMYK, L*a*b*)
- EPS, PDF
- Photoshop (PSD)
- Illustrator (AI)/Freehand(FH)
- MOV, MPEG, AVI, DV
- AIFF, WAV, MP3
- 3DS, DXF, MAX, MB
- QXD, INDD
- TXT, RTF, DOC, XLS, SXW.

On the one hand, the more flexible your software is in supporting different formats the better. On the other hand, you should avoid using too many formats to make handling and exchange as easy as possible. Always use industry-standard formats and avoid exotic or outdated formats to make sure the assets can be used in the future without time-consuming conversion. Formats not appearing above should be converted into one of the listed formats if possible.

Number of assets

You already estimated the number of assets created per year and their size in the last chapter. Now find out how many assets from previous projects you will need to add to the archive, if you want to build one. Also note their average size.

Number of parallel projects

Another important issue is the numbers of projects that you are working on in parallel. It makes sense to isolate the assets of each project, but to run all asset management through one system.

Quality—resolution, compression and sample rate

Think about which resolution your image files should have. Some years ago, 800×600 pixels were more than enough for a picture used only on the screen. But with the development of

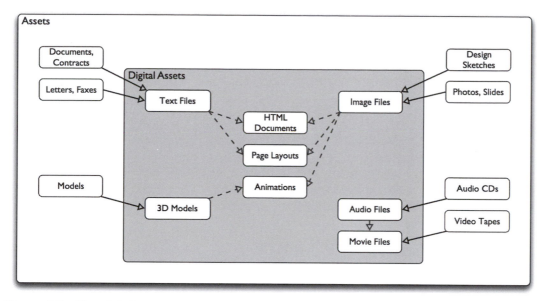

Figure 4.5 *Non-digital assets become digital assets (lines) and may be incorporated into other digital assets (dotted lines)*

bigger and better screens, this is no longer enough. Think of HDTV and print. Is the resolution you are working with today enough for the future?

How much compression do you use? Uncompressed files provide the best possible quality, but lead to extremely large file sizes. You have to find the right compromise—but don't settle for too low quality. If you learn years later that the quality of your files is too low to be used, some of your investment in the DAM system was a waste of money.

If you want to include audio or video, you have to decide which sample rates and which compression you want to keep, similar to the compromise you have to make between quality and size.

Linked files

One major issue to keep in mind is the handling of files with links. Files with links are quite common: HTML documents, page layout program files, 3D model files, and animation files usually have links to other files. If the links have an absolute path, moving them results in broken links that often can't be fixed automatically. There is also the danger that the linked files are not archived. Or, if you have several links to the same file, it is archived several times, which wastes storage capacity, leads to unnecessary network traffic, and can cause confusion when one of the files is changed but the others remain unchanged. The system you choose should address these problems if you have linked files.

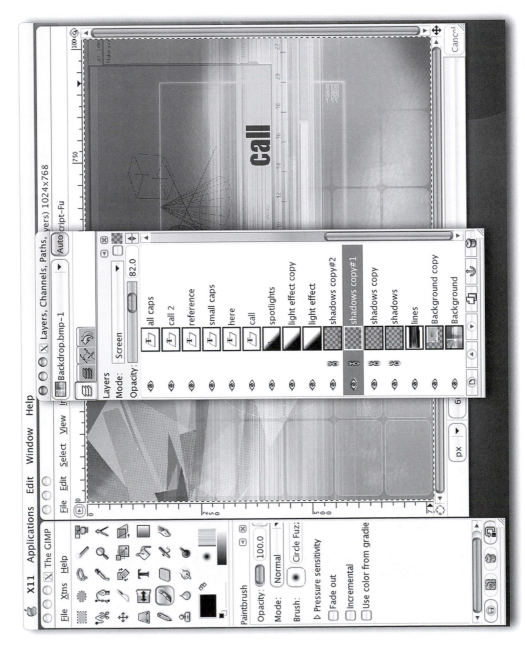

Figure 4.6 *Photoshop and other design software packages like GIMP (shown here) allow the use of hundreds of layers to compose an image. Even the artist who created the work gets lost here once in a while*

Working versions

Do you want to keep all working versions? All designers create several different versions of their artwork, but usually only one version is used in the end. It makes sense to archive these versions if you want to go back to a previous version later, or the artist wants to recycle an unused version into another project.

If the artists work with a program like Adobe Photoshop, they use several layers to compose each image. This way, it is possible to modify the image later without too much work—for example, to exchange the photo of a person or to correct text that is part of the image file. It definitely makes sense to keep these layered documents and not just the final image file (which is called "flattened" because all layers are reduced to one).

Similar questions arise when you are working with audio and video. Do you need all the raw footage or just the finished films?

Keep in mind that archiving all working versions can increase the amount of data from twofold to tenfold or even more. And retrieving assets from a big repository is always slower for the machines and the users because they have to look through more assets to find the right one.

Change of assets

How often do the assets in the archive change? Do they stay in the database forever or will they be modified? Which version should be kept then? Should all the changes be documented?

Example: Projected number of files and volume for website production—Case study of ProperProduction

Carla, the project manager of the web design firm ProperProduction, looks at the table of file formats and number of assets created during a typical project she compiled earlier (see Chapter 3, "Example: Business processes in web development"). She tries to think of the future formats they might use and adds them to the table. She also enters values for how many different versions of files it is reasonable to keep.

Then she tries to assess how much production volume will increase in the next five years. She feels this is the minimum time for which any system they might buy should be able to handle the volume of data their company creates.

For this, she introduces a growth factor, which indicates how many fold the number of assets increase in five years due to growing project size and to a higher number of employees. Then she sums up the values for the number of assets created in each project and the total size in megabytes. She finds out that both will increase approximately tenfold in the next five years. For each project, there will be about 14,000 files, totaling more than 3 GB (see Table 4.2).

The table Carla compiled was only for one project. But ProperProduction has about six projects each year, with at least two projects running at the same time. This means that the volume of data a Digital

Table 4.2 *Format, number, and size of digital assets produced during a typical project at ProperProduction—today and projected for five years later*

	Today			In five years				
	Formats in use	Number of assets	Total size (MB)	Future formats	Average number of versions to keep of each asset	Growth factor over five years	Number of assets	Total size (MB)
Production manager	.doc, .xls, .mpp	500	20	.sxw, .sxc	3	2	3000	120
Information architect	.doc, .outline, .vsd	25	30		6	2	300	360
Senior graphical artist	.ai, .pdf	15	10	.svg	6	3	270	180
Animation artist	.fla, .swf	62	6	.svg	10	5	3100	300
Production designer	.psd, .gif, .jpg	300	253	.xcf, .png	2	4	2400	2024
HTML coder/ programmer	.html, .css, .js, .cgi	300	4	.xml, .wml	4	4	4800	64
Tester	.doc	2	0.5	.sxw	2	2	8	2
Total		**1204**	**323.5**				**13,878**	**3050**

Table 4.3 *File formats, linking, modification frequency, and potential for file re-use at ProperProduction*

	Formats in use	Linking of files	Modification during production	Potential for re-use
Production manager	.doc, .xls, .mpp	None to low	Seldom	Low
Information architect	.doc, .outline, .vsd	None	Seldom	Low
Senior graphical artist	.ai, .pdf	Low	Not too frequent	Low to medium
Animation artist	.fla, .swf	Medium to high	Often	Medium to high
Production designer	.psd, .gif, .jpg	Medium to high	Often	Medium
HTML coder/ programmer	.html, .css, .js, .cgi	High	Often	Low
Tester	.doc	None	Never	None

Asset Management system used for production has to deal with is double the values indicated in the table. For archiving, it has to handle the sixfold values each year.

Carla is aware that this calculation is shaky since it is based only on her personal assumptions. If her company grows much faster, these numbers will be too small. She will have to discuss these figures with her boss; maybe he has some plans she doesn't know about yet. Also, if new file formats are added that increase the data volume considerably, her projections will be wrong. For example, if it becomes common to have large video files on the websites they produce, these numbers will be obsolete. But she thinks that her educated guess is better than jumping ahead blindly.

As a next step, Carla rates how much the file types in use rely on linking to other files, how often they are modified during production, and how much potential they have for re-use (see Table 4.3).

With all this information at hand, she feels she knows her assets well enough to take the next step—finding out what her co-workers need to handle these assets better.

Of course, it is difficult to make assumptions about your company's future growth and the evolution of the industry, or predictions regarding file formats and end-user or client demands. But who could do it better than you? You know your company, you know your business, and you know your plans.

TO DO

Take the table with the formats and numbers of assets you create during a typical project, which you compiled in the last chapter. Now it is time to decide what you will need in the future.

Write down additional file formats, resolution, number of working versions you want to keep, and file size. It might also be a good idea to note usage of linked files and frequency of asset changes.

4.3   What do your users want?

In recent years most Digital Asset Management solutions implemented were content management solutions for managing websites. One reason why so many of these implementations failed is that nobody talked to the intended users before buying the software solution. Don't repeat this mistake when introducing DAM in your company. Ask the people who will work with the system day to day. Talk to team leaders, hold workshops, and/or do a survey to increase the chances that you will get them something they want to use.

How many users do you have?

Note how many users are working in your company right now. Project ahead and estimate the numbers in five years. How many of these people will work on a project in parallel? How many will access the same asset at the same time?

What is their experience?

What experience and expectations do your users have? A seasoned page designer has more computer skills than a typical temporary worker entering data. A graphical artist has different expectations than a hardcore programmer.

Respect egos

Many software implementers in mid-sized to big companies find that often there are some users that just don't like the system. They keep complaining that it is inflexible and hinders their natural way of working. But as soon as they feel involved in the evaluation process, know that they have the ability to set options or customize new software, and really understand how the basics work, they can become its most ardent supporters. The changes can be small—sometimes it is even enough to modify the shape and color of some menu elements according to their proposals.

This might sound funny, but it happens more often that you would expect. Just try to understand the psyche a bit. The users are the experts, so they know best how to do their work. If a boss just shoves a new solution at them which they have to work with, but which they have no influence over, they will feel misunderstood and resentful.

Sometimes a system is even loved by its operators *because* it is so inflexible and so hard to use. It took the users a long time to learn how to use it and they know things many of their colleagues don't know. They can impress others by hacking a few lines of cryptic code using a keyboard attached to a monochrome terminal and getting an equally cryptic result, which they can easily interpret. It reminds them of when computers were wardrobe-sized boxes housed in large rooms without windows, often in the building's basement. Everyone just whispered there; the main source of noise was the humming of the huge air conditioner. Serious-looking men wearing white coats operated these computers and accepted calculations only if given to them on the proper forms. They handed over the results to you on a printout some days later, giving you the feeling of receiving a holy gift.

This time seems long gone, but some of the essence of it still remains today. Sure, the command line makes doing certain things easy—that is why programmers love it. Some file operations are done in an instant when using a graphical interface for this would take much longer. But another important angle to consider is that knowing how to do this operation with a command line tool by typing some hard-to-memorize commands makes you different; it makes you part of a group of insiders. It's the same as a Photoshop wizard impressing bystanders by switching tools, opening inspectors, changing settings, clicking here and there with enormous speed, and presenting an impressive picture seconds later.

Some of these artists even use keystrokes to invoke certain operations, which makes it impossible for you to see exactly what they are doing. This is where programmers and artists are similar—they both use hard-to-follow actions to work faster—but neither group likes to acknowledge this common ground.

In conclusion, when you are implementing a DAM system, try to respect the egos of the prospective users. Involve them as early as possible. Consult them when considering starting the evaluation phase. Ask them what they think would be good to change, and what their personal preferences are. This gives you valuable feedback, and it provides the additional effect that the team feels involved, which will help in securing their support.

Inform them about the progress of your DAM implementation project and let them know the reasons for your decisions. Explain at every step what you did and why. For example, if you decide not to further pursue examining a DAM software one of the prospective users suggested buying, make clear why it is not suitable. This might seem like too much time and effort, but it is definitely worth it. It's no use having the best system if the team is reluctant to use it.

4.4 What your new workflow should look like

In the previous chapter we looked briefly at the current workflow in your own company. Now we'll examine it in more detail to find out how it should be ideally. This helps you to streamline production by making processes less error-prone and more efficient.

TO DO

Take the overview of your current workflow you created in the previous chapter. With the help of the following suggestions, discover how it could be improved and write down your ideas.

DAM software can drastically change the way you work for the better—but don't let the software dictate your workflow. The software should be flexible enough that it can be adapted to your optimum workflow, yet enhance it.

Remember, asset management is more than software; it is about the entire process. As a first step, identify what you like about your workflow. What has proven to be effective?

As a second step, identify what you don't like. Where do problems arise often? Which parts seem too slow or error-prone?

Do a bit of research on best practices in your industry; maybe ask friends at other companies how things work there. How do they handle their assets? Also take a look at the Appendices in this book for further information on how others work.

Questions you should ask

How are the assets incorporated into the system? Are they created digitally? Or are they first created on paper and then scanned? And when is it done, is it possible to do it earlier to enable version control from the start and provide easy access to all team members? Does it make sense to have special machines to digitize the files—for example, a scanner with automatic document feed? Could it be useful to have OCR (optical character recognition) to convert them into text documents?

Is it necessary to include metadata describing the assets for later retrieval? Who creates the metadata now? Could this be done by someone else who can do it faster or who has a lower hourly wage? Is there a way to automate this process? (Usually there is not; automatically generated metadata is often close to useless—whatever vendors might tell you. Test these features extensively with your real assets if you plan to use them.)

Collaboration

Do the users work together on the creation of the assets or can they work independently? How much communication is necessary, and how does it take place at the moment? Is it documented in any way? How do they hand over the assets to each other?

Think how communication could be improved. Sometimes it is enough to introduce simple rules or guidelines. Sometimes new systems like instant messenger, intranet forums or the like could do the job. And sometimes it is just a matter of enforcing discipline to make sure nothing gets lost in the process of communication.

If your workflow is complex, it might be useful to have a DAM system that supports tracking progress and making approval and hand-over easy. But keep in mind that such features sometimes seem appealing only to the project manager—the people who have to use it daily might find it cumbersome to manually edit status data for every single file they work on. But if the feature really saves them time, they will readily adopt it.

How often are assets retrieved?

How often an asset is needed can vary greatly. For example, during the development of a product dummy in industrial design, the sketches and design studies are accessed frequently for reference. The textures and models for the creation of the different parts of the dummy are

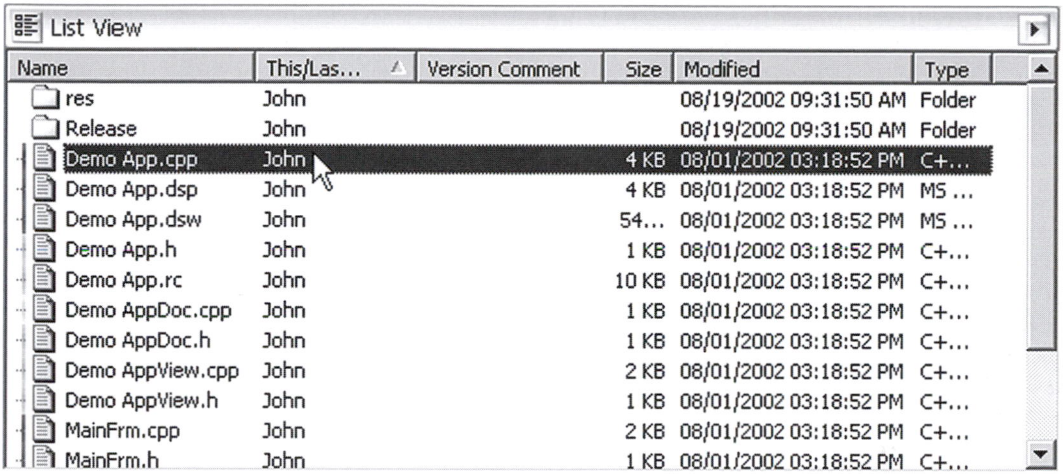

List View						
Name	This/Las... △	Version Comment	Size	Modified	Type	
res	John			08/19/2002 09:31:50 AM	Folder	
Release	John			08/19/2002 09:31:50 AM	Folder	
Demo App.cpp	John		4 KB	08/01/2002 03:18:52 PM	C+...	
Demo App.dsp	John		4 KB	08/01/2002 03:18:52 PM	MS ...	
Demo App.dsw	John		54...	08/01/2002 03:18:52 PM	MS ...	
Demo App.h	John		1 KB	08/01/2002 03:18:52 PM	C+...	
Demo App.rc	John		10 KB	08/01/2002 03:18:52 PM	C+...	
Demo AppDoc.cpp	John		1 KB	08/01/2002 03:18:52 PM	C+...	
Demo AppDoc.h	John		1 KB	08/01/2002 03:18:52 PM	C+...	
Demo AppView.cpp	John		2 KB	08/01/2002 03:18:52 PM	C+...	
Demo AppView.h	John		1 KB	08/01/2002 03:18:52 PM	C+...	
MainFrm.cpp	John		2 KB	08/01/2002 03:18:52 PM	C+...	
MainFrm.h	John		1 KB	08/01/2002 03:18:52 PM	C+...	

Figure 4.7 *Some DAM solutions offer workflow support. Here you see a directory view in Alienbrain, where the files are marked with a color bar at the left side to indicate their status*

modified on a daily basis. But when the project is finished, the assets will probably be accessed only a few times, if at all.

In contrast, the assets in a stock photo website are accessed regularly over the years, but there are no such phases of intensive access of particular items.

You might think of ways to ensure that an asset is changed as little as possible. This reduces search time and the potential for errors.

How do your users search?

How does a user search for an asset? Which queries does he enter if there is already a search tool? How often do users search? How much expertise and experience do users have in searching? How long does it take? How could it be improved? Maybe thumbnails or other preview tools would do the trick. Maybe a complex combination of search criteria would help. Or maybe the search operation simply should be faster because people spend too much time waiting for the system to run a complete search.

Determine the search functions needed

The more assets you have in your archive, the better your search functions should be. One important factor is response time. Another key factor is how well the search functions help the users find the assets. There are several approaches to this problem:

Browsing
Browsing through an electronic catalog of assets often makes sense when you are looking for a non-specific asset (for example, the image of a tree, but you don't have a particular one in

mind). This is effective only if your assets are categorized so that the user doesn't have to go through too many pages and if only the relevant results are given.

Full text search

If you search for information in text documents or databases, full text search is an option. It requires a lot of expertise to compile search phrases that find the needed item and don't bring up too many irrelevant results. The greater the amount of texts, the more difficult searching becomes with full text search.

Keyword search

Keyword search is often the most effective search, but it depends mainly on the quality of the metadata entered when the asset came into the system. Only if metadata is complete and concise can the asset be retrieved. Without good metadata, the assets are close to useless because they cannot be found again.

Phonetic searching

There are systems that try to find certain phrases in audio or video files based on the phonetics of the phrase. This makes it possible to search for files that have no metadata. The quality of the results varies. These systems are expected to improve in the future with the progress in algorithms and computing power, but in the next few years this method certainly can't compete with good metadata entered by a human.

Visual searching

For photos, there are systems that find photos similar to a selected one by comparing colors and shapes using the search function.

Analogous to phonetic searching, there are systems that try to filter out certain key visuals from video. This technique is still under development, and in the next few years it will mainly help in finding sequences, cuts, and shapes. However, in the near future, these systems may help find content in long videos lacking manually entered metadata.

Printed catalogs

In some cases you will also need to publish printed matter. If you publish a printed version of the asset catalog or a part of it, you will need a system that supports assets with different image resolutions and/or can export the data in a way that best fits your print workflow. Also examine how cooperation with external contractors like the print shop could be improved. Do you still send out CD/DVD-ROMs? Do you manually select the files that should be transferred and upload them on the printer's server by hand?

Simplify the workflow

Trying to simplify the workflow is usually the most successful plan of attack. Are there double cycles that can be avoided? Is it necessary to let a manager approve every single asset, or can they be submitted all at once as a package? Or maybe the person who created an asset can decide for himself whether it is OK.

Is the workflow iterative in review and rework cycles? Who is involved in these? Is this the most effective pipeline or can it be simplified? Perhaps it makes sense to limit the number of rework cycles by default to avoid so-called "gold plating"—the phenomenon that an asset or feature is polished over and over, adding little to the overall quality of the product.

TO DO

Finally, write down how your new workflow should look. You can find sample diagrams for inspiration in this book:

- For web design, in Chapter 3 (Figure 3.3, page 52)
- For game production, in Chapter 2 (Figure 2.8, page 37)
- For 3D animation, in this Chapter (Figure 4.8, page 77).

Our diagrams are quite general in order to fit as many firms as possible, but try to make yours more specific for your company. It is also a good idea to include the names of the people who handle the assets—or at least their job titles.

After you create this diagram, you'll be able to check it easily against the workflows that different systems support, as presented in the next chapter.

Integration with existing software

If you already own software that has to work in combination with the DAM system, decide how the systems should work together. Do you just need certain data imported when you start using the DAM system? Or do you want to synchronize data with other applications/databases on a regular basis? Do you have custom programs that should integrate with your new solution?

In game production, for example, it is quite common to have proprietary tools that are created for a particular project. They make the team members' lives easier by running batch processing or applying certain manipulation to the assets—perhaps transforming images into a special format the game engine in use needs. Make sure that the DAM system you choose integrates with such tools if you use them, or if you might want to use any in the future. The sales engineers at the vendors should assist you in determining if their systems can be customized to handle these special requirements.

Digital Rights Management (DRM)

If you sell your assets, you probably need Digital Rights Management support. It makes sure that only users who have purchased permission to access the assets can do so. Such a system should handle these permissions and also the payment for the usage of the assets.

Maybe you want to automatically include watermarks in the preview versions of your pictures or video, or you want to create low-resolution samples of your pictures. In other cases, maybe you need 30-second low-quality clips of your songs. Think of all the features you need in place to let users access what they want in the format they want without expending much effort on the company's part for each transaction.

For example, Getty Images, one of the world's biggest stock libraries for photos and video, uses a DAM system (Artesia Teams) to provide via the Web a fully searchable database of digital assets containing more than two million images and 80,000 video clips—and they add about 2000 new assets per week. Of course, usually you won't have eight million visits to your website every month like Getty Images, and it is unlikely that you need to deliver two billion thumbnails per month. But even if you are a photographer and just want to provide access to the images you made yourself, the use of a DAM system is imperative to provide fast and easy access, ensure that no one uses your assets in a way which is not intended by you, and save you several hours a week of converting, saving, and sending images around.

Keep the intellectual property rights of others in mind; you might have to secure permission to use their assets. For example, maybe you bought the right to use a video clip from a stock footage library in a certain production. The file is probably still sitting somewhere in your system. But everyone should be aware that re-using it would mean that you have to purchase the license again. If not, time-consuming rework might be necessary when this point is discovered and the material has to be replaced, or even worse, you get a legal notice when the library finds out you used their footage without permission. Therefore, consider how a DAM system can support you in managing permissions if you use outside assets frequently.

Example: The new workflow for animation film production— Case study of ProperPictures

Richard, one of the project managers at ProperPictures, was asked to investigate how DAM could help end chaos during production. He analyzes their workflow and concludes that, in general, their workflow is not far from that of other, even bigger, companies in the field of animation film.

He does notice, however, that Sven, the art director, could do better than his habit of scribbling his first drafts and ideas, and the storyboard of a new film, on random materials and leaving them scattered around; this is not industry standard. Sven will at least have to get used to scanning his drafts and ingesting them into the DAM system they plan to implement so that they are accessible to everyone in the team.

The review and approval procedure in general is OK. Each asset should be presented to Sven and then forwarded to the next person who needs it for his or her work, if any. But during the hectic end phase of the production, Sven sees too many assets for the first time when they are already part of a finished scene. This should change with the help of DAM.

What Richard also plans to do is introduce regular status meetings to make sure he always has an overview of what is finished and signed off. He plans to hold these meetings during the core production phase every Tuesday morning, standing at the bistro tables in the cafeteria to keep them brief.

Richard decides that they don't have to change too much—he just needs to find a DAM system that suits the needs of ProperPictures and gives their animation studio the maximum benefits.

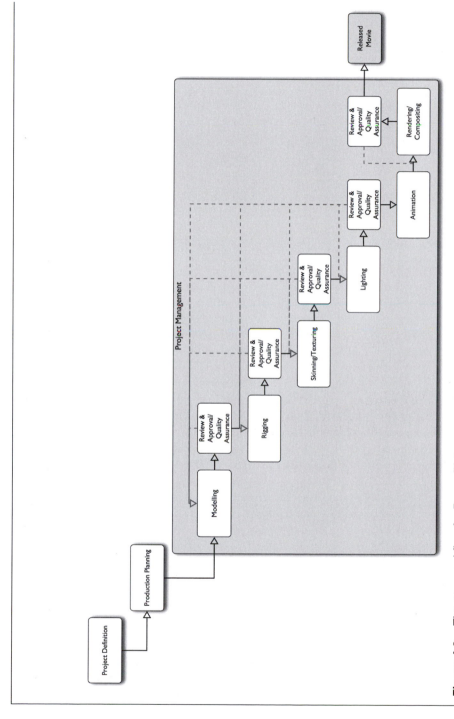

Figure 4.8 *The new workflow for ProperPictures*

4.5   Compile a list of features needed

If you have a clear picture of what you need to improve and how you want your procedures and workflow to run, compile a list of the general functionalities you expect from the Digital Asset Management solution and which features you need.

Next, you'll find a list of key asset management areas, from which you can choose what your system should include.

Centralized storage

Leaving data scattered across multiple user workstations is bad practice. Any team with three or more members should put their data on a central server with access for everyone (even if it is one of the user's workstations) and make sure everything is backed up every day.

A central repository means the content is easier to find because it is in one known place. The content is accessible even if the author is not, and all users can get to the content without interrupting the author.

Backup and archiving

If you have centralized storage, all content is assured to be backed up. So if the hard disk of a user workstation crashes, very little or no work is lost. Archiving also becomes much easier because you have everything in one place. Some DAM solutions also support a wide variety of media for archiving—from CD/DVD-ROMs to magneto-optical discs, data tape, and robot-operated tape libraries.

Another important issue is what should be archived when the project is finished. A good DAM system helps you avoid duplicate files or gumming up the system with files that are no longer used. But what should you do with all the different versions? Does it make sense to archive them all, even if they contain basically the same content with only minimal changes?

You can choose to archive only the latest revision of all files. In most cases these are the only ones that will be needed once the project is finished. But in some cases you will want to recover older versions, and so to archive them all you will need miles of backup tape or large amounts of other storage media.

There are systems which decrease storage capacity greatly by saving only the differences between the versions of each asset, and not the whole file each time it is saved. Because there are usually only small changes, this method can reduce the storage space needed significantly. The drawback is that if the base file is ever broken, the revisions can't be restored either.

Metadata classification and search functions

To make retrieval simple or in some cases just possible, it is essential to tag the assets with metadata. This doesn't seem so important in the production phase, but it's crucial when you're trying to find a file a few months after the end of the project.

Thumbnail generation for image and video files can be one of the most useful search features, and overall features, of a DAM solution. When you have so many images, the time it takes to open several when hunting for a certain picture can add up to an enormous waste of time during the project. The display of thumbnails should be as flexible as possible to best fit the way each team member works. For example, it can be of great value if the program can display two versions of a file next to each other to make comparison easy.

Figure 4.9 *Comparison of two versions of a file in Alienbrain*

The more you archive, the better your search functions should be. They can be very basic, as in Explorer or Finder, or they can be elaborate and allow complex searches with a combination of arbitrary criteria. Saving searches can also be a valuable feature in these cases.

Automatic conversions

Automatic conversions can save a chunk of time and money. If the DAM system is able to convert any asset to any common format on the fly, the need for a person to perform this dull and repetitive job is obsolete. Additionally, you save storage space since you don't have to store a single file in several different resolutions.

An important factor to consider here, though, is that the conversion has to be fast. If it slows down the whole system when someone is retrieving a sizeable file that is yet to be converted, it can hinder production speeds instead of speeding them up.

Catalogs and publishing

The automatic generation of catalogs is one of the biggest time savers, if you publish them in any form on a regular basis. The DAM system just dumps the pictures and texts you select using certain criteria into pre-defined layouts. Editing the result, however, should be an option since you usually need to fine-tune the look.

The automatic generation of catalogs is not only interesting if you are in the publishing business. It can be handy to have a catalog with all the assets created last week for a team meeting, for example.

If you also publish on the Web, a DAM system with Content Management capabilities can do a lot of work for you by generating HTML pages using templates.

Local sandboxes

To provide change isolation, each user moves files to their local sandbox (sometimes called workspace) before editing them. That means that the users copy the files they want to edit and the dependent files to their local hard disks and edit the copies to test the changes they want to make.

This ensures that the files on the server are never changed in a way that breaks other files that rely on them. Each user can experiment and can easily revert to the previous version if they want to. Only when they verify that their changes are OK do they commit them to the server. It is also possible to restrict the commit option to only one person—for example, the project leader. This is an additional security measure to make sure only tested assets find their way into the central repository.

Check-in and check-out

To avoid access collisions, file locking is used. In combination with local sandboxes, this adds up to check-in and check-out functionality. Digital Asset Management systems that focus on production conveniently combine these two steps into a single operation.

This is the single most important feature to prevent overwriting other people's work. The system makes clear that a file is checked out and may not be modified until it is checked in again.

Version control

Through the check-in operation, backup versions are automatically generated on the server. A Production Asset Management system handles this transparently for the user. Just decide how many old versions you want to keep, but remember that they can take up vast amounts of storage space in a short time.

One of the main results is the ability to roll back to a previous version quickly. This is extremely useful if a change had severe consequences that are discovered much later.

Labels

A feature especially useful for long-term projects is labeling. It allows you to tag all or some assets as being part of a set at a certain time. For example, if you create a preview version for your customer, you can label all files that are part of this version with "Preview March". If the customer comments on this version in May, you know which assets in exactly which state the customer has seen, even if development has progressed much further by now.

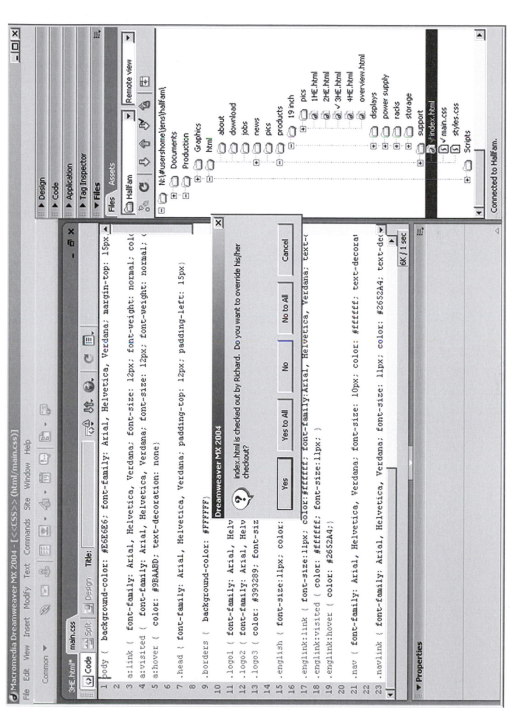

Figure 4.10 *A basic tool like the HTML editor Macromedia Dreamweaver also provides check-in and check-out to make sure team members do not overwrite each other's work*

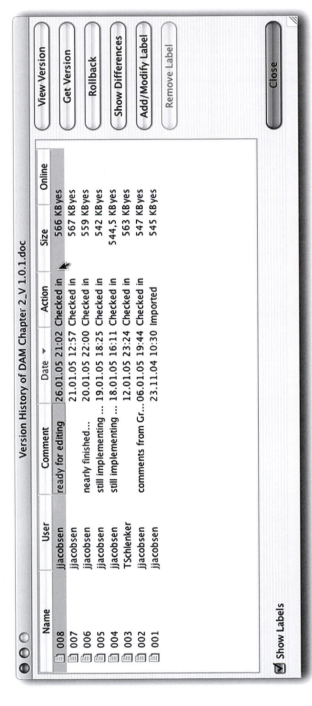

Figure 4.11 *Version history in Alienbrain. Here you see all the versions of the file, when they were checked in on the server, who did it, and the user's comment*

Configurations

To handle different configurations for different languages, standard and professional versions, etc., configuration management is used. A DAM system offering this feature keeps track of all the files that are specific for a particular configuration and makes collecting all required files easy and virtually error free; forgetting files or including incorrect language versions doesn't happen.

Branching

In programming, when you need to work on two versions of the same part of a project in parallel, you "branch" the main code. This means that two (or more) developer groups work on independent copies of the main project so that development is faster. Later you have to merge the branches to get the work from all groups combined into one final product. Luckily for programmers, this can often be done automatically for code.

Change sets

Change sets report all the changes that were made to a project's files to accomplish a specific task. For example, one change set can describe the adjustments made for a feature request from the client, while another change set describes corrections done to fix a bug.

Reference management

Linked files can be a headache to track. If you use HTML documents, page layout program files, 3D model files, or animation files extensively, your system should help you with this task to avoid inconsistencies and/or missing files, as well as orphan files with no references to them.

Change request/bug tracking

Virtually no file remains unchanged after someone other than the creator looks at it. The art director wants an image altered, the programming head wants a change of the functions, the beta testers found a bug, or the client wants a variation of the implemented functionality.

Usually these change requests and bug reports pile up rapidly and it is difficult to keep track of them. If this happens in your projects, a production-focused Digital Asset Management system can offer a bug tracking function to help you out. This feature is most valuable if you develop complex products like computer games or websites that include a lot of scripting or Java applets. The system can even be made accessible to external testers or clients so you no longer need to transfer their bug reports manually from e-mails.

Messaging/notification

How do you notify your co-workers about changes? Is your current mode of communication the best productivity-wise? You should use a formal and reliable way of communication once your projects become sizeable. E-mail and instant messenger are good, but some DAM systems provide tools that make referencing and linking files in messages simple to ease communication.

Example: The features needed for animation film production— Case study of ProperPictures

Richard, one of ProperPictures' project managers, reckons the most important DAM features for his firm are:

1 Ensuring that *no files are overwritten*
2 Keeping *old versions*
3 Providing a way to *get a quick overview* of what is ready and what still needs work.

Richard thinks that *labeling* would be a big advantage. If he could mark assets as "test", he wouldn't be afraid that they would accidentally be used in rendering and someone would have to spend hours re-rendering the entire scene.

If the DAM system could also support *tracking of references* for all files, it would be clear which files are co-dependent. This way the team wouldn't agree to make changes which are much more work than estimated because the implications were not clear. Therefore, Richard thinks this feature should also be provided.

He favors a DAM software that has *workflow features*, which could significantly streamline production. The software should enable each team member to mark an asset as finished and to automatically forward it to his or her leader for approval. If it's rejected, a notice should be sent back to the team member along with the reviewer's comments or requests. When it is finally approved, it should be forwarded automatically to the next person who needs the asset. This would ensure that no time is lost because items that are not approved are included in a scene, which then has to be changed and re-rendered.

Richard concludes that these features are the most relevant for his company. He is open to experimenting with other features a DAM system might bring, but the ones described above are the most important in his mind. So he's ready for the next step: looking at what the systems on the market have to offer.

Of course, what Richard at ProperPictures concludes is based on his particular needs—the most valuable DAM features will vary from company to company depending not only on your products and on the way you work, but also on the systems you already have in place. For example, if you already have a bug tracking system that all team members are happy with, you might be better off sticking to it and using it in parallel with your new DAM system. Or you might be able to integrate the two systems.

However, in any case, clarify what you need most before you start looking at all the DAM system features. It is all too easy to get lost in the huge feature lists, the impressive marketing collateral, and the many buzzwords used when you don't have a clear target.

TO DO

Write down the features that you think are essential, the features that could be beneficial, and the features that are just nice to have.

4.6   Other important features of asset management systems

Performance

Poor performance can be a major hurdle in the acceptance of a Digital Asset Management system. Users will work with it every day, so it should not give them the feeling of hindering their productivity. The performance depends on the hardware, the DAM software, and on the volume of network traffic your work results in. Also think about what happens when the access is via WLAN or the Internet.

Make sure the solution you consider installing is tested with the number of users and the amount of data that are typical for your projects.

Extensibility

If you rely on custom tools, which are common in the games industry, the system you implement must support the option to integrate with your own custom tools. It should allow scripting actions to accomplish tedious tasks like converting files into a special custom format, combining certain files, or adding information to a batch of files automatically with the click of a button.

Scalability

It should be possible to extend the DAM system later to support your company's growth. Your workforce will most likely increase, the projects will last longer, more projects will be run in parallel, and/or the number and size of files will increase.

Make sure the system can grow with you.

Reliability

Any system needs to run reliably. That means stable software, but also predictable administration, strong support, and assistance in finding solutions when unforeseen problems occur.

Check up on the vendor of the system you are considering installing. Since when has it been on the market? What do its users say? Ask friends, colleagues, visit conferences, and read newsgroups.

What impression do you get from their support? Do they offer to build special features for you?

Ease of use

Usability is a major consideration. The amount of time users need to become accustomed to a system can add up to a huge loss of efficiency, which has an impact if you often have to train new users or if some of the users are not very experienced. Also, less user-friendly systems lead to more mistakes and lower acceptance of the DAM solution.

Don't rely solely on your own gut feeling. Show some prospective users the prospective system and let them try some tasks. Observe them doing this and ask them their opinion of the program afterwards. Were they able to accomplish the tasks without error? How fast did the system seem to them, and how fast was the operation actually? Did they like the program? What did they think was missing?

4.7   The most important consideration: focus

Based on your research of how much benefit you will get from each of the DAM system components (Chapter 3), prioritize desired features according to their strategic value. Determine the three to five changes that add the most value; this is what you should focus on during implementation. Decide what to implement now, what to implement later, and what not to implement at all.

Avoid "gold plating"; don't try to find the most comprehensive solution ever, but the solution that will bring the most to your company with the least overall effort.

5 Find the right solution

5.1 Types of DAM solutions

In this chapter, we will take a look at the DAM systems on the market. It should give you an overview that will enable you to narrow down the vast number of different programs to a few that fit your needs. You can evaluate these as a next step to get a good basis for your final decision.

Many vendors claim that their software offers Digital Asset Management, but what each vendor defines as DAM varies widely. As a comparison, a simple text-editing program such as Notepad or Wordpad might be considered a word processing application, although it is nowhere close in functionality to applications such as Microsoft Word. With Digital Asset Management this is a bit different, and almost opposite—Windows or Macintosh file systems can be considered DAM solutions, but usually aren't labeled as such. There are, in fact, quite a lot of applications that are not categorized as DAM but offer DAM functionality nevertheless. Image libraries, for example, usually aren't filed under that category, but they clearly are DAM solutions.

For an overview of the different types of DAM solutions, see Chapter 2, Section 2.5. Now we will look at the scale of different DAM solutions.

In the first part of this chapter, the systems are differentiated by the number of users they support. In the second part, they are differentiated by their complexity and their capabilities. The most commonly used category names will be explained here. Finally, in the third part of this chapter, three sample scenarios with typical use cases for the application of DAM are considered:

1 An advertising agency introducing an image library
2 A web agency introducing an image catalog and an SCM tool
3 An animation studio introducing a Production AM system.

Single-user solutions

Single-user solutions are the operating system's file systems and basic programs like iPhoto, iView Media Pro, or ThumbsPlus for image files. They can only manage a fairly small number of pictures (hundreds to thousands of assets) and remain usable, quick, and reliable.

Most of these solutions specialize in handling images and other rich media files, but there are also simple version control programs like Aladdin FlashBack or RCS.

Single-user solutions can be implemented even for larger companies if there is only one person managing the assets. They don't provide teamwork features and are subject to manipulation and data loss due to mistakes in operation.

On the other hand, these solutions are not expensive—from freeware to about $100 (US). They are easy to install and maintain and it is easy to learn to use them.

Workgroup solutions

Workgroup solutions store all assets on a central server. This makes access control, centralized backup, and sharing possible and easy. Such solutions can be repositories that simply archive the assets, but often they also have more or less advanced features for version control. They keep track of the changes made to the assets and offer the possibility to retrieve older versions later.

For archiving there is the option to use offline storage like CD-ROM, DVD-ROM, or tape backups to free up space on the server.

Most solutions in this category are media libraries like Portfolio Server and Cumulus. They store media assets, enable simple ingestion into the system, provide powerful search functions, metadata entry, and export of custom catalogs.

Costs start around $10,000 (US) for a 20-user license.

Process-oriented workgroup solutions

Some workgroup solutions offer features for collaboration. For example, they might allow the project manager to assign, prioritize, and track tasks. Communication between the team members is supported as well as tracing an asset's history over the course of the project. Here, Digital Asset Management becomes Production Asset Management.

This is especially useful if your workflow requires tight collaboration. For example, for a CG feature film, an artist may draw on paper a sketch of an animal stalking in the woods. The sketch is given to a modeler, who creates a clay model of the animal, which is scanned with a 3D scanner. With this as a foundation, a 3D designer creates the digital wire frame of the animal and hands it over to the texture designer. The texture designer creates the fur and gives his textures, together with the 3D model, to an animator. The animator creates the movements of the animal and finally hands his animation to the sequence director, who places the moving animal in the woods (which were created in parallel by another team of artists). In most steps of this workflow there are sequences of approvals, change requests, and corrections.

Even if your workflow is not so complicated, you can benefit from Production Asset Management features—the more people that are involved, the more the management functionality of such a system can be leveraged.

Software can greatly simplify such a process. Your workflow is normally quite specific for the industry you are working in. The best bet is to choose a solution that is already used by other companies similar to yours. Be sure to examine closely whether the collaboration features the software offers fit your own workflow though.

Examples of such systems that help improve workflow are Avid Alienbrain, Picdar Media Mogul, or North Plains TeleScope. The disadvantages of systems like these are that they need high-speed networks, high-performance hardware, huge amounts of storage capacity, and that they demand higher costs to set up and maintain them. Last but not least, these systems can be 10–50 times more expensive than plain catalog/library systems.

In recent years, production management features like simple version control also appeared in more basic programs like image catalogs. This trend is expected to gain momentum, so we will see more and more of these functions in low-price software in the next few years.

Enterprise solutions

Enterprise solutions are systems that manage all kinds of assets in a whole enterprise, often with offices scattered around the world. Thousands of users access such systems every day for a broad variety of purposes. Attorneys review agreements, accountants work on spreadsheets, managers edit reports, quality assurance staff write checklists, human resources managers provide promotion guidelines, designers create brochures, and so on—virtually all assets can be managed by such systems.

Often, the wish to provide consistency in the promotional and marketing collateral is the starting point for introducing DAM in big companies. There are stories of blue-chip companies that found out that there were 29 different versions of their logo used for the vast amount of brochures, ads, catalogs, and films. Or they discovered that the same picture was bought several times from a photo agency by different departments for use in the same company.

A Digital Asset Management system can be a great repository and a means of communication for all the employees, external contractors, and agencies working with assets or creating assets for the company.

However, managing these files is often only the start. Soon the companies realize the benefits of DAM and decide to introduce it also for documents, reports, spreadsheets, contracts, and much more. Sometimes all assets in the enterprise are managed by one single DAM system. The manufacturers of such solutions expanded their products to meet the demands of their customers over the years, so today they offer an overwhelming number of features.

Examples of such enterprise solutions are Artesia Teams and Documentum. The software costs for such solutions start at around a quarter of a million US dollars and can easily add up to more than a million. The cost of implementing and maintaining such a big system is also a major factor. You have to cooperate closely with the vendor or hire a consultant for this task. But it is worth the effort if you truly need such a solution—remember all the advantages that will overall save much money and lead to better results, described in Chapter 2.

E-commerce solutions
E-commerce solutions comprise a special subcategory. They have to serve thousands of users at the same time, provide the customers the information they want, and process their orders.

If the assets themselves are sold to the users—for example, images, music, videos, or software—the system has also to provide the possibility for the customer to receive the assets bought.

Such solutions are complex, and they have to work closely with banks, manufacturers, storage facilities, logistics, customer relationship management, and many more facilities. They are far beyond the scope of this book, so for this reason we will not look at them in greater detail.

5.2   Complexity and capabilities of the solutions

The complexity of Digital Asset Management solutions varies greatly. To provide an overview, the following section contains a short description of the different flavors of DAM that are on the market today. This will help you determine where to research further to find the system that suits your needs. See Appendix 1 for a detailed description of the most important products.

Unfortunately, the terms and definitions out there can be quite confusing. There are no commonly agreed upon lines that separate the different flavors of DAM. Some of this is due to the similarity of features the solutions offer, and some to the manufacturer's marketing, which is always trying to find flashy or cutting-edge names and to claim that their solution

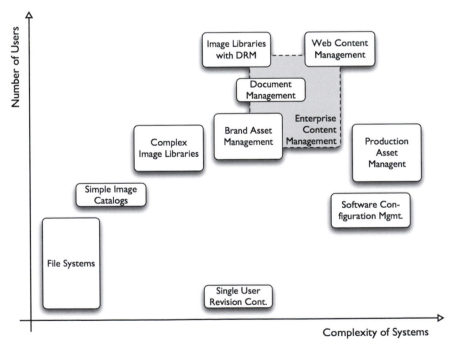

Figure 5.1   *The different DAM systems, their complexity, and the number of users they allow*

offers all the features their customers can think of. To complicate matters even more, most manufacturers acquired other companies to add features that their software did not have to offer. For example, Documentum purchased Bulldog and Interwoven acquired MediaBin to improve their software's capabilities to manage media assets. Expect this trend to continue in the future.

File systems

File systems like those of Mac OS (HFS+), Windows (NTFS), or Linux (UFS, EXT3, ReiserFS, to name just a few) only work as the most basic asset management when a real person does most of the management part. The feature set is quite limited; they just save the assets and provide some fundamental metadata, like creation and modification date. This means that if you want to use file systems for DAM you need clear rules, virtually error-free working, and great discipline of all the team members. A file system is the DAM that everyone automatically starts with.

Pros

- The most flexible system.
- Virtually no installation effort except for the user rights management.
- No additional software costs and low maintenance costs during normal production.
- High performance and compatibility with virtually every system.
- For really large files, like several gigabyte raw video data, this is often the only option, since most systems are not designed for files of this size (files this big do not get lost easily anyway).

Cons

- Works only if everyone follows the rules.
- Offers no or only very limited features for backup, retrieval, workflow management, or archiving.
- Version control features are completely lacking.
- Costs can spiral if files are lost or mixed up.
- Control of access rights is possible but lacks flexibility and needs a lot of work to maintain.

Image catalogs and libraries

There are two types of such systems for image management: simple catalogs and real libraries. Catalogs are additional tools to retrieve and sort files in the file system. They provide thumbnails, metadata features like categories or keywords, creation of different sets (collections/albums), and export features. Some also offer automated archiving and backup. Examples of this software category are iPhoto, iView Media Pro, and ThumbsPlus. They

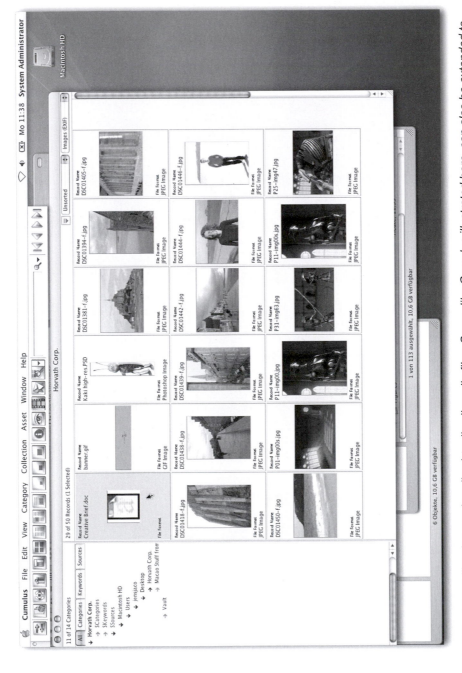

Figure 5.2 *Image libraries can handle virtually all media files. Some, like Cumulus illustrated here, can also be extended to manage other assets like Word or Excel documents*

basically just offer you a catalog including a list of your assets and directions for where to locate them.

The other category these kinds of systems fall into is image libraries. Libraries not only manage *references* as catalogs do, they also manage the asset *files*, so they can control who is allowed to look at certain assets, who can import assets, and who may modify or delete them. Additionally, they have all the same features as a simple catalog. The best-known product in this field is Cumulus.

The use of the terms "catalogs" and "libraries" is not consistent, so it is always necessary to have a closer look at any system bearing one of these two names to know what it really does.

In nearly every company, managers starting to think about the problems that arise with file systems as the underlying software of DAM come up with the idea of using a library system. These work in a way familiar to everyone—you put in assets and retrieve them when you need them. A printed catalog works in a similar fashion, the same way as any basic catalog from the system in the local public library to a phone directory on the web works.

Pros

- Easy installation; not much training is required for the users.
- Software costs are quite low to moderate, depending on the solution's scope.
- The ideal solution for photographers, illustrators, and all others that don't work for a long period on a single asset or cooperate while working on a single file.

Cons

- Catalogs that are based on the file system provide no access control and security features for the actual asset files.
- Most image catalog/library systems offer no features for workflow management, collaboration, or versioning.
- It is often difficult to implement more powerful features later on such a system. Some have a scripting interface but usually you are limited, and switching to another system is necessary if you want certain advanced DAM options.

Brand Asset Management (BAM)

Brand Asset Management (BAM) systems are intended for multinational companies that need to share assets in branches over countries or continents. Usually these assets are logos, pictures, videos, drawings, product descriptions, marketing texts, press releases, and so on.

Brand Asset Management systems put the main focus on managing the assets that determine the reception of the company's brands—like logos, fonts, advertisements, and other marketing-related assets. If the focus is more on managing assets like contracts, reports, spreadsheets, and product data, it is usually called Document Management (see the next section).

Artesia Teams is the best-known product for Brand Asset Management, but note that many other tools can be used for this purpose.

Pros

- Security features are paramount here. The systems allow for exact administration of access rights.
- These systems make sure a company uses the same marketing collateral, product information, and CI all over the world. Therefore, nearly all blue-chip companies in the world use them.

Cons

- Installation and maintenance costs can be enormous (but usually the benefits justify spending this money because they amortize within months or a few years).
- In most cases some training is needed.

Document Management (DM)

Document Management (DM) is closely related to Brand Asset Management. The difference is that mainly business assets rather than media assets are managed. As the name implies, it is mainly about documents—reports, spreadsheets, calculations, minutes, contracts, legal documents, and so on. DM is one of the oldest categories in the field—early in the 1980s companies started to ingest non-digital data like letters and faxes into their computer systems and had to keep track of these and the increasing numbers of documents created digitally. Collaboration features, access control, and archiving are among the most important features in this category.

Such systems are used in traditional non-media enterprises from middle-sized companies to world leaders in fields from insurance to pharmaceutical companies, to governmental agencies. The best-known product for Document Management is Documentum.

Pros

- A system to manage all of your documents with the highest security.
- All legal requirements are met (archiving, restriction of changing some documents if necessary for the record, usage of international standards or formats required by laws).

Cons

- Same as for Brand Asset Management.
- Features for managing media assets are mostly quite limited.

Web Content Management (WCM)

Web Content Management (WCM) evolved when websites grew bigger and more complex at the end of the 1990s. It allows companies to maintain large sites, keep them up to date, and automate the publication of texts, pictures, and other media. The main idea behind WCM is to separate content and its representation. This is achieved by managing content (mostly text) in a database and filling it into pre-defined templates to generate the HTML pages seen by the user. The content can be filled into several different templates to allow personalization or for display on different devices, such as standard web browsers, PDAs, and cell phones.

Such systems also support publication workflow with features like automated notification of changes, review and approval management, and automated archiving.

Examples of WCM solutions are RedDot CMS and Imperia.

Pros

- Makes publication easy.
- Gives the control of the content of a website back to the people responsible for the content, and takes it away from IT staff and designers.
- Prevents offline time and outdated content.

Cons

- Pages maintained by a WCM system tend to appear all the same.
- Innovative design and special features are limited by such a system, although this becomes better from year to year.
- Sometimes people use creative workarounds—which in turn can endanger the integrity of the system. WCM focuses on content, not on files, so the management of assets is often rudimentary. Today, handling of images, audio, video, and PDF files is supported, but versioning features are mostly missing.

Enterprise Content Management (ECM)

The distinction between Brand Asset Management, Document Management, and Web Content Management is close to impossible to discern. The reason for this is that they all manage assets and that large corporations tend to stick to a software system once they have made the decision to have one. Also, the manufacturers continue to expand the scope of their DAM solutions to find more ways to help their customers—and to win new ones.

To make things even more complicated, the term Enterprise Content Management (ECM) became fashionable to describe systems that offer features of Document Management, Brand Asset Management, and often also provide some Web Content Management functionality.

Because discrimination between these systems is so difficult, it is better to have a close look at the actual functionality than at the name with which the system is sold.

Enterprise Content Management is intended for big corporations that have to deal with a lot of files, want to manage all their assets with one system, publish catalogs, newsletters, ads and the like, and that maintain a large website and perhaps an intranet.

Vendors who label their products as ECM are Interwoven and Vignette.

Pros

- Compared to the effort of introduction and maintenance of three separate systems for brand assets, documents, and the website, there is tremendous potential for cost savings.
- Ideally, every single digital file in all branches all over the world is accessible to anyone who needs it regardless of location, when it is needed, and over which system.

Cons

- Such a system is extremely complex and therefore its introduction can take years, block the everyday work of many employees, and require several consultants to work in the company for a long time.
- It is nearly impossible to test the system under real-life conditions because it involves several thousands of people.

Single-user Revision Control

Revision Control or Version Control is the management of file iterations to keep track of the changes that are made to them. Revision Control systems came up in programming when projects became so complex that it was difficult to keep track of which changes were made when and for what reason. If there is more than one person working on the code, Revision Control becomes imperative to avoid conflicts. But even when working alone, it can help when the project is large in hunting down bugs or comparing different versions. It enables you to fix bugs in a release version of your software and work on the new features for the next version at the same time.

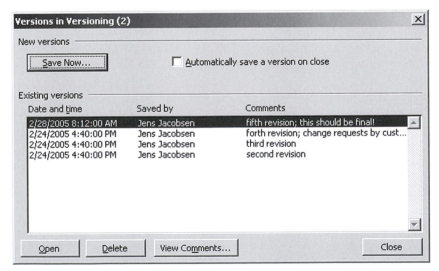

Figure 5.3   *Even Microsoft Word offers simple version control. Here all the revisions are stored in the .doc file itself*

Most Revision Control systems even allow developers to work not only on the same project, but also on the same file at the same time. This, of course, is only possible with file formats that can be merged together later on. In the case of source code, this is often quite easy since the files have a clear structure and are human readable. Revision Control applications can do this because the system does not store the complete file every time you save it. Instead, it notes who you are, tracks everything you change, and when you did it, and saves only the changes made in increments. Thus it is very easy to find out which changes were made to each file simply by looking at the differences stored by the system.

The Revision Control System (RCS) is best known for Single-user Revision Control. Software like Concurrent Versions System (CVS) or Subversion can also be used for this.

Pros

- Helps keep track of changes and prevents overwriting files or losing old versions.
- Makes bug tracking easier.
- Most software is available at no cost.

Cons

- Revision Control systems are comfortable to use only for source code or, with some restrictions, for text.
- The interface of these tools is the command line and no one other than a programmer will use its cryptic commands naturally. Although there are graphical interfaces for these programs, they are also designed for programmers and require some effort to get used to.
- In most cases the single-user approach is not appropriate today.

Software Configuration Management (SCM)

Software Configuration Management (SCM; sometimes also referred to as Source Code Management) includes all the functionality of Revision Control and more. Like the former category, SCM is also a system derived from software development and includes managing all files developed for a specific application in such a way that they are always consistent, in sync and fitting together. It enables you to keep all team members up to date, prevent overwriting each other's changes, and to automatically extract different versions of the application for testing, demo purposes, and for the final version(s).

Pros

- Helps enormously to develop software. Its powerful functions make comparing versions, merging work of two or more people, and building working versions of the software easy, especially in larger teams.

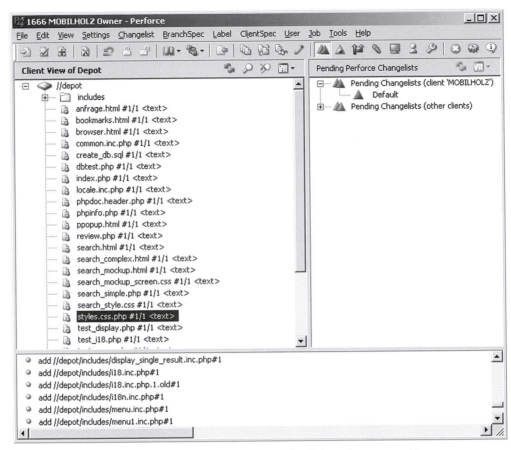

Figure 5.4   *SCM tools like Perforce allow you to control collaboration on any file*

Cons

- As with Revision Control, these systems are made for programmers and the management of program code. They offer only restricted functions for management of text, spreadsheets, and media files.

Digital Asset Management (DAM)

Often, the term Digital Asset Management is used in a stricter sense than in this book. Some use the term DAM only if the system can natively manage media files like images, audio, video and the like, and offer thumbnails, streaming previews, metadata extraction, and other special features to make working with such files easy.

DAM systems are common in publishing houses, media companies, and video production firms. There are several solutions for the broadcast industry and TV news specializing in the management of video for archival/retrieval, creation, and broadcasting, which are beyond the scope of this book.

Production Digital Asset Management (ProdAM)

Production Digital Asset Management (ProdAM; sometimes also called Digital Production Management) concentrates on production workflows. It helps with the management of all the files and supports media files of most types. Often, these systems have archiving functions.

Basically, they are very similar to SCM tools. The main difference is that ProdAM tools can handle binary data effectively. Program code is stored in plain text files. These are small and therefore you can easily store, transmit, or compare hundreds to thousands of them without much effort. With all other assets, this is not the case. 2D and 3D programs, sound and video

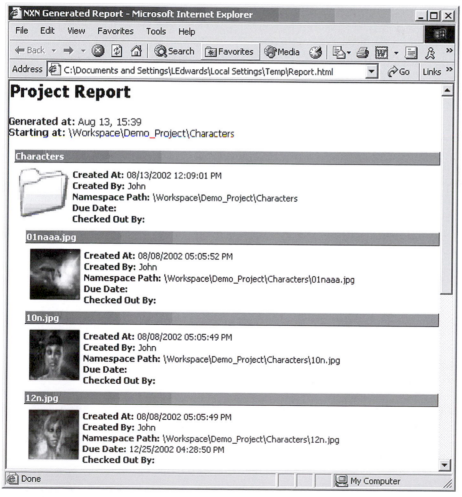

Figure 5.5 *ProdAM systems like Avid Alienbrain manage all types of media files and support production workflow (EVE Images. © CCP HF)*

editing systems all store their data in binary files, not in text files. The same applies for word processing, spreadsheet, and project management applications.

These binary files are magnitudes larger than program code's text files. Even for a complex project like a computer game, all the program code with all revisions, interim versions and so on could easily fit on a single CD-ROM (which contains up to 700 MB). However, one Photoshop file alone with several layers, as is common today, can easily take up 30 MB. So if you were to store several previous versions of this file, it would not be uncommon to end up with 350 MB storage space used just for one art asset—that is half of the capacity needed for the complete program code of the entire project!

Simply applying the features suited for program files to binary files leads to unacceptably slow performance and often even to errors because the tools are not created for handling files of this size. Another reason why SCM tools are usually not well suited for the management of art assets is that many features that are great for source code control simply do not work for binary files. For example, if two developers worked on the same part of the code, the SCM tool detects this when the second change is checked in (the programmer tells the tool that he is finished with his work and says his work is ready to be integrated in the project). A good SCM tool automatically resolves this conflict in most cases because it has a built-in logic that can decide how to integrate both changes in a way that they work together. In some cases the two changes do contradict each other, and then the programmer sees the two contradicting parts of the code next to each other on the screen. He can now decide which version is to be kept. This process simply does not work on art files. There is no use looking at the binary data directly to resolve conflicts, and automatically mixing two versions would lead to unpredictable results. In artwork, usually there is something wrong with the processes that needs to be resolved if two people are working on the same file at the same time.

SCM tools lack features essential for visual files. Seeing even a small thumbnail usually helps more to identify what a file contains than reading pages of descriptions. That is why ProdAM tools offer preview, which might not seem like a high-end feature but which is actually one of the most important features. It can save a lot of time when you don't have to open several versions of a file to see what is in each of them. This is even more important if the files are large and transferring and opening them leaves you enough time to fetch another coffee.

HTML files are a special case to consider in this context. They are plain text files like program code files and SCM features can be used for them with benefit. But, on the other hand, they describe HTML pages, which are in part a quite visual thing—they usually even contain several other files with graphics, audio, or video. That is why for HTML it is great to have SCM features as well as preview features from ProdAM systems. If you are working with HTML, keep this in mind when having a closer look at the DAM system you are considering buying.

Pros

- Can provide one system for all team members—programmers, 2D and 3D designers, animators, sound artists, and project managers.

Cons

- Programmers might want to stick with the SCM system they are used to, which might even offer more features or easier access for them.
- Requires huge storage capacities, fast networks, and enough server capacity.
- Depending on the system used and the scope of the solution, the installation phase can last a long time.
- All this effort may not be necessary when production cycles are short, and teams are small and work closely together.

Other categories: "... Management" buzzwords explained

There are some other category names you will encounter from time to time that we don't consider to be separate categories. To give you an idea what these mean, here's a brief explanation of these buzzwords.

Digital Rights Management (DRM)

Digital Rights Management (DRM) solutions usually are not systems on their own, but part of another software like a Web Content Management system or an e-commerce database. They manage the access rights a customer has for files, usually media. DRM is commonly used today in software for media playback like Apple's iTunes, which makes sure you can only listen to AAC files that you bought yourself in its web shop. In the same way, Microsoft Windows controls the handling of WMA files that are locked by WM DRM (Windows Media Digital Rights Management).

Customer Relationship Management (CRM)

Customer Relationship Management systems are specialized for the management of files and information related to customers, like e-mails, calls, faxes, letters, orders, and so on. They can be a separate application or they can be part of an Enterprise Content Management system or something similar.

Knowledge Management (KM)

Knowledge Management is a name for the process of collecting and distributing information within a company, and is not a name for a certain technology. For Knowledge Management, several technical solutions can be used such as Document Management, a company intranet, data mining, or cooperation features like forums, online meetings, and so on.

Enterprise Information Portals (EIPs)

An Enterprise Information Portal is usually the intranet site of a large organization. It offers employees and external partners access to any information they need for their daily work. An EIP is a simple interface to information that comes from several different sources from all over the enterprise.

Media Asset Management (MAM)

Media Asset Management is usually used as a synonym for Digital Asset Management in the strict sense—the management of rich media files.

Digital Media Management Systems (DMMS)

Another synonym for Digital Asset Management.

Records Management (RM)

The term Records Management is used for the process of working with any record that exists in an enterprise. Often, the term is used when compliance to legal demands has to be met to make sure everything is well documented within a firm. For Records Management, usually Document Management tools are used, while there are systems that are specialized for Records Management. Discrimination between RM and DM is very difficult.

Learning Management (LM)

Learning Management specializes in delivering and keeping track of e-learning content. It presents the appropriate lessons or tests to the users and records their progress. It is closely related to WCM, and therefore some call LM systems Learning Content Management Systems (LCMS).

Catalog Content Management (CCM)

Also known as Product Data Management (PDM) or Product Lifecycle Management (PLM). It encompasses the management of all product-related data—from first sketches, CAD drawings, production instructions, packaging information, and legal documents to product shots. The focus is on the product; therefore, CCM is mainly used in the production industry.

5.3   Which size fits for you?

You already have an idea of what you need from Chapter 4. Now, earlier in Chapter 5, you learned which types of DAM systems are available. Now it is time to decide what is right for you.

TO DO

Take the list of desired improvements you made in the last chapter and compare to see which of the solution categories described in this chapter best match. It is unlikely that you will find a single category that fits all your needs, but don't despair. The descriptions above are quite general and chances are that you will find one or even more solutions that fit your top-priority needs. Concentrate on these because often the products available offer features from neighboring categories or can be extended.

When you know which solution category is right for you, continue with this chapter or have a brief look at the product overview in Appendix 1 first to get an idea of which programs could be candidates for your purchase.

5.4   What if there is no suitable system?

The more features you want and the more complex these features are, the less likely it is that you will find a system that fits all your needs. If nothing on the market looks right, you're left with these possibilities:

- Extend an existing system yourself
- Let a system be modified for you
- Combine existing systems
- Create your own system
- Rent a system.

Extend an existing system

Many DAM systems can be modified or extended to fit your specific needs. The manufacturers often offer additional modules or third-party plug-ins. Several programs can be customized by scripts (Visual Basic, AppleScript), which are relatively easy to develop.

This approach is feasible if you only need some adjustments, you use commonly used tools, and your workflow habits follow industry standards. Of course, the more unique your needs, the less likely it is that there is already an extension available and the more work customization will be.

If this is the case, you may decide to plunge into plug-in development. A few existing solutions have APIs that make it possible to write your own integration routines with C++ or Java. This is usually a major task. Before making a decision to do this, find someone who can handle this task and let him or her examine the documentation, support options, and survey newsgroups. This is important, because when there is not enough information available, these development efforts can become frustrating and consume a lot of time and resources.

Let a system be modified

Some manufacturers will modify their system for you or include features that are not yet implemented upon request. Especially if the product is relatively new, the manufacturer is small, or your company is interesting as a reference customer, chances are that you can hand them your wish list and they will make these wishes come true—or at least a few of them.

However, when you make such a deal, keep in mind that you will be the beta tester of the new features. Don't make tight schedules that rely on the availability of these features, or better, don't even rely on the whole system without thorough testing, because it is possible that the new features don't work in a way that you can use under real-life production conditions.

Combine systems

If you can't find a single solution that fits your needs, it is also possible to combine two or even more systems, but keep in mind that this requires that both systems can work together seamlessly and that you will have to install and maintain two systems instead of one. Additionally, the users will eventually need to learn how to use two new systems.

A possible scenario for this is to use a workgroup solution for archiving—for example, an image catalog for the management of artwork. On top of that, during production you could use a custom project management tool that helps you control the creation of the artwork and keep track of the project's status.

In game development it is also quite common to use two independent DAM systems: one for source code and one for all other assets—images, 3D models, audio, video, text documents, and so on.

Create your own system

Building your own Digital Asset Management system seems tempting to many at first thought. You can implement all the features you can dream of, integrate it with any other system you need to, and save the often tremendous costs of buying a commercial solution.

While all of this is true, the biggest disadvantage of building your own system is that experience shows that most of these projects have failed. It usually takes too long and tends to become a never-ending story. Too often you hear: "It would have been the best possible solution anyone could dream of—but it never got finished." You take all the risk, and you will have to learn for yourself all the lessons the manufacturers of DAM systems learned over the last two decades.

If you are sure you can handle this, look at what companies that succeeded in creating their own systems have done (for example, read the success story of Scholz & Volkmer in Chapter 7). You can identify these success factors:

- The companies that succeeded are close to technology and had the experts that built the system already in-house.
- They had experience in developing software.
- They started small. It is better to create one part of the solution after finishing another. Each part needs a clear objective. (For example, it should just handle the images that are sent in by the customers. As a next step, you can add features for archiving these, and as a third step maybe you can add workflow support.)
- The tools were intended to solve some problems that they clearly understood from every-day practice.
- The companies were relatively small—they had from 30 to no more than a few hundred employees.

Choose your tools with much foresight. Using a media-enabled database like FileMaker has the advantage that you get results quickly, but first carefully consider whether it will work for you in the long run. Databases are not the best way to manage assets since they are built to manage textual information in the first place. FileMaker is great for setting up DAM prototypes, but many firms dropped their custom FileMaker solution fairly quickly and switched to a professional DAM system.

5.5 Rent a DAM solution

Buying a large DAM solution can cost tens to hundreds of thousands of US dollars. Setting it up can be even more costly, because a large team has to implement the system, which can take weeks to months if it is an enterprise-wide solution. For large companies, therefore, using an Application Service Provider (ASP) is an option.

Mainly companies whose core business is not generating digital assets choose this option. Media companies, publishers, game producers, 3D animation firms, and web design agencies are usually better off with an in-house solution.

The biggest advantage of an ASP Digital Asset Management solution is that you can get your system up and running within a few days for a fraction of the cost. You can concentrate on your business and don't have to become an expert in DAM system implementation. You save personnel and hardware costs. If the asset types you have to deal with change, the data volume grows or shrinks, or you venture into new fields of business, it is relatively easy to accommodate your DAM system at an ASP to meet your changed needs.

The downside is that all your file operations go through the Internet. This requires a high-speed connection and brings all work to a halt if the line is broken or the remote server is down. All your data is stored offshore, so you have to fully rely on the ASP for backing up and maintaining security.

5.6 Don't over-engineer

One of the most important bits of advice when choosing a DAM solution is not to aim too high. It is better to start with a simple solution that works than to aim high and miss, because working with the system is more a burden than a blessing. Resist the temptation to get the best possible solution, and try to implement only what seems realistically manageable within a limited time. Don't over-engineer the solution but, instead, after careful planning and consideration, just dive into your new system with a small pilot project.

TO DO

You should now know which categories of DAM tools are suitable for you. Now, examine your favorite candidates by looking at the product overview in Appendix 1, at the vendor's websites, and by installing demo versions if available.

To assist you, you can use the checklist below. Cross out the items that do not apply to you. Then make a column for every product you are reviewing and enter $-$, $+$, $++$, or $+++$ for each feature of each product.

- Compatibility with existing hardware
- Compatibility with existing operating systems

- Integration with existing software/databases
- Supported formats (cataloging and preview)
  - Image formats
  - Page layout program formats
  - PDF, EPS
  - 3D program formats
  - HTML, XHTML, XML, text
  - Scripts, program code
  - Word, Excel, PowerPoint, diagramming, and project management file formats
  - Audio and video formats
  - Flash
- Indexing
  - Automated metadata generation
  - Support for EXIF, IPTC, XMP
  - Custom fields
  - Shared keyword lists
- Search functions
  - AND/OR search
  - Wildcards
  - Search in multiple sets/catalogs/projects
  - Savable queries
- Collaboration and workflow
  - Central repository
  - Check-in/check-out
  - Exclusive locking
  - Versioning
  - Configuration management
  - Labeling
  - Branching
  - Differentiation/merging of source code
  - Messaging
- Project management
  - Setting status of assets
  - Assigning owners and due dates
  - Automated notification and sign-off
  - Automated report generation
- Extensibility
  - Scripting
  - APIs
  - Open plug-in architecture
  - Use of standard protocols
- Backup and archival
- Export
  - HTML catalogs
  - Catalogs for offline viewing (CD/DVD-ROM)
  - Printed catalogs
  - E-mail files

- Access
  - Definition of users and user groups
  - External access via Internet
  - Access via browser or free viewer application for all platforms
  - Secure transfer
  - Bandwidth
- Stability and performance
- Usability, training effort
- Support
- References in your industry
- Price (installation; server and client licenses).

5.7 Questions to ask potential vendors

After you select the potential systems that suit your needs, ask some questions to the vendors—either directly by contacting sales reps or by querying their websites, technical papers, and marketing collateral.

- Can they prove that their system will work for you? If possible, use your own data for demonstration. Include every type of file you want to manage. It is valuable to see the system work with sample data, but you can only be sure it works for you if you test it under real-life conditions.
- Will they help you improve your workflow? Is there a consultant to do so if you don't have the expertise and/or manpower to implement the system yourself?
- Will they help you with system integration?
- What is the state of the company from which you plan to buy? How long has it been in the market? Can you expect it to develop the product further and to provide support in the future?
- Which additional hardware do you need? What network infrastructure is necessary? Will the system perform well on your existing hardware?
- Which storage solutions are supported for backup and archiving?
- How much manpower do you need, for example, for setting the system up and for ongoing administration?

Do some additional research and ask colleagues. Call or even visit reference customers the vendors give you. Search newsgroups to find out the experiences users have with the software.

5.8 Sample scenarios for the application of DAM

In this section, we will look at three typical sample scenarios. The software chosen here is not a direct recommendation for your case. Instead, we'll explain which factors led to the respective decision for it in the company. If you follow the same decision-making process, you will find the software that best fits your special needs.

Example: Advertising agency introducing an image library

AmazingAds, a sample company we have not considered in the previous chapters, has 18 employees and an asset management problem—the usual hassle with lost and overwritten files, data spread all over the computers, removable media all over the office, and too much time spent searching by all employees.

Amanda, the founder and owner of the company, decided to introduce a Digital Asset Management system to solve these problems. She is also a gifted photographer, so she plans to ingest and catalog all the images she shoots with her digital camera into the system to make them accessible for everyone. She no longer wants to be the only source of information when someone needs a picture for a certain campaign.

Candidate 1: FotoStation Pro

FotoWare's FotoStation Pro is widely used in the publishing industry, so Amanda gets a demo version of this software (for details, see Appendix 1, Product overview). She imports some images she just shot from her digital camera to test it. She thinks the process is painless and the keywording functions seem alright to her. After setting some options in the preferences, she manages to get the files placed correctly in a folder on the server to which others also have access.

Amanda is impressed by the image-editing features that FotoStation has to offer. It makes many corrections possible without having to open Photoshop. She especially likes the dodge/burn tool, although it is clear to her that she and her co-workers would not actually need it too often. Nevertheless, she is a bit disappointed to learn that these functions are not available in the Macintosh version, and the Quark guys at AmazingAds are working on Macs.

Candidate 2: Portfolio

The next software Amanda examines more closely is Extensis Portfolio. She immediately feels at home in its neat interface. She thinks the automatic request for the input of metadata is helpful. She likes the way keywords are organized and that a context menu lets her add files to Portfolio directly from the Explorer without having to start the program. She also thinks that the floating palette is great for searching and placing images directly in QuarkXPress.

She does miss the functions that FotoStation has for directly editing images in the catalog—Portfolio can only rotate the images. But overall she likes the look and feel of the program. She thinks it will be easier to learn, which is important because there are usually three interns, who stay for only a few weeks at AmazingAds. They should help her with cataloging new files on a regular basis.

Candidate 3: Cumulus

After talking with Reno, her system administrator, Amanda also gets a demo version of Canto Cumulus. After working with Portfolio before, she is a bit deterred by the interface of Cumulus. It just doesn't look as nice. Ingesting images and indexing them works fine though. She thinks the search functions are good, especially the option where you can add the results of a second search to your search results.

When Amanda plays around with Cumulus for a while, she becomes more and more overwhelmed by the vast features this program has to offer. But, on the other hand, she becomes more and more overwhelmed by the overwhelming number of options scattered through the numerous dialogs. She has to consult Reno several times to set up some functions—which is usually not necessary because she is quite a power user with enough skills to help herself. For example, getting the File Vault running for version control functionality takes even Reno an hour.

But this is the key feature for Amanda. With it, she can manage her conceptual documents and always have access to all old versions without having to take care of properly naming and archiving them. It will also come in handy for the different draft versions for ads they create and their changes after discussion with the clients. The Quark documents can also be handled with it. For photos this feature will not be so important, because there will always be an unchanged master file and only a few modified versions, which are to be saved into the respective project folders.

Last but not least, Cumulus can handle PowerPoint and Excel files—it even indexes their contents and has multi-page thumbnails for PowerPoint presentations.

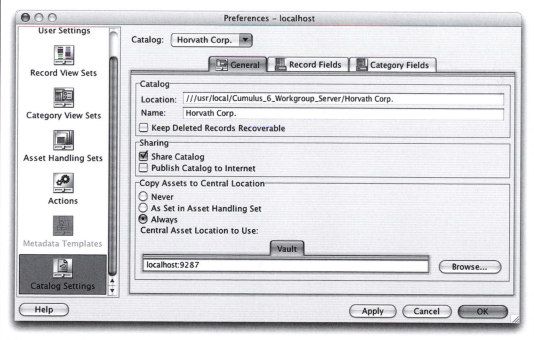

Figure 5.6 *Cumulus offers so many functions that finding the right options in the dialogs can be daunting*

After some long thinking sessions and some discussions with Reno, Amanda finally decides to buy Cumulus. She is well aware that it is much more expensive than its competitors, it is more difficult to use, and requires quite a lot of administration effort on Reno's part to set up everything for all the users. But she thinks that it is worth it because Cumulus can actually handle all the file types they are working with at AmazingAds, and it offers version control for all of them. Of course, a product with more options leads to more complex implementation, but day-to-day use is not too complicated.

Six months later, she reviews her decision and still thinks it was the right one: the typical production chaos disappeared; her own photos are used more often for their ads, which led to lower cost for licensed photos from stock libraries; all previous versions of conceptual documents and layout files are in order and can be retrieved with ease when necessary.

Example: Web agency introducing image library and SCM

For this example, we'll check back with our sample company ProperProduction, which you already know from the previous chapters.

Since they just won a large customer who wants to display online several detailed pictures each of all the hundreds of products they offer, they feel they have to act quickly. This website project is chosen as a pilot, and the project manager, Carla, gets the task of taking care of this.

It was clear from the beginning that the website itself would need a Content Management System. But for the management of production in-house, they could not find a CMS that would suit their needs.

Carla had already asked several colleagues working in other companies about the way they work. She attended a three-day workshop on project management for IT professionals and read two books on this matter. After these efforts she was sure that the general workflow they had at ProperProduction was OK, so they had to find a software solution that would support this workflow.

Candidate 1: Zope

Together with Jason, the programmer with the most experience at ProperProduction, Carla discusses the possibility of using a CMS built on Zope (see the product overview in Appendix 1 for details) and extending it with custom asset management functions they would program in-house. Soon they decide against this option, because none of the programmers has experience with Zope and they don't want to set off on an adventure into completely unknown territory. Since there is a fixed deadline for the project, Carla strongly dislikes this option, although Jason would prefer giving it a try.

Candidate 2: RedDot CMS

For the management of the final website, they choose the RedDot CMS (also see product overview in Appendix 1). The main reason for this is that they already used it for another project and everyone on the team therefore already knew its strengths and weaknesses.

Candidate 3: iView Media Pro

Carla and Peggy, the senior graphical artist, install trial versions of iView Media Pro (also see Product Overview) on their computers. Colleagues had recommended the program because of its

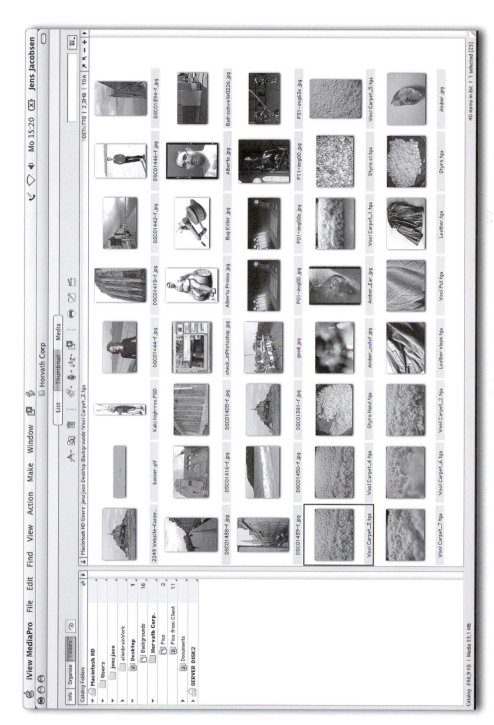

Figure 5.7 *iView Media Pro has a clear interface that makes it quick to learn*

gentle learning curve. Since the project is about to begin soon, this is a major prerequisite. They immediately like the program and are impressed by its features.

After some time playing around with it, though, Carla also finds some drawbacks. The versioning features are not as mature as she expected. They basically only work for Photoshop files—and this requires opening the files via iView Media Pro, which she considers error-prone. There is no support for Word, Excel, or OmniGraffle files in iView Media Pro.

Nevertheless, they decide to use the program for managing the pictures they get from the customer and the Photoshop files they create. She prepares a short handout for the graphical artists, describing how the versioning features work.

Candidate 4: Subversion

In the meantime, Jason from programming gives the Software Configuration Management tool Subversion a try. He knows its predecessor CVS from his previous job and has already heard much acclaim for Subversion from colleagues (details for both systems are given in Appendix 1). One big advantage he sees is that Subversion is free. He also thinks it is so common by now that any new programmers in the firm will probably know how to use it.

Jason liked Subversion because it works similarly to CVS. You only have to learn a few basic commands and the underlying principle of repositories, and then working with local copies should be clear for any programmer. But to Jason, it was obvious from the beginning that the graphical artists would not like Subversion. The graphical user interfaces available would make using it a bit easier for them, but nevertheless he thought it is too much of a programmer's tool.

When he now shows it to Carla she agrees, but she still likes its versioning features. That is why she discusses using Subversion for managing the Photoshop files during production. When she learns that Subversion offers no file locking, though, she drops the idea. For image files, it is essential to lock write access to the file as long as someone else is working on it. For program code or plain text files, this is not necessary or can sometimes even be counter-productive. For such files it is often possible to merge changes made to different parts of the document automatically. If changes were made to the same part, there is always one solution that is better than the other, so the person who is checking it in can resolve this conflict easily. This is not the case for images.

So Carla and Jason decide to stick with iView Media Pro for the management of images and to choose Subversion for the management of Java, JavaScript, PHP, and HTML. All programs, scripts, and HTML templates are to be managed with Subversion. Only at the very end of the project will the necessary files be transferred to the CMS for implementing the final site. Jason goes on to write a script for automating this process, which will come in handy when they have to create prototypes for functional testing and usability testing.

Candidate 5: The file system—and discipline

Carla presumes that the most pressing issues regarding asset management at ProperProduction are now covered. But one important thing is still missing: the management of her own files and those of the information architect, Louis.

She thinks about using Subversion but then she decides against it because her and Louis' files were only changed by one single person. Most of the files will have several versions, but she prefers naming and archiving these by hand. She prepares a detailed scheme containing a naming convention and directory structure, which she discusses with Louis and Jeff, the second information architect. She compiles a list of everyone on the team and defines which access and modification rights to which directories on the server he or she should have. She also develops a plan for how to archive all project files from the server holding her files, those of the information architect, the code, and the graphical files once the project is finished.

In the end, ProperProduction has several Digital Asset Management systems instead of one. But everyone on the team is happy and the fatal problems that appeared during previous projects will probably be avoided. The final cost is low, since the only software they have to purchase is iView Media Pro, which is not expensive and installation efforts are minimal.

In fact, the sample project finishes six months later within time deadline and budget. Of course, some problems occurred, but they could be resolved later with relative ease, and the client is happy. Carla really is satisfied when she takes three DVDs to the copier room feeling assured she knows exactly where and what to look for on the discs in case she has to find an asset later.

Example: Animation studio introducing ProdAM

ProperPictures, the sample animation studio already introduced in previous chapters, just finished a big project complete with the usual hassle. Everyone is exhausted—but the project manager Richard is determined to end this sort of chaos. He has already compiled the list of features they need to get a grip on in the production so he looks at the systems on the market. Since his focus is on asset management during production, the selection soon boils down to two programs: Perforce and Avid Alienbrain (see product overview in Appendix 1 for details).

Candidate 1: Perforce

A friend working at a game producer recommended the Software Configuration Management tool Perforce to Richard. He downloads a trial version and plays around with it a bit. Perforce can handle all types of files and offers check-in/check-out with exclusive locking. This means that everyone has to check out the file he or she wants to work on before starting to edit. Until the file gets checked back in, no one else is able to modify it. This would prevent one of the most pressing problems during production at Richard's company. The versioning features would also help a lot.

Perforce works faster than Richard had imagined, even with the large files they often have to handle. He is happy to learn that there is a visual client for Macintosh OS X. He thinks this will make persuading the artists using the tool much easier.

Candidate 2: Alienbrain

From reviews in animation magazines, Richard knows the Digital Asset Management tool Alienbrain. He gets a trial version of this program too for closer examination. It has check-in/check-out and locking like Perforce. He is quite impressed by Alienbrain's visual client. It offers thumbnail views of all the files in the central repository—for virtually all the file types they use at ProperPictures. This makes it easy, for example, to locate a certain texture among a great number of files without having to open one after another.

And, what is even better, the version history view of the files also lets you compare different versions visually so you can see with a glance what has changed. Alienbrain tightly integrates with the artist's tools like Maya and Photoshop. The functionality can be accessed directly and easily from these programs.

As a project manager, Richard is especially fond of the workflow features. He can assign files to team members, who in turn can change their status so that it becomes clear when they are ready for review. When the files are finally approved, they can be locked. Richard can easily generate a report about how many files are overdue, who has checked out which files, and so on.

He discusses his impressions with Sven, the art director, and the two artists, Liz and Bill. Together they test the two programs thoroughly, simulating most common tasks. Finally, they decide that they want to give Alienbrain a try for the next project. It is more expensive than Perforce, but because of the special features it offers for working with visual files and its workflow capabilities, they think it might promise a bigger improvement to the way they work.

Figure 5.8   *In Alienbrain you can compare different versions of a file visually (© Pixelspell Animation Studios. All rights reserved)*

ProperPictures' next project—the test drive for Alienbrain—is a five-minute special effects sequence for a feature film. It is completed within five months and delivered only one day late. This happened because Richard got the flu in the last week and mistakenly sent the hard disk with an old animated product commercial to the producer. Anyway, the team was happy and only slightly overworked at the end of this project.

6 Implement the solution

This chapter will point out the possible pitfalls when implementing a Digital Asset Management system to help you avoid these common mistakes. Likely you will run into some problems regardless of your precautions, but this guide will help you to handle them and find feasible solutions.

Implementing a Digital Asset Management system requires careful planning. The system and its implementation will impact everyone who touches it. If a DAM system is introduced too slowly or without a high degree of importance, you will have users still storing data in other places, making the data inconsistent. If it is introduced too quickly, without appropriate instructions for the users, problems may occur which force them to use workarounds (even such as not using the system!). Both cases can render your DAM useless from the user's perspective and you will have a hard time consolidating all data in the DAM. Good planning and well-structured implementation are therefore extremely important for the success of your DAM system. Don't try to introduce your new DAM piece by piece because you are not confident it will work—your users will pick up on this and, besides, it will work!

In this chapter we will run through the most important things to take into account when implementing an asset management system: the planning, evaluation, training, and setup.

6.1 Planning

Before investing any time in the implementation or testing of the DAM system, make sure that you know what you actually need. Look at your requirements and the specifics of the system that you want to use. Here are some important questions to consider beforehand:

- What kind of system do you want to use?
- Who is going to use it?
- How is it going to be used?
- What do you need to run the system you want to use?
- Who is responsible for maintaining the system?

Setting up such a system without taking time to predict a user's behavior (daily usage, access needs, asset sharing, etc.) and without considering how the data should be structured for the long term is a typical mistake.

Most importantly, make sure that the ownership of maintaining the system is clearly defined. If there is a problem with the system, everyone should know who to contact so there is minimal work time wasted.

Directory structure and access rights

One very important aspect to consider for a DAM system is the user or team structure. Users of asset management systems can perform very different functions and responsibilities, and it is important that you know beforehand who is doing what. Then you can consider by group what type of access rights users need, depending on the types of files they need to access.

The underlying idea is to be as restrictive as necessary but to give as many access rights as is smart. Restricting access, mainly write access, reduces the probability of accidentally changing, deleting, or overwriting data. It also makes sure that team members only modify files that they are allowed to, with the expectation that they understand the implications of what they are doing.

No one on the team should get the feeling of exclusion or secrecy unnecessarily, so it is better to give read access liberally. So, for example, give artists access to the project management area in general and hide only documents that contain calculations, contracts, and confidential information.

On the other hand, hiding data from users makes it easier to find the files they are looking for. Find a balance between the two extremes and decide on the access rights suiting your project, team structure, and experience of the team members.

As an example, consider a website production. You will typically have:

- An information architect
- A project manager
- A technical manager
- Programmers
- Artists/designers
- Content creators/writers.

Depending on the size of the project this can be a more or less hierarchical structure. Let's assume that in this case each of the types of users works quite independently, with the project manager taking care of communication and coordination, and the technical manager taking care of the technical implementation and planning. This means that the data produced can be divided into five groups:

Project management

This section contains all general information about the project. This could be project plans, contracts, communication with the customer, and budget plans. Some of this information must be available for all, and some should only be available to the project manager. In general, only the project manager(s) should be allowed to edit information in this section.

Website

The website itself is also stored in the asset management system. For a web project this is the place where it all comes together—code written by the programmers, graphics prepared by the artists, and HTML pages written by the designers. Depending on the complexity of the project this could be a read-only area, which can only be changed by the technical manager, assembling all parts into a running system. Or it might be created by all technical users and controlled by the technical manager.

Since this is a critical part, it should always be clear (and controlled) who is allowed to make changes here to prevent users from accidentally breaking things. In this example, the website directory is not a work area where users can try out ideas, but a storage directory where only final data should be stored.

Code

Depending on the type of project, the programmers might not need their own area. In a simple PHP-based website, the code does not have to be compiled and can be stored directly in the website directory itself. In these cases you will only need a code directory to store test code.

With more complex technology such as JSP, on the other hand, you will have a distinct separation between source code and compiled code. When writing Java servlets or other types of CGI programs you will need a working directory for the programmers. In these cases development itself should only be done in the code directory, and only what is necessary for the website should be copied into the website directory.

The code area should always be secured for the programmers. Since even small changes in code can have disastrous effects, make sure that only those who know what they are doing have write access to the data.

Design

In general, creative work takes a lot of trial and error and iterations, and artists need a storage area where they are free to try out different ideas. Usually it makes sense to give every artist and designer their own work area in which they can store whatever they want. Having this work area on a centralized asset management system instead of the local hard disk has the added advantages of facilitating idea sharing and improving data security.

Depending on the nature of the project, it may be necessary to make each artist's work area private. This makes sense if there are competing designs and the final results have to be compared.

Content/text

The information architect creates the site structure. The content creators or writers will produce storyboards or raw text which has to be made available for the page designers who will put the content on the website. Although this data itself is probably the least complicated in the project, it is the most important for the customer. Tracking the development and approval of the documents can be very beneficial in the long run.

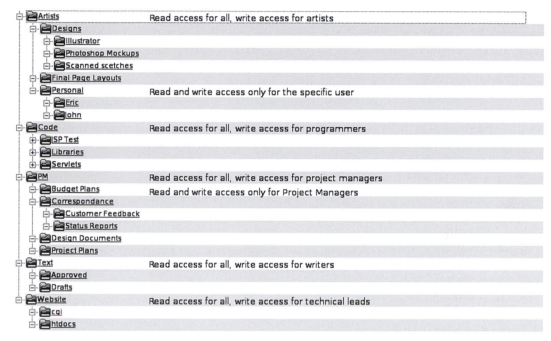

Figure 6.1 *Try to keep the file structure as simple and clear as possible*

Database responsibilities

Depending on the size of the installation you are planning to implement, there will be different user groups performing tasks to maintain the system.

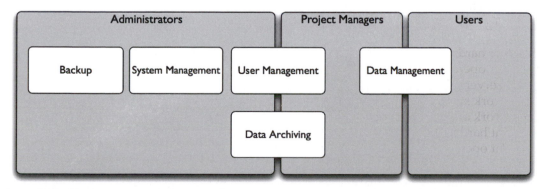

Figure 6.2 *Responsibilities should be given to the appropriate users; some can be shared*

Of course, in most smaller installations this will be done by one or two people, but it is important that responsibilities are clearly delegated and that there is always at least one person available at all times who can work with the ins and outs of the system.

In general, the scope of system maintenance is too often underestimated. If you start putting all your data in one place, this should be a secure and well-kept place. Make sure that administrators are aware of everything this job entails. If you are unsure that certain areas are being covered thoroughly, do regular reviews on the system status to find out if something is developing in the wrong direction. It is far easier to fix these types of problems sooner rather than later.

Typical problematic areas are:

- *Disorganized or even incomplete backups.* This often becomes an issue towards the end of productions when there is more data to back up than the backup system can handle. If this occurs, don't try to somehow work around the problem with an incomplete solution. If in any way possible, extend your backup system to meet the new requirements. Don't skimp on this; in an emergency, a good working backup can be priceless.
- *Badly maintained user lists.* In some systems, maintaining the user accounts can be cumbersome, especially if you have a number of freelancers. Make sure that the user accounts are always up to date and that users that are no longer needed are deleted or at least deactivated as soon as possible.
- *Too finely-grained user definitions.* In larger projects, especially when employee turnover or the involvement of freelancers is high, it can become quite a headache if user rights are defined too minutely. Don't make the mistake of trying to plan for each and every eventuality, or you'll spend too much time adapting the rights again and again when frustrated users can't work properly and always have to ask for a modification of their access rights.

Technical requirements

DAM systems have very different and sometimes very specific technical requirements. As a first step in the implementation, make sure that you have sufficient information about all the requirements and can actually satisfy them. These requirements typically involve the following:

- Server hardware
- Server operating system
- File server
- Network system (Windows domain, LDAP server)
- Network architecture (network bandwidth)
- Client hardware
- Client operating system.

The specifications are often broad (Windows server) but can become quite specific in certain cases. Make sure that you read all relevant documentation and get your questions answered if anything is unclear.

Scalability

Having a system that will handle the amount of data that you currently produce is a no-brainer, but you also have to anticipate the amount of data to be produced in the future and find a suitable system. Depending on the DAM system, scalability can be largely dependent on the type of hardware you choose. Make sure that you get a hardware platform that you can extend later on if you need to, or invest in the future and pick one that is already powerful enough to support you for the next years. Moving your DAM server to a new machine during production can be very painful, and it will probably cost you more than the initial investment in hardware. Even a small upgrade can stop production for a day—in a team of just 20 users, that's one man-month lost. Think of a team of 200+ users! The cost in time lost is often larger than the cost of the hardware.

The vendor of your DAM system should provide you with a rough guideline for what type of system you will need for the kind of projects you are working on. You can also do some test runs in your evaluation phase, but simulating a real production environment is next to impossible. Try to find other users who are running similar setups to get recommendations or try to get some real-world examples from the DAM system vendor rather than resorting to guesswork or synthetic numbers.

Timing

Implementing the DAM system can take a long time for larger installations. If this includes client setup or software installation on your production servers, try to perform the installation when there is no production running or make sure that the time needed for installation is short enough not to interrupt production.

A good way of planning the amount of time you will actually need is to perform a test installation on a system similar to your production system. This will provide a rough estimate of how long it will take to actually install the software. If you have to install client software, take into account that there is always at least one machine that will have some sort of issue.

6.2   Testing

As you already know from reading the previous section about the planning phase, there are many things you can only be sure of if you do some testing in an environment as similar to real-world use cases as possible. If you are planning to depend on a DAM system for years, you should take the time to thoroughly test the system you are going to use. Most software vendors provide test installations of their software if requested, and you should use the time to both test the system's functionality and to get enough experience with it to set it up for production later on.

A simple way of testing a DAM solution is to set up a simulated use case and play around with it until you feel that you have tried everything relevant to your production. This will give you a feel for the product, but it will not give you concrete information about how it will work with your real projects with real data.

To make sure that the DAM system you are looking at is the right one for you, test it with a real project. Depending on the type of projects you are running this can be quite simple; if you run small, short-term projects simply use the DAM system from beginning to end in your next project.

If your projects are too large or last too long to test the DAM system through a full project life cycle, at least try to use it in part of a project. Give a representative group of users access to the system and let them manage their data on it. Make sure that you test your most demanding scenarios. If, for example, you have users that produce very large amounts of data, then one of these users should be on the test team. If you run extensive data processing, then test that these processes work with the DAM system.

Always make sure that you throw a realistic load on the system. If you have team sizes of around 100 people but test the system with just three people then you will have no idea if it will actually work when used in production. If integrating a sufficiently large group of users into the test is not an option, then ask your IT department to run automated tests from the users' machines outside of work hours to simulate the load you will have later on.

While for the users the testing of the software should be as non-disruptive as possible, for the system administrators this is the big chance to test all special use cases that they might be unsure about. This includes backup, recovery, installation, and failover.

You will want to make sure that the administrators test all worst-case scenarios that they can think of to enable them to handle these gracefully if they do occur during production.

Preparing for a test

Before you start installing and running a test system, think through and map out all aspects of the test:

- Who should participate?
- How long should the test run?
- What kind of project do you want to test on?
- Which features have to be tested specifically or intensely?
- What environment is to be simulated?

Of course, if you are unable to test on a real project then you will only be able to simulate a real-life situation. Make sure, though, that all relevant members of the team are involved in the testing, especially in heterogeneous environments where each group of users might have completely different priorities.

Executing the test

While the test is running, frequently synchronize everyone on the testing team and ask how it's going—is anything going wrong, or are any expected features missing? Some users tend to hold back comments until specifically asked for information. Giving everyone a chance to discuss shortcomings and advantages alike during the process will give you a much better picture of the system than getting a summary of issues at the end, when thoughts may have been forgotten.

Often, users either blame issues on themselves, thinking that they are using the system the wrong way, or blame the system, expecting the software to work around every mistake they make. In both cases this can lead to a wrong impression of the DAM system and, even worse, decrease the efficiency of the DAM system if these problems are not resolved.

To help the users in evaluating the system, conduct short meetings to discuss these kinds of issues. Different perspectives help clear up confusing areas and can be considered when drawing conclusions. There are two approaches to getting good feedback: you can either talk to each user directly or have small meetings with all users.

Talking to each user one-on-one is ideal for getting immediate feedback, especially if you meet within their work environment, where they are comfortable. They will easily be able to show what parts of the software they like or dislike, and if they have an issue they can demonstrate it to you.

Team meetings are good for getting users to cooperate, but often the more dominant members of the team may influence the other users and shyer members may not speak at all. Keep the meetings short and make sure that every user has the opportunity to voice their opinion.

One thing to avoid is sending around a feedback form for everyone to fill out and basing your decision on that. Such written feedback might generate good ideas for a meeting, but reports will typically be incomplete.

6.3 Team preparation

The most important part of implementing an asset management system is the preparation of your team. Everyone who has to work with the system should know beforehand what's coming and why it's coming or you won't get buy-in. Releasing an unknown system on an unprepared user can be extremely frustrating for both the user and the system's maintainers. And new, unprepared administrators won't even be able to support the users, since they don't know how to figure out what users have done or what occurred in the system, let alone what they should do to fix it!

As always, the first impression is the most important one. If anyone on the team feels that the system will be more of a problem than a solution, they will not use it as efficiently as possible. They might even try to work around the system to hold onto their old working habits. Changing their opinion later on will be an uphill struggle.

To prepare the team, there are several things that can be done:

- Educate the administrators
- Introduce the system to the team
- Provide guidelines for system usage
- Train "super-users" for each team
- Conduct user meetings.

Educate the administrators

System administrators are extremely important to any DAM system. Since the aim of a DAM system should always be to centralize the data, it is crucial that the data is secure and always available. If an error occurs, there is usually not enough time to wait for a support response from the manufacturer. And waiting for someone to fix the problem on-site can be even more frustrating—you're paying someone to be at your beck and call to get things under control ASAP. A well-trained, knowledgeable administrator is capable of solving problems in the shortest time possible. Ideally, he or she should make sure that they don't even occur.

The easiest way to start getting real-world information to your administrator is to obtain an extensive training package from the software vendor or from resellers of the software. In these training packages, administrators should receive information on what kind of problems can occur and how to resolve them.

Most documentation tries to give a good overview over the system and explain all typical tasks of the system administrator. What it can't cover are all the unexpected problems that can occur in a real-world environment. Networked software solutions can run into problems from many angles; covering them all would mean covering each and every software and system running on the network! To get information about many problems, an administrator either has to rely on information in support systems of the software or on information directly from the supporters of the software.

As already mentioned, the best way to give the administrators time to learn the system is to provide them with a realistic environment in the testing phase. Then they can try out all variations of software setups and simulate all problems they might run into after the final installation.

Introduce the system to the team

When introducing a new system, all users need to learn enough about the system to at least get started using it. No user will pick up a handbook and start reading unless they are extremely motivated or bored, so make sure to provide the basics and also pointers to further information they may find more interesting (or need desperately) later. A quick introductory training/demonstration can be helpful, but it should be short enough to allow everyone to attend. Ideally, the system is easy enough to use that a quick 30-minute introduction is sufficient at the start, and the rest can be explored.

A crucial part of the introduction is explaining what is in it for the users. They may have the impression that the new system means more steps to take, extra work, and restrictions. They have to understand what they as an individual and the team as a whole gains from using the DAM system.

For example, suppose a creative user has been working on his workstation for the last four years using one specialized software package. Since he only has to deliver his final results to the other users, he will have a very personalized workflow which is probably very efficient for his way of working. When centralized storage is introduced, he will be less than thrilled since he has to change his ways and, even worse for him, he must make his drafts public. On the other hand, storing his files in centralized storage and being able to simply mark those that are ready for the rest of the team will save him many headaches and huge amounts of time. He can also be sure that all his files will be backed up—something that is hard to do when storing everything locally. If you manage to convince this artist that the advantages outweigh the disadvantages, he will approach using a DAM with a positive and curious attitude. Of course, the easier the DAM is to use, the easier the convincing will be! If users have to spend a week learning basic functionality, they will never use it properly.

Provide guidelines for system usage

Using the software is one thing, using it in the right way is another matter entirely. In the introductory session, you should provide an idea how the system is to be used. This can include anything such as outlining simple naming conventions for the files or giving a detailed directory structure that should be used.

If it is necessary to use a strict set of guidelines in the team, make sure that the users have these guidelines readily available, at least until they know them by heart and they are second nature. Writing down a usage guide will also help you cover all your bases, though after the introduction users will undoubtedly have questions and raise issues that will lead to action items for you, the project manager, or the administrator.

Don't expect that everyone will follow the rules all the time though; as stress levels rise, normal work patterns may fly out the window. Your DAM should be flexible enough to handle these conditions. If you see that your guidelines are not being followed, review them to make sure they actually make sense in the production environment. If not, change them. If they do make sense, then you should take some time to explain them again to everyone and enforce them. If there are only a few users who aren't following the rules, it might help to have individual discussions and get to the root of the problem.

Train "super-users"

A very good way to support all your teams is to make sure that there is at least one person in each team who really knows the product. This is usually much more efficient than giving everyone extensive training. Each type of user has very different requirements and different workflows. While a programmer may have a hard time explaining the optimal usage of a program to an artist, one artist can recognize the problems and challenges another artist faces. Therefore, a designated "super-user" should be responsible for supporting everyone in the team, and can also be the administrator's primary team contact.

If you decide to have one super-user on each team, invest time to extensively train those users and allow them, in turn, to train everyone on their team.

Conduct user meetings

During the introduction phase of the DAM system, getting the user's feedback is important. This gives everyone a chance to talk about what they think is going wrong or what needs improvement. Don't make these meetings too long—if users want to discuss specific aspects of the software that don't affect everyone else, have one-on-one meetings with them. Just make sure that everyone has the opportunity to voice their opinion. For larger productions, let each team leader collect the feedback from their users and then hold a meeting with the team leaders only.

If there are serious issues with the software, make sure they are tracked and resolved. Forcing users to work around a bug will not improve their confidence in the DAM system.

6.4   Workflow integration

Depending on the type of project you are working on, there may be a high potential for process automation and optimization. While this is not necessarily something to worry about from the start, it is one of the ideal ways to profit from a DAM system. Any kind of automation also has the advantage that it results in improvements for the users, giving them a reason to appreciate the extra work that they have to put into using the DAM.

How processes can be automated and improved depends largely on the DAM system you are using. Even if you are only using a well-managed directory structure on your server, you can still write scripts that maintain and control data.

Use metadata

Many DAM systems offer metadata storage. Metadata can be used to provide the users and the system with information about the assets stored in the database. The most common example is EXIF information stored in images made by digital cameras. This typically includes detailed information about when and with what settings the pictures were taken, but it can also tell the system how the camera was held when the picture was taken. This allows an image viewer to automatically rotate the image to display it on screen.

Metadata is either automatically generated, as in a digital camera, or it can be added by the user. If you create an asset library with thousands of images, it's sensible to use metadata to describe the images so they can be found easily later on.

If you want to automate data management, you can also use metadata to tag files in your asset management system. For example, if you mark all files that should later be used for distribution, it is then very easy to set up tools to search for this information in the database and automatically extract all the assets that are tagged accordingly.

Adding metadata can be a tedious task, and getting every user to faithfully add the relevant information can be difficult. Therefore, try to make this as easy as possible but also make sure that users can't work around the process. It helps to give users pre-defined values that they can choose from. One good way to encourage metadata entry is to use popup dialogs that ask for specific information upon import.

As an example, think about an image library. You want to make sure that images have enough metadata to be located quickly later. Using a text field that can be filled with any kind of description may lead to unsearchable information—words could be misspelled and descriptions may be subjective. Decide beforehand which criteria can be used to describe the

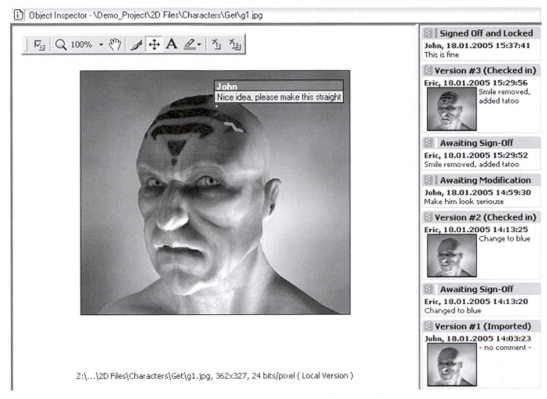

Figure 6.3 *Some DAM systems provide annotations: metadata that is used to mark change requests in assets*

images and then use selection boxes to allow the user to pick from these options. A free text field should only be used for additional information.

Having incomplete information in your DAM will make it unusable, and if the users ever get the impression that the metadata is incomplete they will stop relying on it. When rolling out your DAM, make sure that any kind of metadata you want to use in there is already defined, and that it is clear to users what they are supposed to provide the system and what they can search for.

Automate repetitive tasks

Repetitive tasks are the first thing that can be automated once you have a well-defined data structure. Imagine that you are creating textures for 3D visualization. This is typically done in a 2D application such as Photoshop and the result is then exported to the format of the 3D engine being used. Most 3D engines prefer textures in a specific resolution and bit depth, and in some cases you even need different resolutions of the texture. For users, this means that after they complete a change they have to save the original file, then make sure it is converted to the correct format, and finally move it to the correct target locations.

Most of this can easily be automated; you can even have scripts to check the result. All users have to do is to save their changed files and then tell the DAM to do the rest. With proper logic, the script can even check the texture for the correct format and send the user an error notification if anything is wrong.

Automating with scripts is very easy even for the inexperienced programmer. Start with the single steps that you want to automate and then slowly build a set of tools to take the burden away from the user. Most operating systems have built-in automation tools that can interface with applications on different levels. Examples are Shell scripts on Unix derivatives, the Windows Scripting Host, and Apple Script.

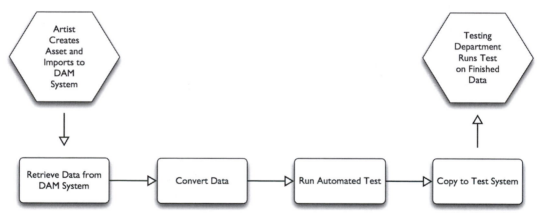

Figure 6.4   *An automated conversion or compilation pipeline can automate data exchange between departments*

Integrate your tools

Having external scripts helps the user significantly, but it is even better if the applications being used can directly interface with the DAM system. Many companies that work with in-house formats create their own tools. This is especially true for game companies and large CG productions. Since these specialized applications are created by the users, they can change any aspect of it that they want to. If the DAM system you are using is open enough, these in-house tools can directly interface with the DAM, ridding the user of the need to work outside of them.

As soon as the content creation tools are tightly integrated with the DAM, production can also benefit from the additional information that they can store in a DAM. If the DAM supports some kind of meta-information storage, the integrated applications can add information that it needs to "understand" the assets.

To use 3D data as an example again, once a 2D application has finished exporting an image to the DAM in all required resolutions, it could then add information about the file it came from

Figure 6.5 *Alienbrain offers plug-ins for most major 2D and 3D tools*

to each resulting image. If after two years of working you suddenly realize you have to change something in the exported texture, you can simply click on the texture in your DAM-integrated tool, and it will tell you which original file has to be modified to perform the changes you need.

Although integrating tools with a DAM creates an extremely powerful solution, it is only feasible for companies with experienced programmers. Most applications and tools require C++ programming experience to customize, and writing good and usable tool integrations requires much experience in the tool's use.

Integrate your workflow

Some DAM systems provide specific workflow support with varying degrees of flexibility. To determine how a DAM will accommodate your project, first analyze how data is created and modified in your projects, and then think how this data moves through the projects. If each file is only handled by one or two people, the workflow is pretty simple—trying to model it in the DAM probably wouldn't afford much added benefit. But if the data has a number of interdependencies and is modified and used by many team members, implementing a suitable workflow might lead to quality improvements.

Depending on the DAM system you are using, "workflow" has a variety of meanings. Systems geared towards software development usually make a distinction between different versions and branches (variations) of the files and folders, and the workflow is all about controlling the dependencies of these files. In document-oriented systems, the focus is more on controlling who has access to the files.

You should never try to force a brand-new workflow on your production, rather look at how you are currently doing things and then try to reinforce and bolster these existing workflows using your DAM system. This is a good chance, however, to think about workflow and how it could be improved; perhaps this is the right moment to introduce some enhancements. Especially if the DAM system chosen is tailored for a specific industry, it should reflect best practices in its defaults, so think before changing the factory workflow settings, but don't keep them if they don't fit your company's working culture.

One very logical place to integrate a workflow is at the end of the production, when it comes to reviewing the data that the content creators produced. With a DAM system you can mark the files that have been finished and approved to ensure that nothing leaves your company that has not been reviewed by the employees responsible.

Another typical usage is in asset creation. The lead artist has to review each asset that is produced to make sure that it fits into the general look of the production. Without a DAM with workflow support, this means that each artist has to show each asset to the lead artist, either on his machine or by sending him a link via e-mail. With a workflow system, all the artist has to do is to mark the asset as finished, automatically triggering a notification to the lead artist. He can then review the asset in the DAM and, if necessary, reject the asset, asking the artist to make some changes. This tracking guarantees that assets used in the later production are actually reviewed and approved.

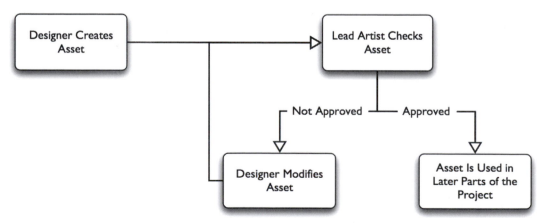

Figure 6.6   *Typical approval process for artwork*

Similar workflows can, of course, be extended through the whole production pipeline, depending on the capabilities of the system. If you are unable to model your complete process with the DAM tool of your choice, then try to break it down into manageable parts. Even controlling short processes like the approval step can help the production tremendously.

Example: Implementation plan in game production—Case study of GreatGames

This short example follows one typical implementation of a DAM system. While this example won't go into too much detail, it contains enough information to serve as a rough guide. All of these topics are covered in this chapter, so if you need more help with each step, refer back to the previous sections. Information about choosing the right product has already been covered in previous chapters and won't be discussed here.

- Test the solution
- Prepare the setup
- Prepare the users
- Deploy the software
- Automate your processes
- Integrate your tools

We are once again looking at GreatGames, discussed in previous chapters. They are a mid-sized company with 50 users and a mixed setup of mainly Windows XP and some Mac OS X machines. The server will be a Linux machine, with a dedicated file server running Samba.

Testing the solution

After reviewing the requirements, GreatGames decides to use Superbranch, a (fictitious) Open Source SCM able to manage binary assets. The main advantages are the cost of the software (it's free) and good support of development tools. Since there is no specialized support for artists, their feedback is especially important during the testing.

Since GreatGames is not able to test a whole production spanning two years' runtime, the team decides to set up a small group of users who are going to test the software with assets from the previous production. Since there is currently a bug fix—a patch—in production, the users decide to produce the patch with the system.

The team consists of:

- Two programmers
- One 2D artist
- Two 3D artists
- One project manager.

Adam and Albert, the administrators, set up the server with the data from the previous project, and everyone on the test team gets a client installed on their system.

During the test it becomes obvious that the system is difficult for artists to use, since some of the system's functions are geared towards programmers and source code.

Adam and Albert run extensive load tests on the system, using automated command line clients. The software behaves quite well under load and seems to handle the amount of data from the last project without any issues. Questions regarding the configuration and backup of the system are quickly answered with the help of the large user base on the Internet.

Peter, the programming leader, reports that programmers are extremely satisfied with the functionality and the integration into their programming tools. Most things work as expected and even though there is some missing functionality, what is there is enough for them to work with the system.

The project manager, Sam, is not convinced though, since there are few tools to help him to monitor the progress of the project. The patch is produced without any problems however, and after getting feedback from everyone, Sam gets the impression that even the artists were able to get used to the system after a while. Since the artist team at GreatGames is used to learning complicated tools, it seems it will not be such a problem for them. Although there are many missing features, the administrators report that the system is very stable, so Sam decides to give the software a try in the next project.

Preparation of the setup

Once the decision has been made, Adam and Albert start setting up the production server. Since they have already been through the configuration process, they finish quickly. But the production of the next project has already started, and they realize they can't just spend a day copying over data onto the production server and then installing the clients on each machine. Therefore, they decide to move the data onto the asset management system team by team. This allows them to install only a few machines per day, making sure that, at worst, only a few users are prevented from working.

Using the database from the software test, Adam sets up a backup system with both tape backups for long-term security and hard disk copies for fast data restoration. Since the data volume is quite high, he also updates the network backbone to a faster standard.

After running some tests on the system, doing backups, and trying out how long it takes them to restore a damaged system, Adam and Albert are confident that the system will work during production.

Preparing the users

Albert installs the clients on each machine. Since at least one user from each team participated in the test, these users are asked to train everyone on their team. Using the test setup that is still running, they explain all the features that are useful to their colleagues and conduct tutorial sessions with each of them. After a day of training, everyone is confident that they can start working.

Deployment of the software

With the clients installed and the servers ready, Adam starts moving the data to the DAM system. As soon as the move is started, the old file servers are made read-only, so changes will have to be made on the new system.

This works smoothly until he gets to the artists. The amount of data is so large that he has to halt production for half a day. Luckily the team is still in the concept phase and the artists can easily spend a productive workday using paper and pencils. From then on, Adam and Albert relocate data during the night, eating pizza and drinking plenty of coffee.

Review of the system

After using the new DAM for a month, Sam, the project manager, starts evaluating the setup. As he had already seen during the testing phase, the programmers had no problem with the system at all. Some artists were annoyed in the beginning though, and tried working around the system as much as they could. This led to situations where data was missing on the central server.

Sam spends some time in discussions with these "problematic" users and their team leaders and finally convinces them to accept the system. It takes some additional training and a few configuration adjustments from Albert for them to realize the system's benefits and start using it properly.

Some bugs in the software itself are slowing down production in some cases, and Adam starts looking on Superbranch's website for fixes. Since none can be found, he compiles a list of these issues and gives them to each user. With this list all users are able to work around the issues most of the time.

On the administration side, there were no serious issues except for one crash of the RAID system, which was replaced within two hours. With the hard disk backup, Adam was able to restore the system quickly, with only the data that was created within the six hours before the crash lost.

Automation of processes

When it becomes clear that the system itself is working well, Sam sets up a list of process improvements and automations together with David, the lead artist, and Peter from programming.

Peter then writes a set of scripts with the help of Adam to automate these processes. Not everything runs as desired, but some of the most tedious tasks can be automated. Sam decides to accept the fact that some things still have to be done manually.

Integration of tools

One big issue left is that the artists have to cope with unfamiliar tools and thus they are not working efficiently. Since the DAM system chosen is not artist oriented, they sometimes even have to use command line-based tools to submit the data they are working on. In some cases they produce large amounts of files, which then have to be selectively imported into the DAM. To solve these problems, David pulls in two programmers who have been working on the in-house tools before. Together, they design an integration that helps the artists to store and access data in the DAM without having to worry about the details. This actually works quite well, but the task consumed a large amount of the programmer's time. And even after one month of usage there are still bugs that the programmers have to fix. But the artists are mostly happy!

Conclusion

Looking at the implementation at Superbranch, it becomes clear that not everything is ideal. For example, the DAM system was not the best solution for the artists, forcing them to get used to a complicated work environment. The additional time spent integrating the in-house tools cost large amounts of work time. On the other hand, there were few problems with the system itself, and the production was able to finish without any issues.

7 Success stories

7.1 Lionhead Studios

About Lionhead Studios

The computer game production firm Lionhead Studios was founded by Peter Molyneux in 1997. Previously, Peter created famous games like *Populous*, *Magic Carpet*, and *Dungeon Keeper* at his former company Bullfrog Productions, which he sold to Electronic Arts in 1995.

All logos used in this chapter are copyright of the respective companies and are reproduced here with kind permission.

Lionhead Studios is located in Surrey (close to London) and today more than 200 people work there. Their first title was *Black & White*, a strategic game where players decide how to rule the world as a god—spreading peace and loving support to virtual people, or lashing out in anger and instilling fear. The game was a worldwide best-seller because of the new level of freedom the player is granted and because of the great care that was spent on every single detail—from dialogs to landscapes, items and characters. In 2005, the long awaited sequel *Black & White II* will be released.

The following success story was shared in an interview with Paul McLaughlin, Head of Art at Lionhead Studios.

Evolution of the industry

Ten years ago, a few people could design a game in a few months. Today, this is no longer possible. Consumers expect not only a great idea and perfect gameplay, but also stunning graphics, interesting dialogs, exciting sound, and elaborate technical features. Game buyers are not a forgiving audience.

For these reasons, projects have developed exponentially. With just 20 people on a team, assets for a production can be contained without special tools. Perhaps even with a strong project leader, you don't even need a producer. Hiccups during this type of production are game oriented, e.g. the game is not playable or fun enough. But in today's super-sized projects, the main threats to a project are caused by improper production.

Lionhead's experience

At the beginning of the creation of *Black & White*, there were only six or seven people. This increased to about 25 in-house staff plus several external testers by the end of the fourth year production run. The Pentium IIs in use back then seemed pretty advanced (and expensive) at the time, but the specifications would be laughable these days. That said, the *Black & White* team created literally thousands of art assets and countless other files.

For subsequent projects, the team sizes and asset count have risen significantly. Currently, Lionhead seems to settle on about 40–50 people in-house for each title in full production, with additional resources found elsewhere as required.

For the next round of titles, Lionhead thinks that the team size could, in theory, rise to 100 people. But they prefer to keep their core teams around the current size and support them with other external or central (Lionhead-employed but non-team-specific) means.

All of this puts increasing demands on their asset tracking and management. It's particularly difficult when communication is spread across more parties and even across different locations.

Development process

The development of any game starts with a basic concept and ideas on how it can be the most fun. With *Black & White*, it was just six lines of text. Usually, in this "initial phase", concept art is also developed and some technical tests are done.

Figure 7.1 *Sketches for temples in* Black & White II*: (left) the good one; (right) the evil one (© Lionhead Studios Limited. All rights reserved)*

Figure 7.2 *The same temples as they appear in the game—here you see some information from the game engine for testing in the upper left corner (© Lionhead Studios Limited. All rights reserved)*

Then, the next 12–18 months of the project are focused on content art, tools, the game engine, and artificial intelligence system. In this "middle phase", the aim is clear and the working process rules are defined.

The "last phase" lasts six months or more and is used to make the game fun. Extra development time adds value to the game. No new concepts are introduced; the game will just be polished.

Team

People who know how to make games are selected for the team. Their abilities and experiences with project management vary greatly, so it is necessary to adjust project

Figure 7.3 *One of the good characters in* Black & White II *(© Lionhead Studios Limited;* Black & White II, The Movies, *Lionhead, and the Lionhead logo are trademarks of Lionhead Studios Limited. Screenshots used with the permission of Lionhead Studios Limited. All rights reserved)*

management to suit the team members, not vice versa. The core teams are focused on design and creation.

Other aspects like asset creation, which doesn't require project vision or strong creativity, are outsourced to external companies or freelancers. When the artwork comes back in-house, someone must track it, let the necessary people know it is available, and find the means to make it available to them. This team member must have a broad project overview and also be able to set priorities for the outsourced team.

Teamwork and project management

The project leader must ensure that everyone in the team has the assets and tools needed for the job. Most of this can be done by walking around, observing faces, and talking to people to see what's up. It is always important to monitor the motivation level.

Problems occur if someone is waiting for work to be finished by a colleague, so the producer has to set the schedule carefully beforehand and make sure that blocks are completed in the right order to avoid problems. This requires experience; no tool can do this for you.

Leaders from different sections like programming, art, and sound meet weekly if not daily to stay on top of the issues that arise in the departments. Verbal communication is key, but large discussions with 20 people or more would be too big to be productive. It is better to hold separate team-building events for the whole group which are not aimed at results other than bringing the team together.

One good way to discover issues during production is to watch e-mail threads and check for consistent comments. These can then be raised at meetings.

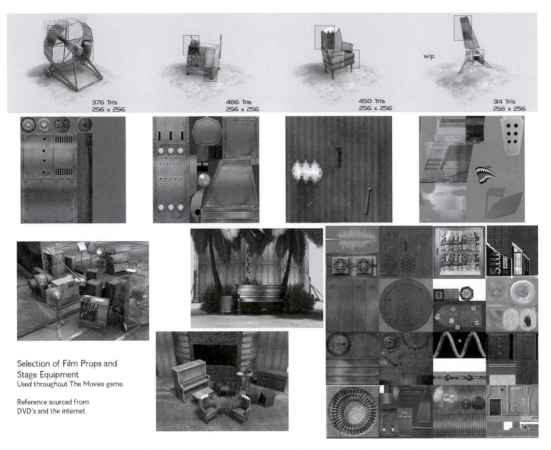

Figure 7.4 *Some props from* The Movies. *There are thousands of such objects that can be used in the game. The creation of the straightforward ones is outsourced (© Lionhead Studios Limited. All rights reserved)*

It's also sensible to invest in process development—at the month's start, management should set goals or ideas for what they would like to get done and maintain daily communication to keep people feeling involved. If the project vision and mission are not clear to all, the approach must be changed.

Work always can and should be delegated in small chunks. This ensures that everyone has a small success as often as possible.

Digital Asset Management

Lionhead Studios design from the ground up, but already start working on the small pieces of artwork before all the basics are determined. They just decide generally what will be in an environment and then immediately start creating things to speed up production.

The artwork is continually reviewed as it is worked on—regardless of whether it is created in-house or externally. All art assets are imported into the DAM system as early as possible, so that they can be reviewed within the game engine.

In the middle phase of game development, when the initial idea is fleshed out and more assets are created daily, proper Digital Asset Management is paramount. Of course, DAM is more important the bigger your team is and the longer the project lasts.

Tip

If possible, try condensing the middle asset creation phase to leave more time for the critical last phase, where the game can be turned from a good one into a great one.

Figure 7.5 *Some sample costumes that can be used when creating your own movie in* The Movies. *You can choose from a wardrobe of hundreds of different costumes—which is one reason the tracking of assets is so critical and so difficult (© Lionhead Studios Limited. All rights reserved)*

Tools used

Lionhead started without any DAM system for artwork. Files were just kept on local machines without any control over versioning, access rights, or the like. Inconsistent or unclear file names and employee absences were highly problematic, since work became inaccessible. Then there were the usual well-known problems: people would overwrite newer versions with old ones, and there was too much guesswork—which file was worked on when and by whom?

Programmers already used Visual SourceSafe (VSS) for version control, so to combat the recurring problems in the art team, VSS was also introduced for managing artwork. But the artists disliked this software since it offered no features specifically suited for their files and has an interface developed for programmers.

Then, for *Black & White*, which was considered a big project at the time, Alienbrain was introduced. They used it mainly to back up and find things. But even with proper file naming conventions, it can still be difficult to identify artwork files, so the thumbnails that Alienbrain offers are key for artists. Their programmers now use Perforce for source code control, but access art through Alienbrain.

Alienbrain's rollback and history features ensure that no more than one and a half day's work can be lost due to an error of any team member. They all feel better with such a safety net.

Accommodating human error

Even the best DAM system can't prevent errors. During the end of *Black & White*'s production phase, when everyone worked till dawn and on countless weekends, accidents happened when overworked people included a bug fix that broke several other things. As a solution, it was decided that only one machine should be used for checking in the changes to the central server. And no one was allowed to check-in the changes alone; they always required another team member to oversee the process to make sure nothing went wrong. But they would never again work without a DAM system because it prevents the real nightmare situations and helps everyone stay organized.

7.2   Sony Pictures Imageworks

About Sony Pictures Imageworks

Sony Pictures Imageworks is one of the world's largest and most successful visual effects and character animation studios.

The studio was responsible for creating breathtaking effects and memorable characters seen in *Spider-Man*, *Spider-Man 2*, *Stuart Little*, and *The Polar Express*, among others. At any time, as many as a dozen major motion pictures may be passing through the facility. Imageworks has contributed visual effects to many recent films, including *The Aviator*, *Cast Away*, *Bad Boys 2*, *Big Fish*, *The Haunted Mansion*, *The Matrix: Revolutions*, *The Matrix: Reloaded*, *The Lord of the Rings: The Two Towers*, and *Harry Potter and the Sorcerer's Stone*.

Since the company's founding in 1992, it has been recognized by the Academy of Motion Picture Arts and Sciences with Oscars™ for its work on *Spider-Man 2* and the CG animated short film *The ChubbChubbs!*, and nominations for *Spider-Man*, *Hollow Man*, *Stuart Little*, and *Starship Troopers*.

Figure 7.6 Spider-Man *Motion Picture © 2002 Columbia Pictures Industries, Inc. All Rights Reserved. Spider-Man Character ® and © 2002 Marvel Characters, Inc. All Rights Reserved. Courtesy of Columbia Pictures*

Figure 7.7 Spider-Man 2 *Motion Picture © 2004 Columbia Pictures Industries, Inc. All Rights Reserved. Spider-Man Character ® and © 2004 Marvel Characters, Inc. All Rights Reserved. Courtesy of Columbia Pictures*

Figure 7.8   Stuart Little *Original Motion Picture: © 1999 Global Entertainment Productions GmbH & Co. Medien KG and SPE German Finance Co. Inc. All Rights Reserved. Extended Television Version: © 1999, 2002 Global Entertainment Productions GmbH & Co. Medien KG and SPE German Finance Co. Inc. All Rights Reserved. Courtesy of Columbia Pictures*

Imageworks has more than 700 employees and is a division of Sony Pictures Digital, which oversees the digital production and online entertainment assets of Sony Pictures Entertainment.

Material for this success story was provided by Bill Villarreal, Sam Richards, and Manson Jones at Sony Pictures Imageworks.

Structure of the studio

Sony Pictures Imageworks is unique among Hollywood's effects studios because it supports a wider range of digital productions than any other facility. Projects range from sets of a dozen visual effects shots requested at short notice by a live-action film studio, to films that require creating realistic digital characters and environments for effects-laden motion pictures like *Spider-Man* and *Stuart Little*, or feature-length performance capture computer-animated movies like *The Polar Express*, and now, with the establishment of Sony Pictures Animation, feature-length CG animation.

Supporting such a wide range of projects requires a very scalable and flexible digital "production pipeline" that can cope with large variations in size and complexity but still leverages commonality among productions as much as possible.

Because at peak times Imageworks may be working on a dozen shows simultaneously, the production processes also need to be able to support multiple parallel production flows and hundreds of users.

Key software systems

At the core of the infrastructure at Imageworks are two software-based management systems. One, called VnP (for "versioning and publishing"), is used for main production asset management. The other, called "TrackIt", is used for task and workflow management. These two central systems are in turn surrounded and supported by more than a dozen additional, more specialized programs and databases that connect to planning tools, financial systems, the render farm, and other asset management databases.

Data flow at the studio

Budgeting and planning

All productions are driven from centrally produced budget and project plans. These are based on detailed breakdowns of the shows coming in and the work that is required for each scene that Imageworks is responsible for. Budgeting and planning are done through a combination of customized Excel worksheets and specialized databases developed by Imageworks for this purpose.

Shot breakdown

Complex shots generally require an elaborate sequence of steps by a variety of artists. To determine the work that is required, each show is broken down into its constituent parts—such as sequences, shots, characters, props, and environments. These production elements are entered into a specialized database and annotated with additional production details.

Task and workflow management

From this database, detailed task lists are generated in TrackIt, the central task and workflow management system at Imageworks. The task lists cover all work steps required to complete the elements and assemble the shots. A 3D character model, for example, must be built, rigged, and textured with reviews and approvals required between each step. Each of these tasks may require a different artist with experience in the corresponding discipline. The leaders of each department or specialty (such as modeling, animation, and lighting) are responsible for assigning tasks to artists or groups of artists. Assignments are based on availability and take into account any special skills that may be needed.

Asset management for reference artwork

To make sure everyone on a show works towards a common visual style and all artists follow the guidelines of the production design, the art department prepares detailed specifications for most aspects of a film. These specifications can include just about anything that helps define the look of a film, ranging from rough sketches, color swatches, and reference photographs of real scenes and objects, to character expression studies and clay maquettes.

Most of these items are digitized and made available to everyone on the production as digital assets through an artwork database called BrowseIt. For this and other asset-tracking functions, Imageworks has adapted Avid's Alienbrain asset management platform.

Content creation

Once tasks are assigned, artists create content for the shots. Numerous content authoring tools are in use at Imageworks and new systems are regularly introduced if new technologies emerge or if the effects on a new show require special software. Commercial tools employed by Imageworks range from Alias Maya for 3D modeling and animation, Maxon Bodypaint for texture painting, and Avid Media Composer for editing, in addition to a wide range of proprietary systems for lighting, layout, and compositing.

The main Production Asset Management system

The digital content produced for each show is stored in folder structures on a central, high-volume disk farm that can hold dozens of terabytes of data. The folder structure is highly standardized and maintained through VnP, a proprietary system for main Production Asset Management. VnP is based on custom software and a very large Oracle database server. VnP is a very complex and powerful system, but on a high level the main responsibilities of any such asset management system are:

- *Maintaining order.* Maintain the centralized storage structure with standardized folder and file naming conventions—artists are generally not required or even allowed to define their own file and folder names.
- *Tracking versions.* If multiple versions or variants of an asset exist, the asset management system will track them and link them to the primary asset object.
- *Isolating changes.* Since several users may work on a shot at the same time and there are many interdependencies between the files they work on, the asset management system also isolates users from changes made by other users until they are officially committed or "published" in a controlled fashion. This way, render jobs do not fail if someone changes a file while the corresponding shot is being rendered.

Other supporting systems

Many other auxiliary systems are employed by Imageworks to streamline the production flow and handle important tasks. Some of the systems that were either created or adapted by Imageworks that play an important role in the production cycle include a time sheet system for artists, a job queuing system that optimizes the workload on the extensive render farm, and a rework request system that tracks and distributes information about changes requested for work that has already made its way through parts of the production pipeline.

Success against the odds

Building or customizing and then integrating such a wide variety of systems and fusing them together into a coherent infrastructure is a challenge for any company. Also, as pieces of the structure are required to continually change in order to meet clients' needs and to accommodate technological advances, the job can become a nearly impossible task. Imageworks, however, has mastered this challenge and has become one of the most successful effects and animation studios ever.

7.3   Scholz & Volkmer

About Scholz & Volkmer

Scholz & Volkmer is a full-service agency for interactive media. It is located close to Frankfurt in Wiesbaden, Germany. In 2004 it employed 47 people and had a turnover of 4.7 million Euros.

SCHOLZ&VOLKMER

They have been crafting interactive applications that stand out through creative concepts, intuitive navigation, and lean back-end solutions. The agency's core competencies lie in the development, implementation, and support of promotional and corporate websites, the visualization of (real-time) data, the development and application of online marketing and CRM concepts, as well as the development and integration of individual back-end solutions.

Scholz & Volkmer work for customers like Acht Frankfurt, DaimlerChrysler, E.ON, Fraport, Ingo Maurer, Linotype Library, Mercedes-Benz, O2 Germany, Rui Camilo, ThyssenKrupp, Toni Gard, USM, and Vogue. For these customers, they produce websites that are innovative, enhance the visibility of the brand, engage the visitor, and are perfectly user-friendly.

Since its foundation in 1994, Scholz & Volkmer has earned over 120 national and 230 international design awards—among them the Grand Prix (1999) at the Cyber Lions in Cannes, the iF Design Award, awards from the ADC Germany, from ADC New York, from the Clio Awards, and from the New York Festival.

Scholz & Volkmer is regularly listed as one of the most creative agencies in Germany and worldwide.

The following success story was shared in an interview with Sabine Schmidt and Thorsten Kraus from Scholz & Volkmer.

A typical project

A typical project at Scholz & Volkmer lasts 3–12 months and involves six people:

- A project leader, who makes sure the concept is good and is properly followed through
- A project manager
- A graphical designer
- A copywriter
- Two programmers/coders (front/back-end).

The phases of a project

In cooperation with the customer, the project brief and the main idea for the new website are created. This is done in a PowerPoint document, because it is always presented to the client. All team members reference this document during production.

The designer creates the look of the site by scribbling ideas in Photoshop and/or FreeHand. This gives a first idea of the colors, forms, and fonts that will be used to create the experience of the prospective site.

The programmers use UML tools to model the code basis needed for complex, dynamic sites. From the beginning, they use the Software Configuration Management tool CVS (Concurrent Versioning System, Open Source). The programmers work on Windows, Macintosh, and Linux machines. Most of them use HomeSite for coding; visual tools like Dreamweaver are not in use. These have proved to be unhelpful because of their focus on ease of use, not on lean code that supports all technologies for creating dynamic sites (like PHP, Python, or Java).

The project manager's job is to keep files in order. At the beginning of the project he or she copies a pre-defined directory structure—which is used for every project—on the central server. It contains directories for each department and sub-directories for daily work.

Every person on the team can access only the directories he or she needs. The file system's access rights are used to make sure of this. For example, there is a directory "Final" which contains only assets that are approved—internally and by the customer. This is the only directory members from other departments have access to; the working directories are locked. This makes sure only assets that are actually final find their way to the website.

Storing files locally is not permitted; all files live on a central server. To make this possible, a huge file server is provided, accessed by Gigabit-LAN.

All assets that are sent in by the clients are ingested into an image library. This is a custom-made tool, a web application running on a central Mac OS X server. It transfers the files into the Macintosh file system and indexes the assets. The team members access the database with the commercial program ACDsee.

The images that are purchased from image libraries also go into this central system. They are tagged with metadata like where the image comes from, who has the copyright, and how much it costs, if applicable.

Only import and export of assets from the central catalog is allowed. For security reasons it is not possible to modify or to erase them.

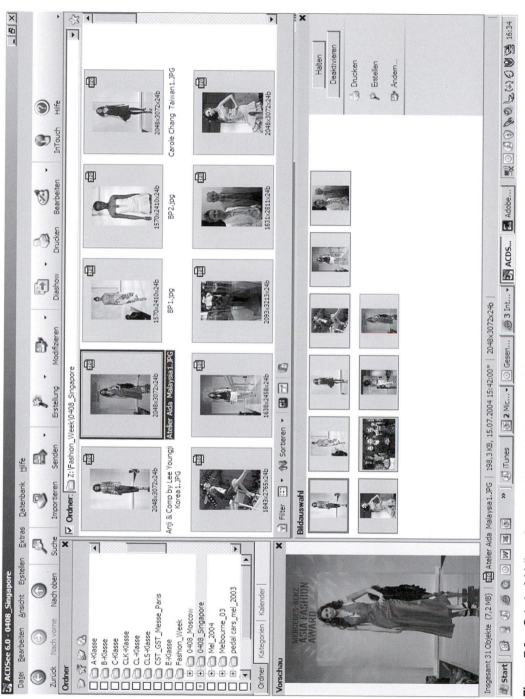

Figure 7.9 Scholz & Volkmer's custom image library uses ACDsee for access (Developed by Scholz & Volkmer. All rights reserved)

In 2004, Scholz & Volkmer conducted extensive research on the image catalogs and Digital Asset Management solutions on the market. In the past it happened that they wanted to re-use an image and found only the low-resolution version of it was part of the website—the hi-res original image was somehow lost in the vast amount of project data.

The evaluation team came to the conclusion that Cumulus was the best software for their needs and they examined it closely. It is often considered the most professional solution for image management. But Cumulus also seemed too expensive, mainly because it offers so many features that were not needed in this case. In the end, Scholz & Volkmer decided to create their own tool for image management because this made it possible to adapt it exactly to the way they work. The self-created image library runs on a Macintosh OS X server and is accessible by clients from Mac, Windows, and Linux systems.

For approval, Scholz & Volkmer use another custom-made tool. It is based on PHP and mySQL and serves as an intranet to support the workflow. Artists upload their drafts to it, and others can comment and/or approve them. Parts of the HTML and other code are also uploaded here.

In the final phase, some parts of this system are made accessible for the customers so they too can see how their site is progressing. However, important things are always presented in person—for example, the first drafts for the look of the site.

The system has no automated notification features. The project teams are small, so everyone knows the milestones. In this case, such features would complicate matters more than they would bring benefits.

For bug tracking in the testing phase, yet another custom-made tool is used. This automatically notifies the person responsible when a bug is entered so he or she can take immediate action. The tool offers only the features that are needed for testing websites. Commercially available bug tracking tools are created for programmers—but testing at Scholz & Volkmer is also done by non-programmers who are representative of the prospective users. They just have to enter what happened, what they did to cause the issue, which system they used, plus they can include a screenshot if they want to.

An example project

As an example, Scholz & Volkmer created the website "Mixed Tape" for Mercedes-Benz in 2004. Mixed Tape is an online platform for free legal music download. The concept was created in cooperation with the music agency Renommee Music Consulting.

It addresses new target groups for Mercedes-Benz and tries to encourage repeated visits by offering a new mixed tape every eight weeks. Each set contains about a dozen songs from international artists of different genres for free download.

For the website, a simple Content Management System (CMS) was created that enables the customer to upload new images and MP3s.

The creation of the initial site and the CMS took five months and involved three employees from Renommee and 10 from Scholz & Volkmer: two for design, six for programming/coding, and two for project management.

Eingeloggt: Andreas Klinger

Dateien hinzufügen | von O2 | von S&V | Texte zur Freigabe S&V > O2 | Texte final | alle

Anzeigen: Die letzten 20 Einträge | Alle Einträge

Dateiname	Datum / Uhrzeit	Größe	Benutzer	Kommentar
banner050208.zip	08.02.2005 15:36:15	168979	Hannes Kober	Banner Dateien, swf und html mit den Popup Codes. MMS-Fotodienste, Buli, Registrierung, MusicFotodienste in 2 Versionen eine für Testserver und die andere müsste immer funktionieren
14_handy_service_guide.jpg	07.02.2005 18:16:55	22920	Dominik Lammer	Banner, Bilder, Teaser // 050207 / Die Handy Services von o2
Banner_Bilder_Teaser_050207.zip	07.02.2005 17:58:11	382798	Dominik Lammer	Banner, Bilder, Teaser // 050207
Banner_AktuellerStand.pdf	04.02.2005 11:55:48	1037877	Hannes Kober	Mobile Multimedia: Panorama-Banner und -Bilder; Aktueller Stand
mobilemultimediabanner.pdf	03.02.2005 17:20:08	1227005	Hannes Kober	Mobile Multimedia: Panorama-Banner und -Bilder
o2_WebStyleguide_v2_050201.pdf	02.02.2005 18:35:52	4458772	David Hofmann	
MobileFun_Start_050201.jpg	01.02.2005 15:59:09	579058	Dominik Lammer	Mobile Fun // Startseite
o2_Media_Player_050201.jpg	01.02.2005 15:49:26	105703	Dominik Lammer	o2 Media Player // Update
050131_o2demo_GK.ppt.zip	01.02.2005 10:10:30	12925403	Dominik Lammer	Mobile Fun Grobkonzept-Präsentation
handylogos_050131.zip	31.01.2005 15:53:07	13844	Hannes Kober	Teaser-Package Handylogos in 3 verschiedenen Formaten.+ callto action "Jetzt downloaden"
050127_myWap_o2online.ppt	28.01.2005 14:57:14	1102848	David Hofmann	myWAP Konzept 1
o2_Media_Player_050128.jpg	28.01.2005 02:15:23	97419	Dominik Lammer	o2 Media Player
Handymodul_050128.zip	28.01.2005 01:30:20	1154605	Dominik Lammer	Mobile Fun // Startseite + Integration Handymodul / 2.
o2demo_myo2_050126.zip	26.01.2005 23:40:08	1847734	Dominik Lammer	o2 Mediac // myo2 / Erste Entwürfe/Überlegungen / 3.
Handymodul_050126.zip	26.01.2005 16:18:00	1108878	Dominik Lammer	Mobile Fun // Startseite + Integration Handymodul
o2demo_myo2_050125.zip	25.01.2005 20:55:52	1419247	Dominik Lammer	o2 Media // myo2 / Erste Entwürfe/Überlegungen / 2.
o2demo_myo2_050124.zip	24.01.2005 17:57:38	1480729	Dominik Lammer	o2 Media // myo2 / Erste Entwürfe/Überlegungen
player_demo.zip	20.01.2005 18:10:00	280230	Dominik Lammer	Banner, Bilder, Teaser Player
022005-03.zip	20.01.2005 15:59:35	512068	David Hofmann	Bundesliga Special Update 2
022005-02.zip	20.01.2005 13:07:45	5158102	David Hofmann	Bundesliga Special Update

Figure 7.10 A screen from the custom tool for file uploading. You can see the file's name, upload date and time, its size, who uploaded it, and what comment was made (Developed by Scholz & Volkmer. All rights reserved)

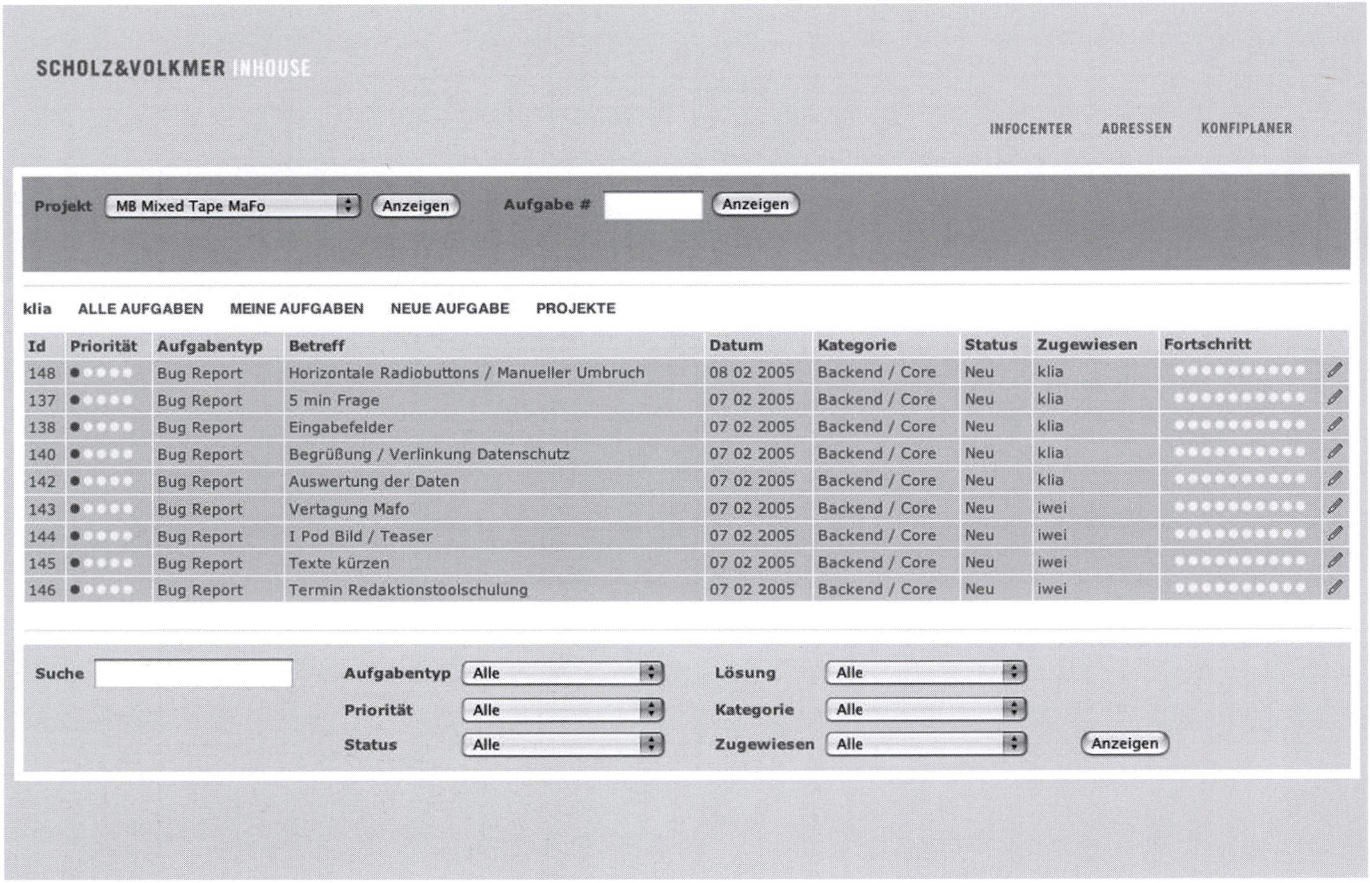

Figure 7.11 *The bug tracking tool of Scholz & Volkmer (Developed by Scholz & Volkmer. All rights reserved)*

Figure 7.12 *The customer view of the exchange platform (Developed by Scholz & Volkmer. All rights reserved)*

Figure 7.13 *The start page of Mixed Tape (Developed by Scholz & Volkmer. All rights reserved)*

Figure 7.14 *The main page of Mixed Tape, where you can select tracks for listening or download (Developed by Scholz & Volkmer. All rights reserved)*

The CMS has to organize up to 15 songs per compilation in two formats (streaming and download); there are five compilations planned—adding up to 150 MP3 files. Additionally, there are the image files for the interface skins, the artist's photos, and the PDF files with the optional cover for a custom compilation CD that can be downloaded.

For the creation of the site, the team at Scholz & Volkmer produced 1400 Photoshop and FreeHand files, amounting to 3.5 GB; 800 PowerPoint, Excel, and Word documents, amounting to 900 MB; 800 Flash files; and 210 PHP documents.

7.4 Framfab

About Framfab

Framfab specializes in delivering digital marketing, information management, and transactional solutions to its global clients. To deliver these solutions, Framfab integrates business consulting, concept and design, information architecture knowledge, and technology.

Framfab's clients include global corporations such as 3M, AstraZeneca, Coca-Cola, Philip Morris International, Nike, Sony, UBS, and Volvo. Framfab's work has been recognized with several international awards, including a Cyber Lion Grand Prix at the Cannes Film Festival.

framfab

Framfab has over 350 colleagues in offices all over Europe (Sweden, Denmark, Germany, Switzerland, the Netherlands, and the UK). In the US, Framfab cooperates with Avenue A/ Razorfish.

The following success story was shared in an interview with Jasjyot Singh (managing director), Bernie Segal (client services director), Kirsty Weston (business strategist), Eliel Johnson (information architect), and Rachel Switzky (user experience leader) from Framfab United Kingdom.

A typical project for DAM implementation

Framfab has assisted several global clients in the selection and introduction of Digital Asset Management solutions. The biggest driver for these clients was to get a grip on all the assets distributed throughout the organization, especially pictures, marketing collateral, video clips, and brand-related assets.

For example, Framfab worked with a global consumer goods company to lead the introduction of a Digital Asset Management system. The client wanted to increase the overall return on their intellectual capital by sharing brand-specific marketing, product, and promotional information across its global markets.

There were four main objectives for the project:

1 To reduce the time-to-market of the central marketing and brand teams by communicating brand, product, and campaign directions faster from the center to each country.

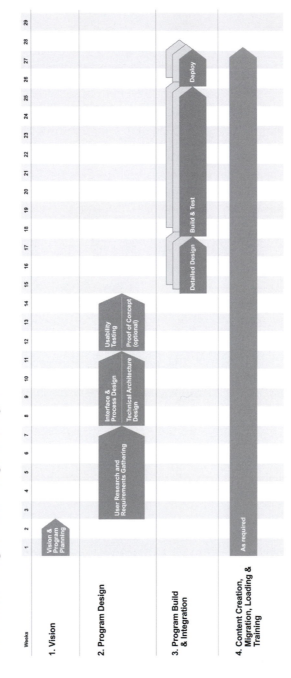

Figure 7.15 *Process diagram for a sample DAM implementation project (© Framfab. All rights reserved)*

2 To reduce the time-to-market of campaign ideas by sharing and re-using brand execution and product promotion results between countries, enabling cross-pollination of ideas.
3 To increase effectiveness in developing new packaging concepts and product extensions.
4 To monitor competitors' marketing activities in each country.

To address these objectives, Framfab designed and built digital libraries of brand and marketing assets that contain best practices, product examples, campaign materials, local executions, and examples of competitors' marketing activities.

Research and requirements phase

Every project starts with user research. The Framfab team conducts phone interviews with the employees that will likely work with the new system. They may also watch them at the workplace to find out about the processes in the company at the moment. Often, there are offline processes that are so informal that no one bothers to mention them explicitly and these can only be unearthed during on-location research.

To assess business drivers for the DAM issue, all the stakeholders are brought together in a day-long workshop. Here they discuss the current pipeline for working with assets, what they like about it, and what they think should change. Other aspects discussed include: When and where are the clients accessing the assets? Who is involved and are there multiple agencies working cooperatively? Are there any bottlenecks? How fast are assets produced? What are the current tools used for searching? How are assets re-used, if at all? What kind of metadata has been used already and how do people define items—and is this categorization system used worldwide or just in the department?

It is always best to get people to talk about their actual work and responsibilities; this is how you learn about the real pain points.

In this sample project, the user research and requirements capture phase for each of the libraries lasted three months. Framfab tested the design with a selection of key users at the end of each of these three-month periods. The detailed design of the user interface and administration interface for both libraries lasted a further two months.

Decision phase

After all the information has been collected from the client, the Framfab team structures the findings and discusses what could be improved. They may create some mock-ups to design how the workflow and access to assets should be handled in the new system. Evaluation is done as to what level of integration is needed—perhaps into the intranet? Should assets be retrieved from the system automatically?

Then the client needs are prioritized and mapped to the DAM requirements that they expect would improve the situation.

The most suitable Digital Asset Management system is selected and proposed. If necessary, Framfab also offers customizations and the programming of extensions for existing packages when there are special requirements that the systems on the market cannot meet. Framfab estimates the effort required to implement these desired improvements.

Then they quantify the business benefits and assess the business and user value provided by these improvements. A detailed Return On Investment (ROI) calculation is done for this. The ROI is an important basis on which to make the decision to purchase a DAM system in every major company.

Design and implementation phase

A pivotal decision is which features of the DAM system selected should be implemented and which should be turned off. Most systems offer so much functionality that it overwhelms users, requires extensive training, and creates errors from misuse. That is why you should disable and hide every single function that is not needed.

In most cases a lot of customization is necessary; a complex product like DAM software is not often an "out-of-the-box" solution. The software has to be modified to fit into the existing IT landscape, to support the existing or desired processes, and most critically to ensure the interface enables users to complete their tasks efficiently.

Additionally, the workflow can be optimized when a DAM solution is introduced. It can structure the whole approach an organization has to getting its work done. This is a process that has to be coordinated with the management strategists because it is such a central part of the company's business. Usually DAM also makes the monitoring of assets as well as the employee's work easier, which is one of the important benefits from the project management perspective.

Another major task is to come up with metadata categories that work within the whole organization. Often, it is difficult enough to do this within a single department, but when the categories need to work for all kinds of different assets, for offices distributed over the whole world, and within all departments, you have to know the exact requirements for all the assets and the needs of all the people involved.

To ensure that the prospective users can actually work with the system, understand how to use it, and actually like using it, some prototypes are fleshed out as a next step. Often, the first prototype is just a paper prototype with the interface drawn or printed. This is shown to prospective users, and they are asked what they would do with this interface to accomplish a certain task. Doing this with several employees of the customer is a fast and efficient way to find out whether they understand how the system will work.

This can be done several times if necessary until the interface developed makes sense for the daily working scenarios. This ensures that the training needed for the users is minimal. The system should be so easy that everyone who only retrieves information should need no special training at all. Only the people who import information or assets into the system or who modify it should need to be trained to make sure the data is always consistent, usually in a session lasting no longer than a day.

During the design phase of the sample project, Framfab also developed a taxonomy containing a set of labels that described the assets stored in the libraries.

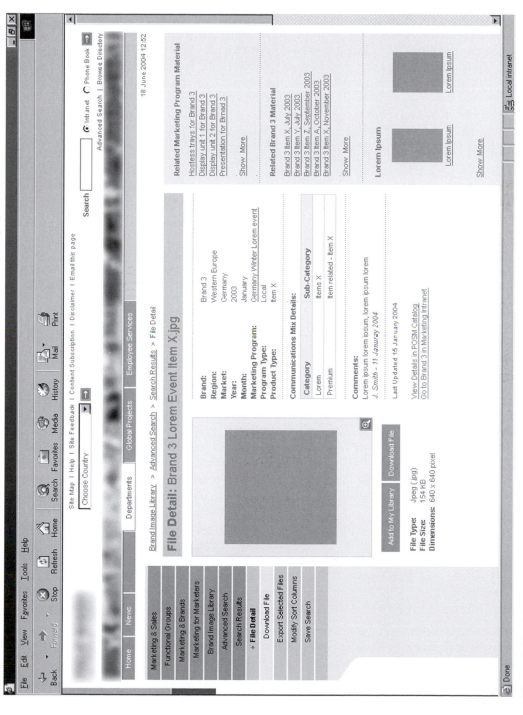

Figure 7.16 *Mock-up of an asset detail page used during development of the sample project (© Framfab. All rights reserved)*

Some key data of the sample project

- Each month, employees around the world add hundreds of images to both libraries Framfab implemented for the client. The library has the capacity to handle millions of images.
- Images in the libraries can range from several hundred kilobytes to several megabytes. Packaging images can include all sides of the product, e.g. front, back, sides, bottom, etc.
- The libraries are accessible by thousands of marketers and employees globally.
- The platform for clients is Microsoft Windows.
- The repository involved is Interwoven MediaBin. This was supplemented by a content management tool, Interwoven TeamSite, and an enterprise class search engine.

Given that the objective was to develop a seamless interface with the global intranet and have a standardized interface across the two libraries, Framfab developed a user-friendly front-end interface for the DAM software.

This was critical as it enables users to search and find images and assets using everyday brand, marketing, and packaging terminology. The user interface design and taxonomy were critical in ensuring adoption and making this project a success.

Since the user groups were the same for both libraries, the interface had to be seamless between the applications so the users would not have to learn how to use two different tools. The libraries also had to have a similar look and feel as the corporate intranet and be consistent with its navigation standards.

Maintenance, improvement, and judging success

The duration of the research and implementation phases together usually adds up to four to six months, depending on the scope of the project. But usually there is a third phase too: Framfab goes back to the customer a few weeks after the DAM system's launch and measures the success.

If modifications are needed or slight improvements can be made (there is always room for improvement!), they are done then. Sometimes it is just the creation of a few more templates. Sometimes procedures have proven to be not as effective as hoped, and they might need to be changed. In some cases the users realized they want to use another feature which was not yet implemented.

In the end, the success can be quantified or documented in varying ways—by recording the number of assets that are now in the system, by charting how the workflow changed, or monitoring the number of assets that are re-used and which types are re-used most often. Of course, the overall feeling of customer satisfaction is the best measure of how the system is working out.

The sample project's main benefits include a reduction in the time-to-market through:

- The sharing of information quickly and efficiently between the center and each country
- The cross-pollination of ideas between countries
- The faster launch of new product packaging initiatives.

The other benefits are that marketers can now monitor competitors' marketing activities in each country and that this information is available on a global basis.

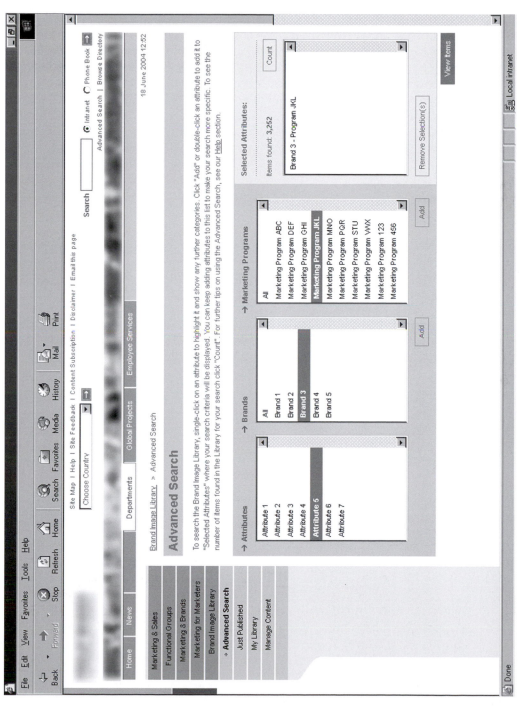

Figure 7.17 Advanced search for the image repository in the sample project (© Framfab. All rights reserved)

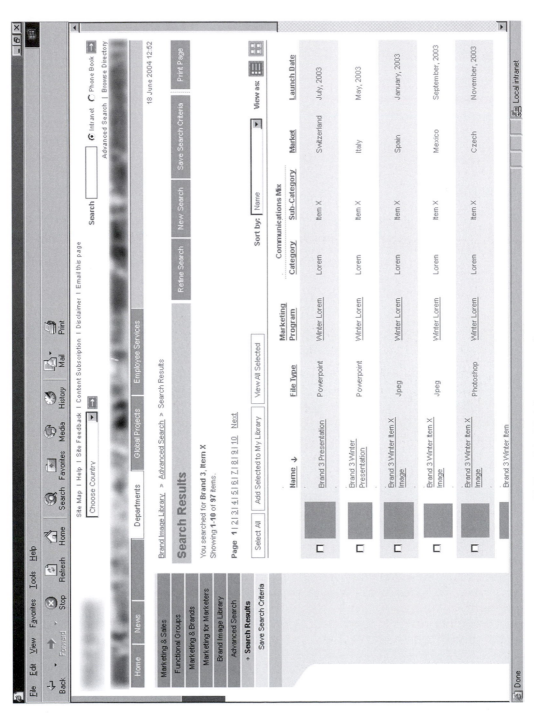

Figure 7.18 *List with search results (© Framfab. All rights reserved)*

7.5   Attitude Studio

About Attitude Studio

Widely recognized as one of the leading companies in computer-generated virtual characters, Attitude offers cost-effective solutions for the delivery of CG animated series, animated feature films, direct to video, video games, and special effects.

Their team of artists and computer scientists has combined state-of-the-art animation systems together with proprietary technology to provide the most emotional virtual characters. From traditional outline rendering to photorealistic characters, the visual diversity of their creations illustrates the *"savoir faire"* they have to offer.

These new pipelines allow for significant cost and time efficiency in the normally time-consuming, labour-intensive process of developing virtual characters for large-scale productions.

Today's animation market is dominated mainly by large North American production companies. Despite this, Attitude Studio has found its place by remaining faithful to its main principles:

- Supplying services for all types of image rendering and formats
- Developing proprietary technology adapted to the main software packages used in the industry
- An industrial production process for creating quality animation at competitive prices.

Choosing a solution

In 2002, Attitude Studio decided to implement an advanced production management model. They decided to select a DAM solution so that they could implement their workflow ideas without having to start from scratch. They needed to have a robust system, capable of having more than 100 people transferring data simultaneously.

At Attitude Studio, the workflow concept consists of so-called "production assembly elements", virtual building blocks corresponding to the typical elements in a production. Since these would be very time-intensive to implement with only a file system or simple database, they decided to use a DAM system as the basis that offered all the data structures that they would need. Using Alienbrain VFX and its element objects, they have implemented an advanced data management tool that allows every user to get a very specific view of the data structures.

With its own dedicated development team, Attitude can implement new management features on top of the DAM system, making features available when they are needed.

Perfecting the pipeline

At the start of each production, Attitude creates an "assembly element", which is a kind of "super-asset" that can itself contain assets and other related information. Each department creates its own assembly elements—for example, the modelers create mesh assembly elements, and the animators create animation assembly elements. They use both in-house software and standard tools such as Maya, MotionBuilder, or FinalCutPro.

Using the typical structure of a CGI project with scenes, shots, characters, and animation data, they create interfaces that allow the user to see the data in that context. Instead of browsing a set of directories looking for a file, the user can simply look for the character assigned to him or her and start working on the 3D file associated with that character.

Setup and configuration

The DAM system is used through the entire production process. As soon as an artist has information to store somewhere, they use the DAM. As soon as data is stored in the system it is flagged with the appropriate identifiers. The work process usually starts with creating sequences, shots, and cameras.

At Attitude Studio there is no set directory structure for the users. Since the ordering and structuring of the data is taken care of by the assembly elements, users can work in any data structure that they like.

All data except for very large production data like rendered layers is stored in the DAM. The larger files are linked inside the DAM and are usable in the interface, but are actually stored outside the DAM's database. This allows Attitude to exclude the data from special DAM functions such as versioning, but still allows necessary information to be added to the data.

Searching for specific files and versions using all the metadata stored in the database is one of the most common uses of the DAM system.

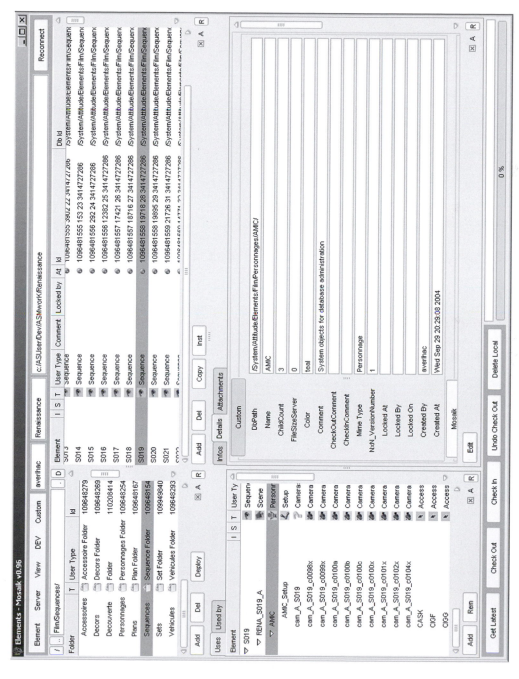

Figure 7.19 *The Mosaik interface to Alienbrain VFX displays detailed information for each sequence with a list of all used items (© Attitude Studio. All rights reserved)*

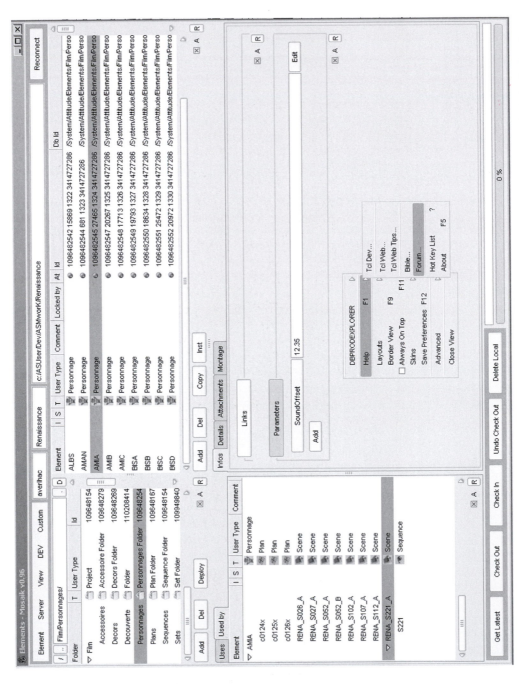

Figure 7.20 *The Dependency Management provides bidirectional links between referenced assets (© Attitude Studio. All rights reserved)*

Recommendations

In many ways the implementation of a DAM system improved communication in the team, since the users didn't have to worry about "what is my scene composed of?" and "what is the latest version of all that content?". Since all information about relationships between the data and the status of the data is stored and available in the DAM system, users can just access the data in a logical manner; they just tell the system "I want to work in shot #, in sequence #, and edit the animation of that character", and never worry about the actual files.

Digital Asset Management improved the pipeline by centralizing the information, and it saves time in the day-to-day work; however, for Attitude Studio the system is not yet as robust as it should be. They may still experience delays in the work schedule, especially if someone has to wait for the information that they need to continue working.

Attitude concludes that if they had to introduce a DAM again, though, they would do it largely in the same way. The major change would be to try to use even more of the DAM's standard functionality instead of rewriting parts themselves. For example, rewriting the search requests and not relying on the VFX features has cost a lot of time and implementation effort. They would also advise companies that want to introduce a DAM to go through several days of training to avoid the trial-and-error stage during development.

7.6   Pixelspell Animation Studios

About Pixelspell Animation Studios

Pixelspell is an Internet-based animation studio. It is a cooperation of more than 50 independent artists from Germany, Austria, Switzerland, the USA, and Japan.

Tom Braun, who had the idea for a distributed Cinema 4D animation film project, founded Pixelspell Animation Studios in 2002. In the same year, work on the film *La Cucaracha* began. It features an animated character, Kaki, a brave cockroach with a big hunger but little luck. This 12-minute short shows a day in Kaki's life with his human roommate in an apartment in 1940s New York City.

The following success story was shared in an interview with Ralf Zender, Producer at Pixelspell Animation Studios.

Development process

Development at Pixelspell is basically the same as at any other animation studio—but with one major difference: team members don't meet in person. Most of them have never even seen each other, but they have been working together happily for years; all collaboration is web based.

Workflow and project management

When an artist starts working on an asset, for example a new character, he uses a typical 3D application, in Pixelspell's case in Cinema 4D. This is a simple and straightforward process that is usually trouble free.

But when the artist starts working together with other team members—for example, when he provides the character to someone else who puts it in a movie scene and does the animation—things begin to get complicated. The artist uploads his work to a server, mails it to someone else, or lets other people access it on his own computer.

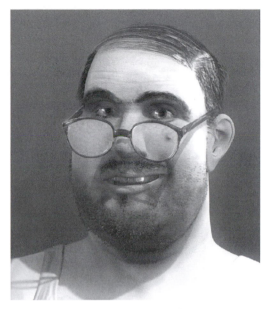

Figure 7.21 *Kaki (left) and his human roommate (right), the main characters of* La Cucaracha *(© Pixelspell Animation Studios. All rights reserved)*

This process soon led to conflicts, lost files, overwritten data, and usage of outdated or incomplete files, so it was apparent that Pixelspell needed to introduce DAM.

First experiences with DAM

Pixelspell started with simple web forums to promote effective communication. They tried three different forums but all failed to make life easier for the artists. They just added an overhead to their work but did not solve their problems.

Next, they built a simple FileMaker application to store their data. This soon proved not flexible enough and was still error prone. One major problem was that FileMaker has no templates for the management of movie assets. For every feature you want, you have to start with an empty database without any interface or options. Some things they needed, like transfer via HTTPS protocol, were not possible with FileMaker.

When these limitations became clear, one team member offered to program a custom solution completely from scratch. The idea seemed attractive at first because it meant that the DAM system would include all the features everyone dreamed of and it would exactly fit their needs. But finally it was decided not to choose this route, since it was obvious that doing so would take a long time—it would involve months of extensive testing, and the danger of losing even more data due to bugs in the system could really slow production quite a bit. Since Pixelspell's aim is to produce animation, not software, the team decided to purchase a DAM solution.

Figure 7.22   *For each scene hundreds of models have to be created and put together into a common scene for animation. This is an especially challenging task if collaborators work on different continents (© Pixelspell Animation Studios. All rights reserved)*

DAM tools used today

Pixelspell compiled a list of features they wanted in their new system—it had to accommodate these fundamental points:

- International distribution of team members
- Remote project management
- Central rendering and post-production (in Cologne, Germany)
- High data volume (especially video files!)
- Secure data transmission over the Internet
- Management of user rights
- Central data repository with good overview for all team members.

They looked at some DAM solutions and finally decided that Alienbrain would best fit their needs.

An Alienbrain Remote Collaboration Server was installed in Switzerland, and Alienbrain Studio Manager Clients and Alienbrain Studio Cross-platform Clients were purchased for all team members so that up to 50 users could work in parallel on their Windows or Macintosh machines.

For Adobe Photoshop, as well as for Microsoft Office, there is a plug-in to make management of these files within the familiar environment easy too. They use Microsoft Office for design documents and project management files, for example.

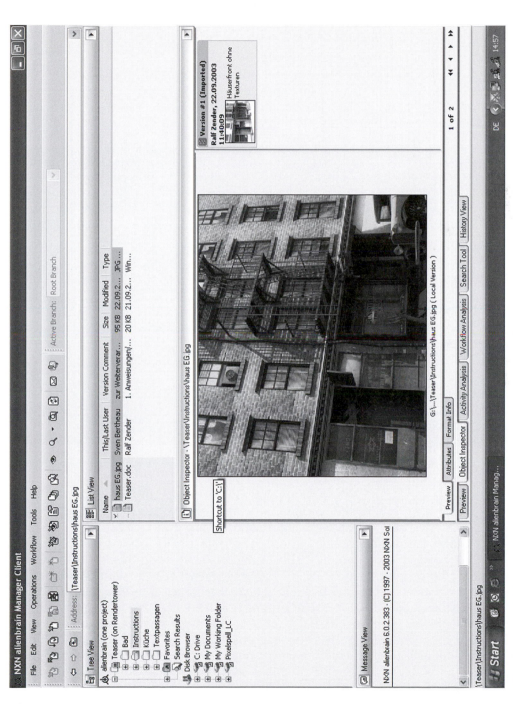

Figure 7.23 In Alienbrain you can see a preview of your modified version (big picture) and the version(s) stored on the central server (small picture to the right). (© Pixelspell Animation Studios. All rights reserved)

Introduction phase

The installation effort was minimal and required no knowledge above what is needed to install any mid-level complexity software package.

Every team member got a short document as an introduction; since people are distributed over continents, in-person training was not possible. Acceptance of the new system was high from the beginning because everyone on the team had experienced the data chaos on different machines before and was eager to improve the situation.

Figure 7.24 *Kaki,* La Cucaracha*'s megastar, in action (© Pixelspell Animation Studios. All rights reserved)*

Everyone tried out the features and began to use what seemed suitable for their role. So in a short period of time, version control, commenting, and sending messages to others with links to files in the system was in use by the whole team. The benefits of the DAM system were soon realized and no one tried to work around it. One main reason for this is that the team consists of highly motivated people that are used to working together in a distributed fashion and therefore they knew how important it is to follow established rules of collaboration.

One thing Pixelspell would like to see improved in Alienbrain is the listing of the directory structure. Currently, it shows all folders for all users—regardless of their access rights. This means everyone can see folders for which they have no access privileges, which clutters the directory and which can be frustrating when you can't open folders that you can see.

There is always room for improvement, but in general the team is using the system without problems. Alienbrain is currently being used for the final production of *La Cucaracha*, a pilot for *ZooZeit* (a TV sequel for kids), and for several shorts.

Appendix 1: Product overview

What you can find here

In this appendix, you will find detailed descriptions of some important applications available today. The market research firm Gistics lists 616 "DAM solution providers" and 1246 "Knowledge Asset Management solution providers" in its 2005 report on the DAM market. Of course, it is way beyond the scope of this book to look at all of them, and it wouldn't make sense to do so either. Since this book focuses on you, working in an advertising or web agency, at a game producer, or in 3D animation, most of the systems listed by Gistics are of no interest to you. Therefore, we've picked the applications that we think can help you improve the way you work.

By the time you get your hands on this book, there might be some great systems developed that didn't make it into our list, since the market is changing rapidly. This collection mirrors what we personally know or what we know has been widely used with good results. Programs that we suspect will be of the most interest are described in more detail. For others, there is just a short description so that you know what they have to offer if you encounter the name.

You are the one who has to decide which functions you really need, how much money you are ready to spend, and how much effort you can exert setting everything up. Go back to Chapter 5 if you need help making these decisions. You'll also find a detailed explanation of the categories in which we group the applications there. Good luck!

Image catalogs and libraries

The focus of all the systems in this category is on handling image files and audio/video files. Most of them don't offer advanced workflow/versioning features. If you need those, you might do better to check the "Digital Asset Management" or "Enterprise Content Management" categories.

iView Media Pro 2.6

iView Media Pro is an image catalog widely used by people working with photographs or other image files. It helps in sorting and retrieving the assets, and lets you compile catalogs that you can output as print, PDF, HTML page, or as a slideshow in a video file. It is acclaimed for its ease of use and it definitely is a good solution for any small team that doesn't need DAM for production, but mainly for archiving and retrieval.

Table A1.1 *iView Media Pro 2.6: general information*

Manufacturer	iView Multimedia Ltd
Type of DAM	Image Catalog
Architecture	Single-user application
Platform	Windows 98, ME, 2000, XP; Macintosh OS 9, OS X
Used by	Photographers, small to mid-size design agencies
Reference customers	Red Door VR; photographers like Jaap Buitendijk, Kevin Foley, Ed Kashi
Website	www.iview-multimedia.com

Technical description

Like other image catalog systems, iView Media Pro uses the file system as a base. It can automatically update the folder's contents so that newly added files are processed. It creates thumbnails from the image files and reads out metadata like the EXIF and IPTC, which are widely used by digital cameras for storing technical information to describe the picture's content. Also, Adobe's Extensible Metadata Platform (XMP) annotations are supported for JPEG, TIFF, PNG, and Photoshop files.

Supported file types

Image file formats supported are basic types like JPEG, TIFF, BMP, PNG, or GIF. Several RAW formats from digital cameras are also supported. iView Media Pro can read the proprietary file formats of Adobe Photoshop, Adobe Illustrator, Macromedia Freehand, CorelDraw, and Adobe InDesign. PDF, EPS, TXT, and HTML files are recognized too. Fonts are displayed with sample text to judge its appearance. AIFF, MP3, WAV, SWF, MOV, and MPEG are among the supported formats. File formats of 3D programs are not supported at the time of writing. They can only be cataloged; thumbnail/preview features are not available for unsupported file formats.

Archiving/retrieval features

The standard EXIF information that records data for digital camera photos—like camera model, date, time, shutter speed, exposure, etc.—can be displayed and searched. You can also add metadata for the retrieval of the files. iView Media Pro uses the standard IPTC standard, which encompasses a broad variety of descriptions and information. You can also define up to 16 custom fields.

All media files can be sorted into catalogs. The catalogs don't move the real file on the hard disk; they only store a reference to it. They can contain up to 128,000 files each and can have an unlimited number of catalogs. They can be organized in unlimited levels of sub-catalogs and it is easy to move references from one to another.

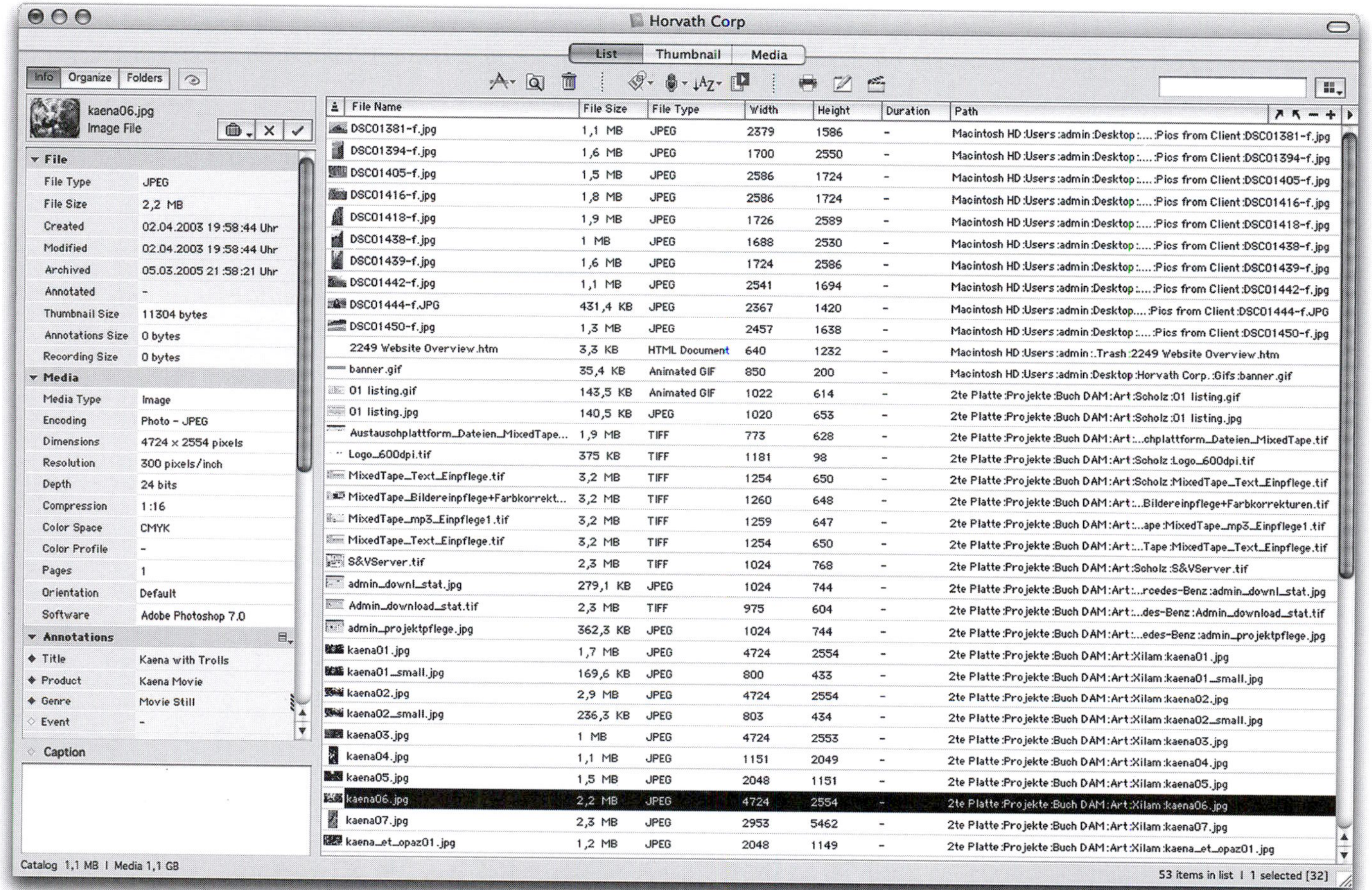

Figure A1.1 *iView Media Pro's main window*

Offline media like CD/DVD-ROM can be indexed and browsed/searched later. Access to the media is only needed when you want the image in full resolution.

Catalogs can be transferred from one computer to another. There is also an extra cost-free application, iView Catalog Reader, that allows sharing catalogs with anyone without the need to give access to the actual files.

A real time-saver is that you can let iView Media Pro watch any folder. Then all assets stored to it will be ingested into a defined catalog automatically. If you choose to, you can let the program signal new files in a folder by showing a special icon for them.

iView Media Pro offers a straightforward search field, like on a website, which simply searches all fields of all catalogs. But it also enables highly complex searches by defining combinations of criteria in a dialog (see Figure A1.2). It can search in up to 50 media attributes and annotation fields. You can save your searches if you have defined complex combinations you need to search for repeatedly.

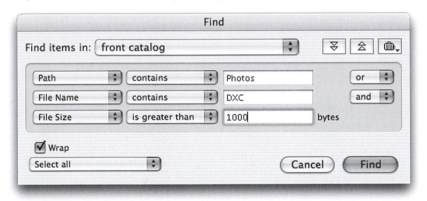

Figure A1.2   *The search window of iView Media Pro*

Backup and archiving options help when storing files on CD/DVD-ROM or other offline or online media (like hard disks on the network).

Workflow and version control

This software offers basic features for version control of your assets. It can back up all old versions of edited files and allows them to be restored later if needed. The feature is integrated with editing applications like Adobe Photoshop, but you need to follow certain procedures for opening and saving to make use of it. This function is expected to become more sophisticated in the next versions of iView Media Pro.

Pricing

iView Media Pro costs around $200 (US) for a single license. Bulk licenses are available upon request.

The program also comes in a standard version (iView Media), which is intended for fairly small amounts of assets (8000 per catalog) and therefore aimed at the semi-professional market.

Figure A1.3   *The version control setup in iView Media Pro*

Portfolio 7

Extensis Portfolio comes as a single-user version, which is quite similar in scope and price to iView Media Pro, but is sometimes considered inferior in terms of speed and usability. But unlike iView Media Pro, Portfolio also comes as a client/server version, called Portfolio Server. In this setup, it supports large workgroups or even corporations—Portfolio positions itself as a strong rival to market-leader Cumulus. It is considered more usable and stable than Cumulus, but is nevertheless not as widely used as its competitor. Portfolio's major drawback is that it doesn't offer the option to manage assets in a central directory—which Cumulus does.

Table A1.2 *Portfolio 7: general information*

Manufacturer	Extensis, Inc.
Type of DAM	Image Library
Architecture	Client/server application
Platform	Windows 98, ME, 2000, XP; Macintosh OS 9, OS X
Used by	Papers, magazines, pre-press houses, mid-size design agencies, marketing departments of large corporations
Reference customers	CNN, Ducati Motors, Ford, Nike, Yahoo!
Website	www.extensis.com

Figure A1.4 *Portfolio's main window*

Technical description

The Portfolio single-user application can also be used to access a central database managed by Portfolio Server. This gives several people access to the same catalog at the same time. Portfolio Server still uses the file system as a base, but it can be configured in such a way that it automatically updates the contents of the folders cataloged. Newly added files are processed automatically, and deletions or renaming of files that were already in the catalog are recognized and the user is alerted. It is also possible to move, delete, and rename files in the file system from within the program.

Portfolio creates thumbnails from the image files and reads EXIF, IPTC, and XMP (Extensible Metadata Platform from Adobe) metadata. EXIF fields can be mapped to custom fields if the imported images are not in standard format. For JPEG and TIFF files, metadata can also be embedded in the images if entered in Portfolio, so it persists when assets are transferred to people not using Portfolio.

Supported file types

Portfolio supports all common image formats, including EPS and Photoshop and several RAW formats from digital cameras. QuickTime and AVI as well as SWF files are played back within the application, and thumbnails are generated. Audio formats like AIFF, MIDI, MP3, or WAV can be played directly.

Adobe InDesign and Illustrator are also supported so that individual thumbnails can be generated. For Adobe Photoshop, Acrobat as well as Microsoft PowerPoint multi-page previews are available.

Portfolio indexes the text in plain TXT files, in PowerPoint files, and PDF documents, so these assets can be retrieved by their contents.

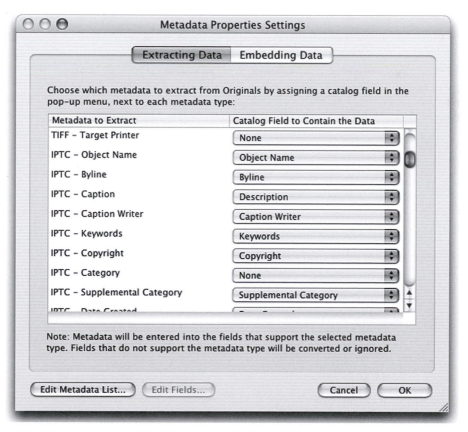

Figure A1.5 *Mapping of metadata fields can be finely controlled*

Archiving/retrieval features

When assets are imported into a catalog, files can be renamed and/or copied/moved automatically. It makes sense to move all assets to a central directory to benefit most from Digital Asset Management. Unfortunately, every user has the ability to change this setting for each import of assets, so this is error prone. You have to rely on team discipline to ensure that all assets are, in fact, stored on the central repository.

Portfolio asks automatically for keywords to be entered. Keywords can also be assigned in batch processing or extracted from file or folder names, for example.

You can organize assets in categories within a catalog to create subsets that are easier to handle. Moving assets within these doesn't affect the actual files and their location on the hard disk.

Portfolio installs a small helper application called Portfolio Express. This floating palette features the search functions of Portfolio so you can quickly find a picture and drag and drop it into any program you are working in without even having to open Portfolio.

Creating a CD-ROM with a selection of pictures is quite easy. Automatically included is Portfolio Browser for viewing the catalog—which actually is the same as the standard version of Portfolio, with a restricted feature set and read-only capabilities. It can be distributed for free with your catalogs to give others access to them.

The size of a catalog in Portfolio is limited to 4 GB. It can be larger if Portfolio is used as front-end to an SQL database, which means you have to set up your own SQL database. The separately available add-in Portfolio SQL Connect Module allows you to use an SQL database instead of Portfolio's standard flat file database used for its metadata. Usually this is not necessary though. You can have hundreds of thousands of assets in a catalog without hitting the 4 GB mark. Another consideration is performance: the bigger your catalog, the slower searching it becomes. Moving to an SQL database increases performance, but usually you are better off just using several catalogs instead of one big one. You can search several catalogs at once with Portfolio.

You can search by using the simple QuickFind option, which just looks for the term(s) you entered as file names and descriptions in the current catalog. You can change the settings for which fields are included in QuickSearch, or use the more complex Find command. Here you can combine up to five criteria with AND/OR. These searches can also be saved for later retrieval.

A neat feature is that you can e-mail the selected files from Portfolio—and you can choose whether you want to send the original files or instead send a smaller sized preview for which you can determine the size in pixels.

For creating HTML pages for presenting your images, there are several templates that can be customized. With a free plug-in you also can publish Portfolio catalogs on your web server to let users search them dynamically.

Workflow and version control

The administrator can determine which users and/or user groups can access and/or modify assets separately for each catalog.

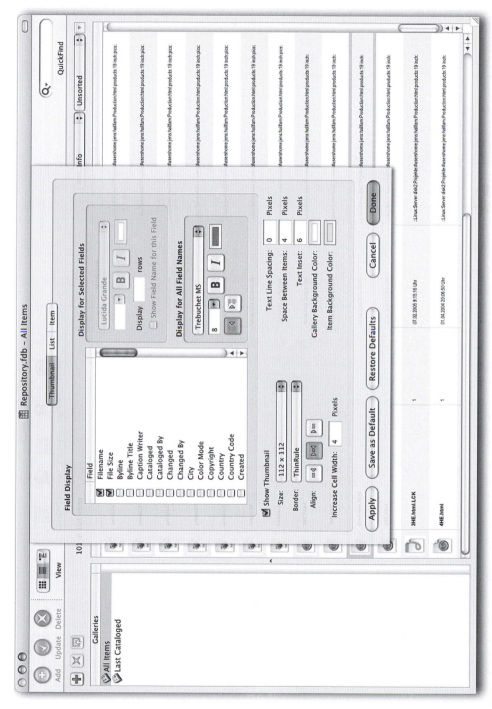

Figure A1.6 *The appearance of any part of the interface can be changed on a very detailed level*

Portfolio records the user ID of the person who imports or modifies an asset in the database, so you know who changed what when. Unfortunately, this function, which is new to version 7, is virtually undocumented.

There are no version control, check-in/check-out, or other workflow features in Portfolio. In theory, you can add these because you can customize Portfolio with AppleScript on the Mac or with Visual Basic on Windows. Or, if you use SQL Connect Module, you can control Portfolio even more by designing your own underlying database.

Pricing

Portfolio, the single-user edition, which is the same as the Portfolio client for access to the server, costs $200 (US). Portfolio Server costs around $3500 (US).

Cumulus Workgroup 6.5

Cumulus comes in three flavors:

- Single-User Edition
- Workgroup Edition
- Enterprise Edition.

The Single-User Edition is a classic standalone program with all the basic functions of Cumulus. The two other editions follow a client/server model.

Table A1.3   *Cumulus Workgroup 6.5: general information*

Manufacturer	Canto, Inc.
Type of DAM	Image Library
Architecture	Client/server application
Platform	Windows 2000, XP, Server 2003; Macintosh OS X; for the server also: Solaris, Linux
Used by	Large photographers' studios, stock photo libraries, advertising agencies, public relations departments
Reference customers	Nielsen Media Research, Apple Computers, Irish News, Lufthansa
Website	www.canto.com

The Enterprise Edition allows customization through writing your own APIs that allow complete integration with almost any workflow. It also offers features that make it possible to track the usage of certain assets and can connect to other databases by ODBC.

The Workgroup Edition is the first choice for all small and middle-sized workgroups. Therefore, we'll focus on this edition of Cumulus.

Canto Cumulus is the most widely used DAM solution for managing images, especially in large companies. It can handle huge amounts of data and is considered fast and reliable. On the other hand, it is not the easiest system to learn to use and to administer. It offers a wealth of functions that might seem overwhelming at first glance. Cumulus addresses this issue by providing handbooks that are comprehensive, exceptionally well written, and easy

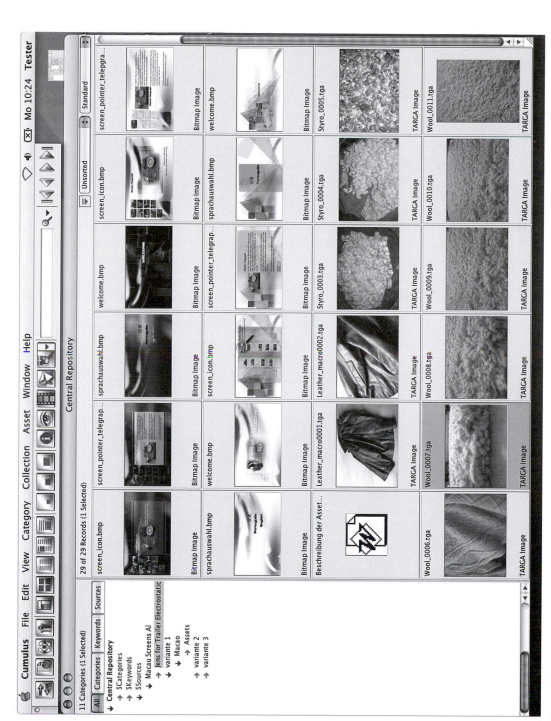

Figure A1.7 *The main view of Cumulus*

to use for learning and referencing. This is also true for the administrator's handbook, which is a real exception for software in general.

Cumulus offers an extension, called Cumulus Vault, which brings version control features and check-in/check-out to the program—making Cumulus the only image catalog on the market with this feature out-of-the-box.

There are several further options for extending the functionality of Cumulus.

Technical description

The Cumulus Server application runs on a central server and manages access from the LAN and from the Internet, if remote access is activated. It uses TCP/IP, so cross-platform compatibility is assured. It consists of three separate servers: the Metadata Server, the Processing Server, and the Asset Server.

The Metadata Server manages a central database with all the metadata for the assets. Some of the metadata, like file type, thumbnail, and existing metadata (for example, from pictures taken with a digital camera), are created automatically. Other types are created by users making comments, categorizations, or the like for assets.

The Asset Server manages access for the asset files. This makes it possible to add different technologies for storage—be it new file formats, new compression algorithms, or new storage hardware like jukebox systems or a new generation of exchangeable storage media.

Finally, the Processing Server converts assets from one format to another or includes watermarks, scales images, or re-samples them in a different resolution. You can apply several filter operations to one or several files at once, do color correction, cropping, or inclusion of borders.

Supported file types

Cumulus supports all common file formats for images, including Photoshop, EPS, and also QuarkXPress files. Support for RAW data from digital cameras is available as a separate option. Cumulus can read out metadata from JPEG files and it can write back metadata into them so if, for example, you change the description of a picture it is not only changed in the Cumulus database, but also in the JPEG file itself. This means that when you transfer the file to someone outside your organization, the metadata is up to date.

QuarkXPress files are also supported and fully indexed when the QXP AssetStore option is also purchased.

There is an extension for Cumulus to handle PowerPoint files (Office Suite) so that the complete text of all slides is cataloged and thumbnails can be viewed directly from Cumulus. The extension also indexes Word and Excel files.

All other file types can be cataloged and tagged with metadata, but there is no preview or cataloging of their contents, though.

Archiving/retrieval features

The creation of catalogs is restricted to the administrator. It is not possible to create new catalogs with the client program. The administrator can define access rights for every catalog separately for every single user.

All files are imported into catalogs. They can then be assigned to one or several categories. By default this doesn't move the actual file on the hard disk, but this behavior can be changed so that moving an asset from one catalog to another also moves the physical file.

Normally, you'll want to copy all of the asset's data when you set up the system so the data is no longer scattered around PCs all around the company. This setting is made in the client software only; there is no setting the administrator makes centrally for all clients.

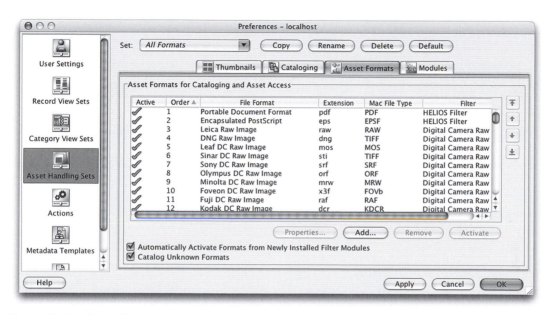

Figure A1.8   *In the Preferences you can dictate for any catalog that all assets are to be managed at a central location*

The number of assets referred to in a catalog is not restricted, but the file size of the catalog itself is limited to 4 GB. The space needed for storing data for one asset depends on the size of the thumbnail, the number of fields, and the values entered as metadata, but usually a catalog needs only a few kilobytes for storing information for one asset, so you can have hundreds of thousands of assets inside a single catalog.

Each catalog can handle assets differently. You can define which metadata fields should be used, what their default value is, whether users can modify it, and whether each of these fields should be indexed.

Cumulus has a simple search function which is accessible from the symbol bar that is always visible. It just looks for the entered term in the assets' names, their metadata, and for categories which contain the term in their name.

The advanced search lets you combine several criteria with OR and AND. A helpful feature is that you can refine your search by searching the results of a previous search. You can narrow your criteria step by step and always get an overview of the assets found. You can

Figure A1.9   *In the Search window you can compose and save complex searches*

even work the other way round: you can add results of a second search to the hits of your previous search. You can also save your search criteria for later retrieval.

So-called collections allow you to create a snapshot of your current selection. All the assets of the category you are viewing or all the assets you find with a search are included in this collection. It is also possible to save the setting with a collection. This means you can define the display of the assets, like the thumbnail size, the metadata that is displayed, and so on. Collections can be saved and sent to colleagues via e-mail.

Workflow and version control
You can export assets in virtually every format, size, and resolution you want. Also, there is the option to save images as a slide show, as a QuickTime video, or in HTML format, for which there are several templates that can be modified by the user.

Canto offers an option called Web Publisher Pro that is purchased separately. With this, you can publish assets on the Web. Functions that allow the end-user to search and sort assets are included, as well as an ordering system that supports licensing and download of the assets.

For version control there is an additional extension called Cumulus Vault. It offers check-in and check-out as well as version control. You can decide for every catalog whether all assets are managed by Vault automatically or whether the user can decide this when importing each individual asset.

Pricing
The Single-User Edition that works without a server is available for $70 (US). The Cumulus 6.5 Archive Server Solution, which includes a Workgroup Server license as well as three client licenses, costs around $3250 (US). Finally, the Cumulus 6.5 Business Server Solution, including a Workgroup Server license, three client licenses, Vault, and Internet Client Pro (enables access to basic functions via standard browser) is priced at about $11,500 (US). For information on the Business Server, contact Canto directly.

FotoStation Pro 5

FotoStation Pro has been widely used by newspapers and magazines for years. It concentrates on their special needs: ingesting, indexing, archiving, retrieving, and publishing photos. It also has several functions for image editing directly in the program.

Table A1.4 *FotoStation Pro 5: general information*

Manufacturer	FotoWare
Type of DAM	Image Catalog
Architecture	Single-user application; optional server add-ons
Platform	Windows 2000, XP; Macintosh OS X (just FotoStation Classic)
Used by	Large photographers' studios, stock photo libraries, newspapers and magazines
Reference customers	Corbis, Getty Images, Time Inc., Irish Times, Reuters
Website	www.fotoware.com

FotoStation is also available as a "Classic" version, which lacks the image-editing capabilities. For Macintosh this is the only available version.

Technical description

FotoStation Pro is single-user software, but it can be configured in such a way that all users work with the same central directory for archiving files. It is possible to create a central preference file on the server that is downloaded by all FotoStation users at each startup.

The image-editing functions include basic things like rotating, cropping, and color correction. On top of what its competitors offer, this software also enables setting white/black points and dodge and burn.

There are several extensions for FotoStation Pro:

- *Index Manager* is a server application that indexes the IPTC fields and also PDFs. It can maintain several online and unlimited offline media. It is essential for keeping good search performance when many users work with a central archive. It runs on a Windows NT or 2000 server and offers access to any Windows or Macintosh FotoStation version.
- *Color Factory* processes large numbers of images to make sure they have the same color standard. This server application can also batch process format conversions like TIFF to JPEG or it can convert RGB images to CMYK images.
- *Distribution Manager* manages transferring files via FTP and e-mail. The files can be processed and indexed automatically.
- *Internet Image Server* publishes pictures on the Web. It creates small previews automatically, includes watermarks, and offers downloadable hi-res versions to users with the appropriate rights.
- *FotoDrop* is an extension for the integration of FotoStation Pro with QuarkXPress.

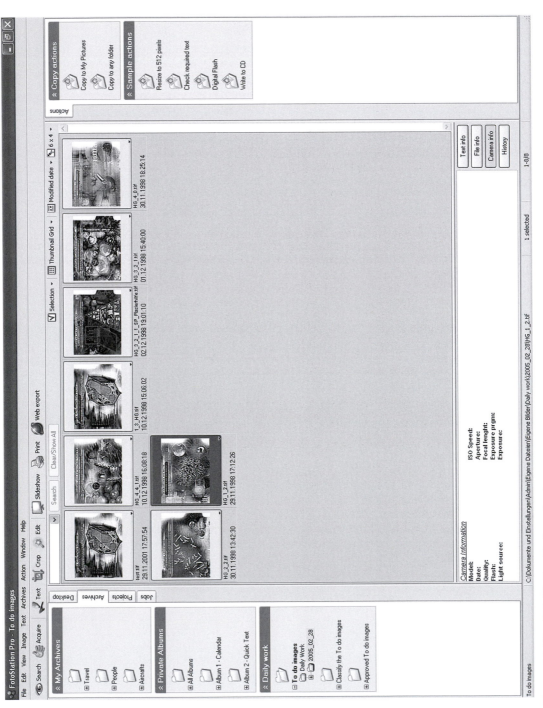

Figure A1.10 *FotoStation Pro's main view*

Supported file types

FotoStation supports all important image file formats.

Archiving/retrieval features

Images are organized in archives. You can also use projects to collect images from different archives and share these with your co-workers.

The software has strong text annotation possibilities for pictures. The IPTC standard is supported for annotations; EXIF data is imported and displayed. You can define your own fields, even depending on file type. To ensure consistent use of keywords you can create your own thesaurus. If Microsoft Word is installed, its spell-checking routines can be used in FotoStation Pro.

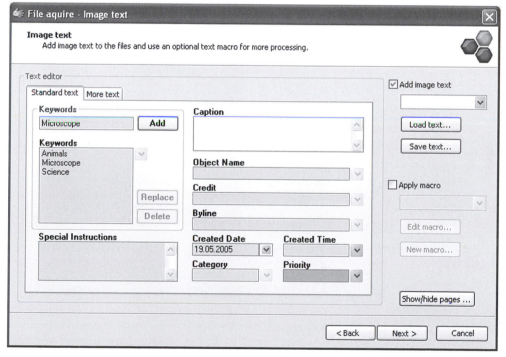

Figure A1.11 *The metadata entry possibilities of FotoStation Pro are very powerful but still easy to use*

You can apply annotations to multiple images in a batch process. The software offers search and replace in fields, so you can update descriptions in multiple files with ease.

Searching is flexible and fast, which is also true for large archives that are used by several people if you have the Index Manager add-on installed. Search over several archives is possible. You can search for file names and all the text fields. In addition, Index Manager also offers you fuzzy, synonym, and phonetic search to find images.

Workflow and version control

FotoStation Pro lets you define actions that can automate tasks like resizing images and loading them to a web server or publishing them to a CD-ROM. Several actions can be carried out in a sequence. With the Distribution Manger, acquiring and delivering files via e-mail, FTP or via specific defined "hot folders" can be automated—including unpacking/packing archive files.

Pricing

FotoStation Pro costs about $600 (US) for a single-user license. For pricing of the add-on modules, please contact the manufacturer.

ThumbsPlus 7

ThumbsPlus is sometimes called the Swiss army knife of the image catalogs. It offers a tremendous number of features and opens virtually every image file format you can think of. Its batch processing is powerful. Performance is not its strength and the many features are not always intuitive to use (and find), but nevertheless this program is widely used by photographers and small to medium web agencies.

Table A1.5 *ThumbsPlus 7: general information*

Manufacturer	Cerious Software
Type of DAM	Image Catalog
Architecture	Single-user application; database can also be managed by ODBC server
Platform	Windows 95/NT (with limitations), 98, ME, 2000, XP
Used by	(Semi-)professional photographers, small to medium web agencies
Reference customers	None listed
Website	www.canto.com

Technical description

Different from most other image catalogs, ThumbsPlus has a strong focus on the location of the files on disk. The program has an Explorer-like window, which mirrors the files on the storage medium. You can directly copy, move, delete, or rename files here if you have write access to the medium. The program only saves the path for each file, a thumbnail, and metadata for it, like description, annotations, keywords, etc., and usually doesn't touch the files.

Removable media can also be indexed. Metadata and thumbnails are always available. When you try to access a file that is not accessible, you are prompted to insert the medium that contains the image.

ThumbsPlus saves this information in a database in MS Access format. This database can also be modified from outside ThumbsPlus. As an alternative, you can also use an SQL

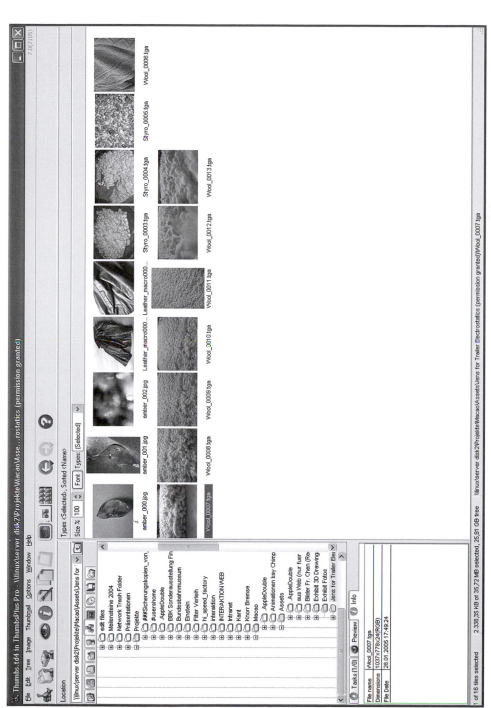

Figure A1.12 *The standard view of ThumbsPlus*

database (MS SQL Server, SQL Anywhere; Support for Oracle and DB2 were announced to be provided in the future). You can make several databases, but you can only access one database at a time. Sharing databases over a network is possible.

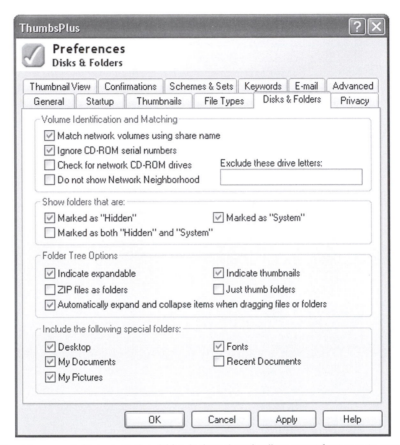

Figure A1.13 *You can define what should be indexed and adjust most features to your preferences*

Supported file types

The software reads 180 image file formats—all the common ones and a few specialities. The Pro version can also read most RAW formats from digital cameras. EXIF data is extracted and can be stored in custom fields. It can be retained when the file is copied, but ThumbsPlus doesn't write EXIF data from its database to any file. IPTC data is displayed. It can also be assigned to images in batch processing. Windows color management is supported. ThumbsPlus plays video files and also generates thumbnails for them.

PDF, EPS, Quark, InDesign, and Microsoft Office files are not supported. They can be displayed in ThumbsPlus, but at the moment there are no thumbnails for them and you can't annotate then.

Archiving/retrieval features

There is no limit to the number of files you can catalog in a database, but the total database size is limited to 2 GB—which is usually enough for more than 100,000 images. If you are using an SQL database, there is no limit for the database size.

ThumbsPlus can watch defined folders so that new or changed image files are automatically added to the database.

You can create galleries that contain references to any thumbnails of files you have on your storage media. There is a wizard for creating HTML pages with thumbnails of selected images. It offers several templates.

The searching function is powerful and includes a feature not found often: searching for visually similar images. With this feature you can find photos that have similar colors and/or proportions as a given one, or you can hunt down duplicates in the database that are stored with different names in different places.

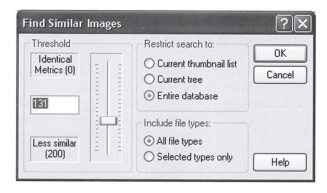

Figure A1.14 *The Find Similar option comes in handy for detecting duplicates on your disks. Unfortunately, this can't be combined easily with normal search*

Workflow and version control

ThumbsPro offers no dedicated workflow or version control features. These can be included by accessing its database.

Pricing

The standard version is priced at $50 (US), which doesn't support RAW file formats and doesn't allow network access of databases and the usage of database types other than the built-in one. The professional version costs $90 (US).

ACDSee 7

ACDSee has been around for more than 10 years. It is a strong competitor of ThumbsPlus. Both programs mirror the file structure on disk and are mainly intended for people organizing images alone or in a small workgroup. ACDSee's usability is superior to ThumbsPlus, but the lack of support for IPTC metadata and its restricted annotation features makes it unsuitable for professional photographers. Additionally, it can't share databases, which is a major drawback for using it in workgroups. If you don't need these features, ACDSee is a good choice because it provides usability and strong performance for a low price.

Table A1.6   *ACDSee 7: general information*

Manufacturer	ACD Systems
Type of DAM	Image Catalog
Architecture	Single-user application
Platform	Windows 98, ME, 2000, XP
Used by	Semi-professional photographers, small to medium web agencies
Reference customers	None listed
Website	www.acdsystems.com

Technical description

ACDSee has a folder view as in Windows Explorer. Here you can copy, move, rename, and delete files. When you browse the files, thumbnails and file information are automatically written in the database. This can slow down browsing quite severely when you are working with folders that contain new files. To avoid this, there is a wizard that allows you to catalog files from different folders all at once. The program also contains a Device Detector that prompts you when a camera, CD/DVD, or any other removable storage device becomes connected. It can automatically launch the Acquire wizard to import the containing files. It is also possible to exclude folders from being indexed.

In previous versions, ACDSee used proprietary "description" files it placed in any folder that it indexed, but now all this metadata is kept in a central database. This database can be exported for backup or for sharing it with other ACDSee users. In the latter case, it is necessary that the referenced files are actually in the same path or they can't be accessed.

ACDSee lets you save files in ZIP, LZH, TAR, or GZIP archives. You can also look into these archives directly without having to unpack them first. The program also helps create CD/DVD-ROMs for archiving or backing up files.

There are some image manipulation tools available, like crop, resize, red-eye fix, sharpen, adjust exposure, and remove noise. It also offers some filters, such as Sepia, Emboss or Oil Paint effects.

EXIF data can be imported—it is accessible for searching and can also be changed in the files themselves. IPTC data is not supported.

The software offers batch processing for format conversion, rotation, resizing, exposure adjustment, setting EXIF info, and a few other options.

You can write your own custom plug-ins for ACDSee. The program accepts arguments when invoked from the command line. For example, you can tell it to open a specific folder and show all files of a certain type it contains. The DDE "open" command is supported.

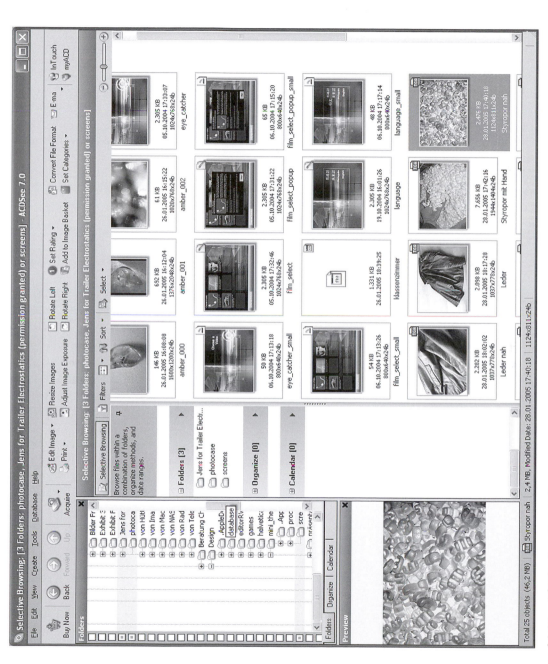

Figure A1.15 *ACDSee's main window*

Supported file types

ACDSee can read more than 50 image and video formats, including Photoshop PSD, EPS (only embedded thumbnail), PDF (when the free GhostScript is installed), MOV, and AVI. RAW formats from several digital camera manufacturers are also supported.

Archiving/retrieval features

You can select several folders on your hard disk and see all the files contained in one single view. For creating custom sets of images, you create categories, which can contain subcategories. They allow grouping images from any location.

Offline media like CD-ROM or DVD-ROM are cataloged and their metadata and thumbnails are available even when the media is offline.

ACDSee lets you search in specific folders by name, date, size, height/width, file format, keywords, or EXIF data.

For each file you can add these metadata:

- Thumbnail
- Category

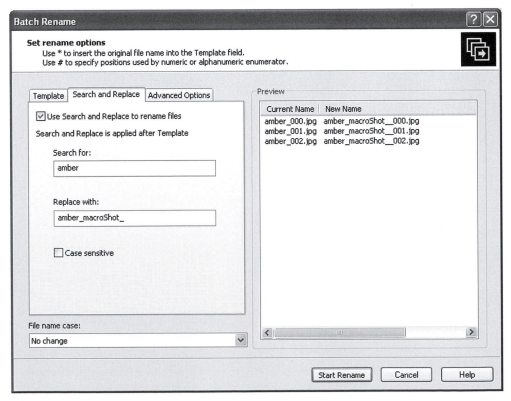

Figure A1.16 *ACDSee has a handy renaming function for files*

- Notes (up to 4095 characters)
- Keywords
- Author
- Date/time
- Rating (from 1 to 5 or none)
- Caption.

In general, the search function is convenient and easy to use. You can also use wildcards. The application offers the creation of slideshows in PDF or Flash format. You can also create an ".exe" file that displays the slideshow on any Windows machine.

Images can be e-mailed directly from within the application; their file size can be restricted in the preferences. ACDSee also creates HTML photo albums, which can be customized within certain limits. Printing catalogs is possible; the options for setting their properties are numerous.

Wizards help you to back up the database with metadata, the files themselves, or archive data onto offline storage media.

Workflow and version control
This software doesn't offer any specific workflow or version control features.

Pricing
ACDSee costs around $50 (US).

ImageFolio Pro

ImageFolio is used for publishing browsable image catalogs on the Web. The images can be viewed in different resolutions, ordered online, and downloaded. It is not an asset management program but more of a catalog manager for online access. It is described here briefly for the sake of completeness.

Table A1.7 *ImageFolio Pro: general information*

Manufacturer	BizDesign Inc.
Type of DAM	Online Image Catalog
Architecture	Server scripts (CGI); accessed by any browser
Platform	Windows 95/NT 98, ME, 2000, XP; Macintosh OS X; most Linux/Unix versions
Used by	Publishers of image data; corporations making images available for contractors
Reference customers	ESPN, National Geographic, Warner Brothers, UPS
Website	www.imagefolio.com

Technical description

ImageFolio is basically a set of CGI scripts (written in Perl) that are installed on your web server. There is no application needed for administration or access—everything is done via configuration files, the browser, and FTP (for file upload).

The process of publishing images is highly automated to ingest the assets in the central repository on the web server. Conversion, cropping, resizing, inclusion of watermarks, creation of thumbnails, and so on are all done automatically. Setting the system up is quite a lot of work though. You have to define what should happen when, which formats should be accessible by whom, how pages should be displayed, and so on.

This system is not suitable for managing your assets; it is intended for sharing assets with other people, mainly customers, over the Web.

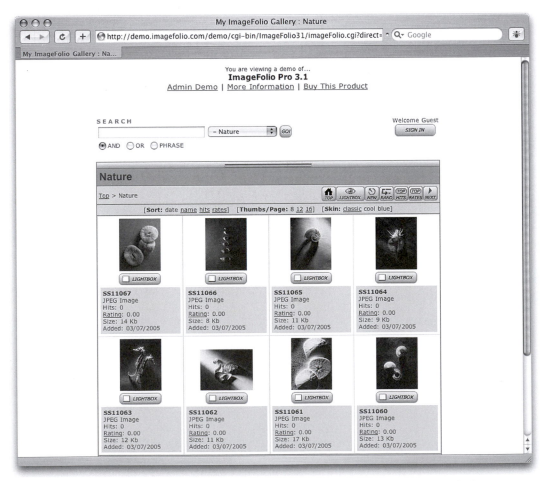

Figure A1.17 *ImageFolio is completely web based. Images courtesy of BizDesign Software*

Pricing

ImageFolio Pro costs about $210 (US) plus $90 for installation. There is a cheaper Basic version; hosting options are also available. Many extensions are available—for example, for sending electronic postcards, for detailed access of user rights, or for a virtual light box.

Software Configuration Management (SCM)

Software Configuration Management or Source Code Management is mainly used by companies that develop software. It is also common at game producers and web agencies that have a strong focus on back-end programming and scripting complex interfaces. More and more, features for the management of non-program code files are popping up in SCM tools. On the other hand, many DAM tools (see next section) can also manage program code.

Feature comparison

To give a brief overview, a comparison of the most important features of all the SCM tools mentioned in this section is given in Table A1.8.

CVS

CVS (Concurrent Versions System) is the SCM all others are measured against. It is a very mature, stable, and scalable software. Due to its broad distribution, there are integrations available for almost every software development tool and for various other software packages.

Technical description

As in most SCMs, the version history is stored on a central server and the client machines can get local copies of all the files the developers are working on. Client and server may run on the same machine. Network communication is only necessary to perform CVS operations, but not to modify the local files.

Table A1.8 *Comparison of the main features of SCM tools*

	CVS	Subversion	Perforce	Rational ClearCase	BitKeeper	VSS
Scalability	+++	+++	+++	++++	++++	—
Speed	+++	++++	+++++	++	+++	—
Security	++++	+++++	++++	++	++++	—
Stability	++++	+++++	+++	++++	++++	—
Handling of binary data	+	++	+++	+++	+++	+

+++++, Perfect; ++++, outstanding; +++, good; ++, sufficient; +, some; −, totally insufficient.

Table A1.9 *CVS: general information*

Manufacturer	Open Source
License	GPL
Type of DAM	SCM
Architecture	Multi-user client/server application
Platform	Windows 98, ME, NT, 2000, XP; Macintosh OS X; Linux; nearly all Unix versions, BeOS, VMS, OS2, DOS
Used by	Mainly by programmers
Reference customers	Bentley, Cygnus, onShore Inc., most Open Source projects
Website	www.cvshome.org

The program follows the copy/modify/merge model. First, a local copy of the necessary files is created, then modified as desired, and finally copied back into the repository on the server. If a file in the repository has changed while it was modified locally, the local and the repository copies of the file will be merged into a new version. Conflicts

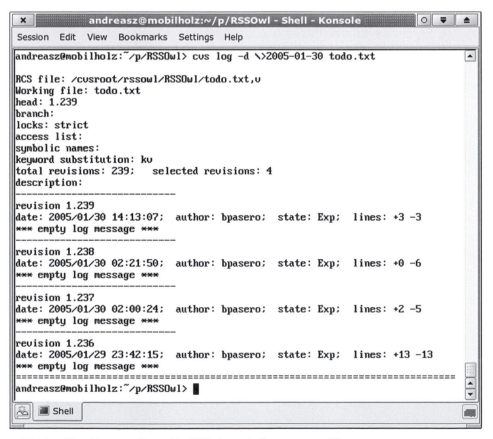

Figure A1.18 *Checking out files with CVS through the command line*

that cannot be resolved automatically require manual action. This model allows concurrent working on the same files and avoids unnecessary serialization, but provides no exclusive check-out, so parallel modification of binary files must be avoided through extra communication.

CVS is a full-featured SCM—it supports concurrent modification of text files, parallel working on several lines of development (branching), and merging branches back together. It is also possible to use tagging so that you can recreate the status at a given point and display the differences between different tags and revisions. CVS supports server-sided scripting for advanced log operations and to enforce site-specific policies like verifying that every commit contains a comment by the developer.

It is also a very efficient system, transmitting only patches to files instead of sending entire files, and further lowering the amount of traffic generated by compressing the transmitted text.

A proper CVS installation provides a high level of network security; CVS can use Kerberos, the industry standard authentication protocol, for authentication or tunnel the entire connection through SSH.

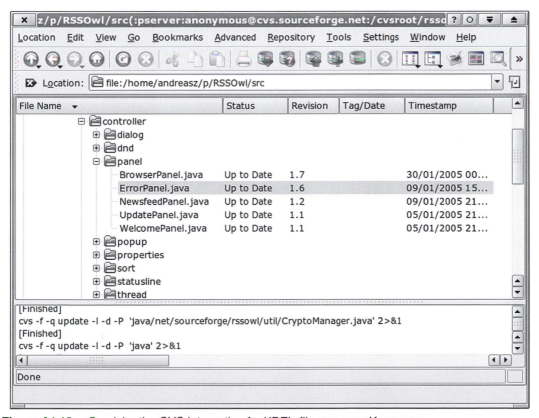

Figure A1.19   *Cervisia, the CVS integration for KDE's file manager Konqueror*

CVS has two major drawbacks:

1 It does not support moving and copying of files while preserving the file's history. (This is possible, but only by direct modification of the repository, which should be avoided.)
2 Atomic commits are not possible, leaving the repository in an undesired state if something fails during a commit. Atomic commits ensure that either all or none of the requests of a commit succeed, therefore preventing inconsistencies in the repository.

Supported file types

CVS was designed mainly to handle text files like programming code files. Using binary files is possible but requires marking them as such.

Tools

Cross-platform front-ends

JCVS is a Java front-end that implements the complete suite of CVS operations: http://www.jcvs.org/.

Available for Unix/Linux, Windows, and Mac OS X, and based on the Tcl/Tk framework, TkCVS provides a graphical front-end for CVS: http://www.twobarleycorns.net/tkcvs.html.

Despite its name, WinCVS offers a set of GUI front-ends for Windows, Linux, and Mac: http://www.wincvs.org/.

Linux front-ends

Cervisia is a powerful, easy-to-use, GUI front-end for the KDE system. It can run as a standalone application or integrated with KDE's file manger Konqueror: http://www.kde.org/apps/cervisia/.

Windows front-ends

TortoiseCVS is a simple, yet powerful, Explorer integration for CVS: http://www.tortoisecvs.org/.

Integrations for IDEs

Almost every IDE already ships with a CVS integration included, except Microsoft Visual Studio. PushOk provides a CVS proxy for the Microsoft SCC API, making it possible to integrate CVS into Microsoft Visual Studio: http://www.pushok.com/soft_cvs.php.

Browser interfaces

ViewCVS creates an HTML summary of CVS activity: http://viewcvs.sourceforge.net/.

CVS Summary is very similar to ViewCVS, except that it produces static HTML: http://sourceforge.net/projects/cvs-summary/.

Pricing

CVS is Open Source and subject to the terms and conditions of the GPL (General Public License, http://www.gnu.org/copyleft/gpl.html). It can be downloaded free at https://ccvs.cvshome.org/servlets/ProjectDocumentList and numerous other locations. Unix- and BSD-type operating systems usually ship with CVS included.

Subversion

Subversion was designed as a successor to CVS and therefore provides similar interfaces while eliminating the drawbacks of CVS. Although it is a relatively new software, it already has a broad and steadily growing user base, and is used in major Open Source projects such as the Apache web server or the netfilter/iptables firewall.

Table A1.10 *Subversion: general information*

Manufacturer	CollabNet/Open Source
License	Subversion License (see "Pricing" section for more information)
Type of DAM	SCM
Architecture	Multi-user client/server application
Platform	Windows 98, ME, 2000, XP; Macintosh OS X; Linux; nearly all Unix versions
Used by	Mainly by programmers
Reference customers	netfilter/iptables, Apache Server Foundation, Connectiva, Absolute Systems, Lexmark (not official)
Website	subversion.tigris.org

Technical description

As Subversion is very similar to CVS, you should read the CVS section first. Differences to CVS are listed in the following paragraphs.

Subversion supports both copying and moving of files and directories. Copies are created with a mechanism similar to a hard link. Instead of copying the entire file, only the information that file X has been copied to location Y at revision Z is stored; therefore, copies need very little hard disk space and CPU time.

Every commit in Subversion is atomic, meaning either an entire commit is successful or the repository remains unchanged. This also enables developers to commit changes as logical entities.

Each file and directory can have an arbitrary set of properties associated with it. It's possible to store any type of text data in these properties. For example, you could create properties for lens, aperture, and exposure time on the files in a photo database. This metadata, like the file it's associated with, is also under version control.

Subversion makes it very easy to implement new network mechanisms. In most cases, an Apache Server module will be used for remote access over WebDAV (Web-based Distributed Authoring and Versioning), but it is also possible to use a standalone server employing a proprietary protocol that can be tunneled easily over SSH. WebDAV is a set of extensions to the HTTP protocol, which allows users to collaboratively edit and manage files on remote web servers. It is a standardized and widely used method for remote collaboration.

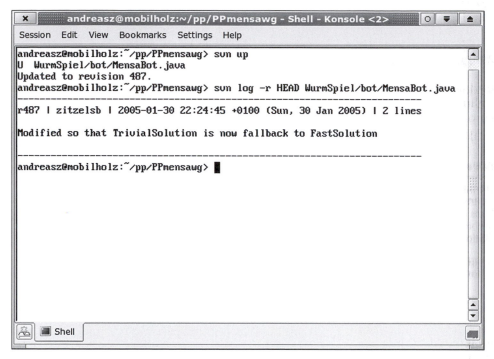

Figure A1.20   *Viewing a file's history with Subversion*

All file types, including binary files, are handled both easily and efficiently. It's as simple as a real version control system can be; image files are treated just like text files. When using a good GUI, it's quite comfortable. Dedicated image catalogs are, of course, easier to use, but offer no VCS features.

Branching and tagging functions are provided; branches and tags are created by creating copies of the project's trunk at a given revision.

Supported file types
Subversion can handle both binary and text files. However, adding and committing large binary files ($>100\,MB$) may take a long time. As Subversion, like CVS, offers no exclusive check-out, concurrent modification of the same binary file should be avoided.

Literature
An introduction as well as a complete reference to Subversion is *Version Control with Subversion* by Ben Collins-Sussman, Brian W. Fitzpatrick, and C. Michael Pilato, ISBN: 0-596-00448-6. It can be downloaded free under the Creative Commons Attribution License (http://creativecommons.org/licenses/by/2.0/). The online version is available at http://svnbook.red-bean.com/.

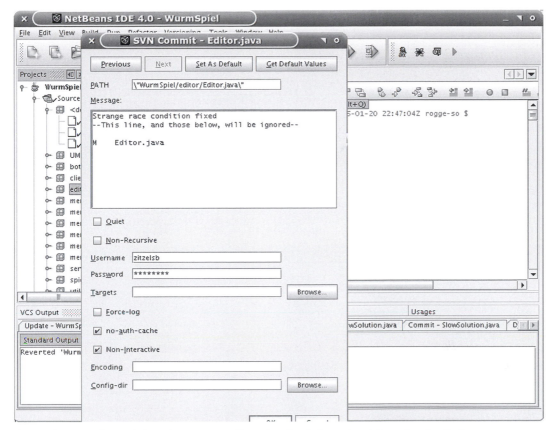

Figure A1.21 *Committing changes to a file using the Subversion integration for Netbeans*

Tools
TortoiseSVN is a good Subversion front-end for SVN: http://tortoisesvn.tigris.org/.

Pricing
Subversion is Open Source and subject to the terms and conditions of the Subversion License (http://subversion.tigris.org/project_license.html). It can be downloaded free at http://subversion.tigris.org/project_packages.html and numerous other locations. Newer Unix- and BSD-type operating systems usually ship with Subversion included.

Perforce

Perforce is an extremely fast, easy-to-use, yet quite powerful multi-platform SCM system. Its undisputed speed and its ability to tightly integrate into software development workflows make Perforce the favorite SCM of many programmers.

Table A1.11 *Perforce: general information*

Manufacturer	Perforce Software Inc.
Type of DAM	SCM
Architecture	Multi-user client/server application
Platform	Windows 98, ME, 2000, XP; Macintosh OS; Linux; nearly all Unix versions, BeOS
Used by	Mainly by programmers
Reference customers	SAP, NVIDIA, Google, Macromedia
Website	www.perforce.com

Technical description

Perforce is driven by a lock/modify/unlock model. This means a client must obtain a lock for a file before it can be edited, and unlock the file afterwards. Locks are usually non-exclusive,

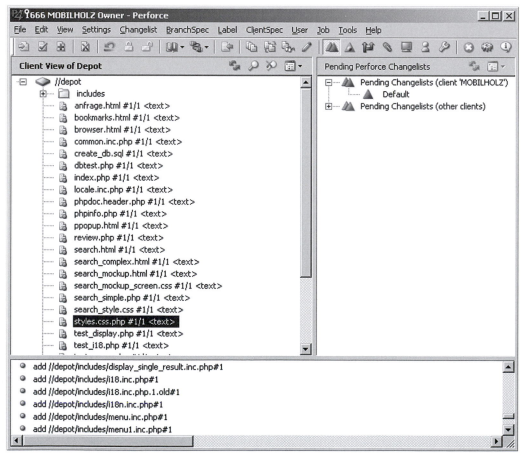

Figure A1.22 *The Perforce Windows client*

so that multiple users can edit a file at the same time. Each user can see which files are currently under modification by other users. It's also possible to lock a file exclusively, denying other users the ability to alter the file until the lock is lifted again. This provides a streamlined way of evading merging binary files, but broken or obstructive clients could seriously thwart the project, since in these cases administrative action is required to lift the lock.

The software also offers atomic commits and it supports branching, tagging (labeling), and merging.

It also has a built-in defect (or job) tracker. With a defect tracker it is possible to maintain associations between the change sets as units of work. This could be, for example, the fixing of a bug. This system is able to integrate with external defect tracking systems.

Being a multi-user SCM system, Perforce offers strong networking support and is able to work over LAN and WAN networks. Secure authentication and transmitting can be archived by tunneling Perforce connections through SSH.

Supported file types

Perforce has no restrictions on file types. As it offers an exclusive check-out (or lock), Perforce is suitable for handling binary data.

Tools

An extensive list of tools and integrations is available in the products section of the Perforce website at www.perforce.com/perforce/products.html.

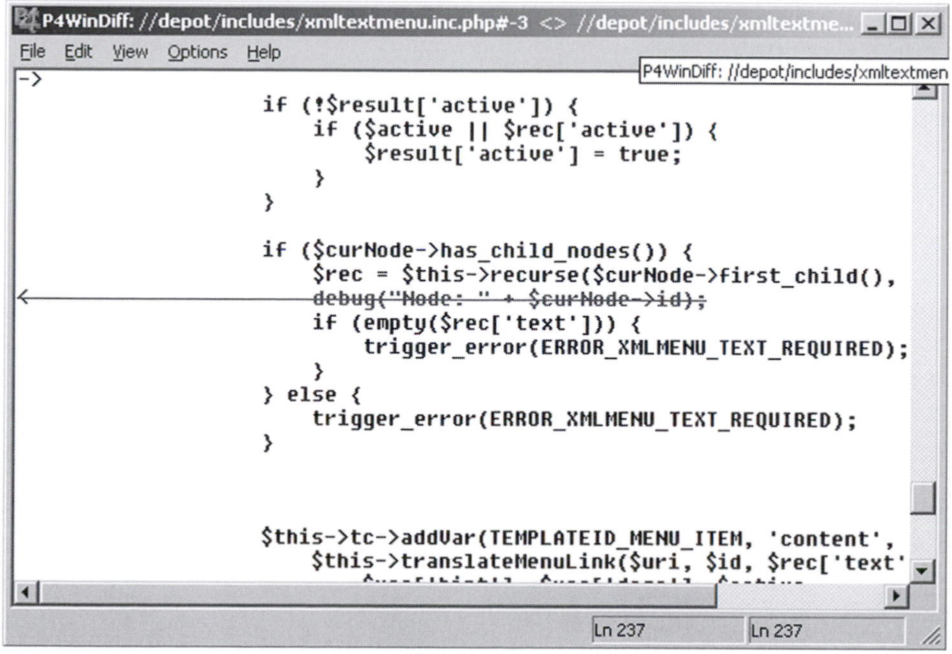

Figure A1.23   *Perforce's built-in diff viewer*

Pricing

Perforce is billed on a per-user base. Prices range from $750 (US) for the first to 20th users, down to $450 for the 1001st + user. Perforce offers educational licenses as well as free licenses for organizations developing software licensed or distributed exclusively under an Open Source License fitting the Open Source Definition (www.opensource.org/docs/definition_plain.html).

Rational ClearCase

ClearCase is a powerful, enterprise-scalable SCM. Since the original manufacturer Rational Software was purchased in December 2002 by IBM, the software has been greatly improved. However, it is still infamous for its complexity and hardware demands.

Table A1.12   *Rational ClearCase: general information*

Manufacturer	IBM/Rational Software
Type of DAM	SCM
Architecture	Multi-user client/server application
Platform	AIX, HP-UX, IRIX, Linux, Solaris, Windows 2000, Windows 2003, Windows NT, Windows XP
Used by	Mainly by programmers
Reference customers	Wells Fargo, CrossKeys, BindView
Website	http://www-306.ibm.com/software/rational/offerings/scm.html

Technical description

ClearCase is driven by a check-in/check-out model, meaning that a file has to be checked out (locked) from the server before it can be modified. Afterwards it has to be checked in again.

It has many features, including atomic commits, branching, merging, and file operations such as moving and copying files and directories. Custom triggers can execute scripts when repository operations such as check-in or check-out occur.

ClearCase client workstations require installation of a proprietary file system called MVFS (Multi Version File System), therefore enabling transparent access to the repository. This adds to ClearCase's negative reputation concerning complexity, as installing a file system is a process requiring deep modification of the host system.

Remote collaboration is only possible with IBM Rational ClearCase MultiSite, available at an additional cost, which supports replication of ClearCase databases to remote sites.

Supported file types

ClearCase has no limitations concerning file types.

Pricing

Pricing starts at about $1630 (US) per seat and goes up to well over $5000 per seat, depending on functionality.

BitKeeper

BitKeeper is an exceptionally powerful, yet small and straightforward, SCM system. It's designed to support heavy distributed development with practically any number of developers.

Table A1.13 *BitKeeper: general information*

Manufacturer	BitMover, Inc.
Type of DAM	SCM
Architecture	Multi-user client/server application
Platform	Windows 98, ME, NT4, 2000, XP; Mac OS X; Linux; nearly all Unix and BSD systems
Used by	Mainly by programmers
Reference customers	The Linux Kernel project, MySQL, SOMA Networks
Website	bitkeeper.com

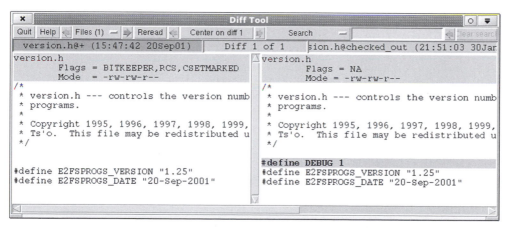

Figure A1.24 *Examining file differences with BitKeeper's built-in Diff Tool*

Technical description

BitKeeper provides all core SCM features, such as atomic commits, powerful branching and merging support, copying and moving of files, as well as a number of advanced features described in the following paragraphs.

It supports multiple repositories, thus making it possible to let people commit their changes to staging areas instead of directly committing to the main repository. A staging area is simply a repository between the client and the main repository, from which changes can be committed in the higher repository. This is especially useful in large software projects, with many developers and teams working together.

BitKeeper makes it possible to trigger custom actions on server commands such as commit and check-out. This functionally could, for example, be used to e-mail a summary of changes to a mailing list, or perform something more complicated.

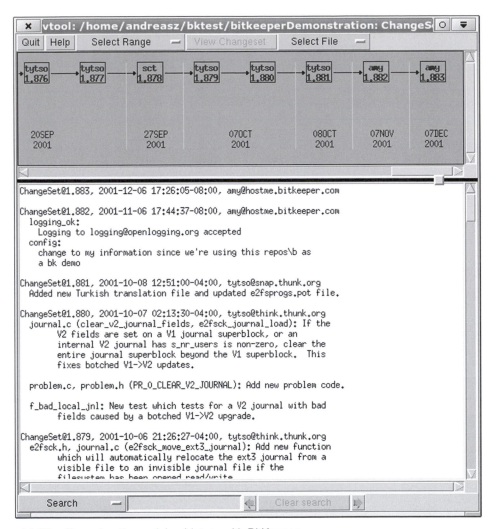

Figure A1.25 *Browsing the revision history with BitKeeper*

The status of a workspace prior to a merge is versioned too. This comes in very handy if a merge has to be undone, which can be a very painful process in other SCM tools.

Supported file types
BitKeeper has no restrictions concerning file types.

Pricing
BitKeeper seem to be very keen to keep their prices secret. Rumor is that at least one person has been threatened with copyright infringement charges for making BitKeeper's price list

public. Therefore, all we can say here is that its prices are usually comparable to those of competitors like Rational ClearCase.

The company also used to offer a free license, whose terms restrict its usage effectively to non-DAM/SCM Open Source projects. Recently this licensing model was discontinued. Additionally, a license with access to the source code is available.

Visual SourceSafe

Visual SourceSafe is Microsoft's SCM product.

Table A1.14   *Visual SourceSafe: general information*

Manufacturer	Microsoft
Type of DAM	SCM
Architecture	File/network share-based solution
Platform	Windows 95, 98, ME, NT4, 2000, 2003, XP
Used by	Mainly by Visual Studio users
Reference customers	None listed
Website	msdn.microsoft.com/vstudio/previous/ssafe

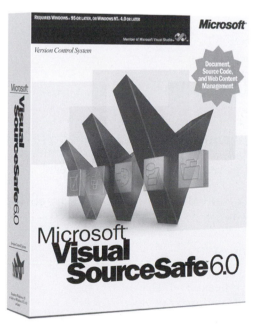

Figure A1.26   *Microsoft's Visual SourceSafe*

Technical description

Visual SourceSafe is, unlike most SCM systems, not a real client/server application, but relies on files shared over SMB, Windows' network share protocol. The result of this is that any malicious or erroneous client can easily destroy the database. This is made worse by the fact that users who require read-only access to the revision control system need write access also.

The system offers basic revision control, locking, branching, and merging support. Unfortunately, due to design flaws, branching is reported as being almost unusable.

Microsoft recommends that the Visual SourceSafe database should not exceed 3–5 GB. This is insufficient for enterprise-sized projects, and makes applications like an image database or even a collection of a large number of Microsoft Word texts impossible.

Remote collaboration is difficult over low network speed, especially on slow networks like the Internet of Visual SourceSafe. To make this problem worse, few administrators dare to expose an SMB server to the Internet, so the only option would be using a VPN connection—further reducing the network speed.

Visual SourceSafe also has a large number of bugs, ranging from stale files to seemingly random database corruptions. Many users report frequent loss of data.

This is the only software that is natively integrated with Microsoft Visual Studio and the Microsoft Office Suite, which most certainly is the reason it is used at all.

Supported file types

Visual SourceSafe can handle both binary and text files. Due to the poor scalability of Visual SourceSafe, having lots of (large) binary files might result in an unusable system.

Pricing

VSS costs $549 (US) per seat.

Digital Asset Management (DAM)

As discussed in previous chapters, the term Digital Asset Management has different meanings; in the broad sense, all the products listed in this appendix are types of Digital Asset Management. In this section, however, we apply the definition in a stricter sense and list only those systems that specialize in managing assets and that are not part of any other category.

As usual, you must look at the individual systems' features and not just the product category to find out what the systems can do for you.

Aladdin FlashBack

Aladdin FlashBack is an application which has no competitor—but was an obvious failure on the market nonetheless. It is no longer developed, although you can still get it from Allume Systems (which is Aladdin Systems' new name) for older Windows and Mac systems. FlashBack offers simple revision control with a graphical interface for single users.

Table A1.15 *Aladdin FlashBack: general information*

Manufacturer	Allume Systems, Inc.
Type of DAM	Single-user revision control
Architecture	Single-user application
Platform	Windows 3.1, 95, 98; Mac OS 9
Used by	Individuals and individual users in any organization
Reference customers	None listed
Website	www.allume.com/win/flashback/
	www.allume.com/mac/flashback/

Technical description

FlashBack is a standard program that should always run in the background. If you want to activate version control for a document, you just drag and drop it into the FlashBack window. FlashBack then saves a new version of this file every time you save it in its original

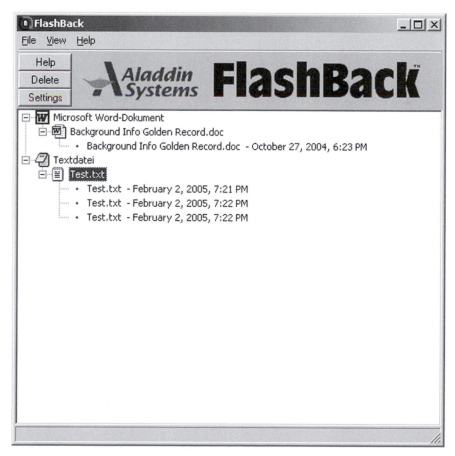

Figure A1.27 *FlashBack's main (and only) window*

application. You don't need any plug-ins or cumbersome routines and you don't need to follow special rules for saving new versions.

This system works with any file type—from plain text, source code, HTML pages and images to Microsoft Office documents, animation files, and video.

The only drawback to this approach is that you need quite a lot of hard disk space if you place large files you change often under the watch of FlashBack. Although the system only saves the differences between versions, you should try not to save your Photoshop documents every minute—or you better buy a bigger hard disk.

When you want to revert to an old version, you simply double-click on it in the FlashBack window to open it.

The program is very straightforward but it serves more as a security net for retrieving old versions than a comfortable tool for managing multiple versions. You can't comment on the individual versions, so finding a specific one is a matter of opening several files and seeing what has changed here.

Pricing

FlashBack costs $30 (US). You can get it directly from Allume Systems.

Quark Content Manager 3

Quark uses its strong market position with its flagship product QuarkXPress to sell their own Digital Asset Management solution, which is tightly integrated with its page layout program. It is intended for publishing houses and large corporations that publish mainly on paper but also on the Web and other media.

Table A1.16 *Quark Content Manager 3: general information*

Manufacturer	Quark Inc.
Type of DAM	Digital Asset Management for publishing with QuarkXPress
Architecture	Client/server application
Platform	Windows NT/2000 Server, Sun Solaris for the server; Windows NT, 98, 2000, XP for admin client; any Windows or Macintosh system on which QuarkXPress runs for standard user clients
Used by	Large print shops, publishing houses, large enterprises
Reference customers	Lenox, The Think Tank (T3)
Website	www.quark.com/solutions/qcm/

Technical description

It is a suite of several applications that can be bought separately. The core modules are:

- Digital Media Server
- Dynamic Document Server
- Workflow Engine

- License Administrator
- Web Application Framework.

The underlying layer is Quark Digital Media Server (DMS—sometimes referred to as Digital Media System), which is set up on an Oracle 9i database.

There are additional modules like Media Portal (to bring your assets to the Web), Review Manager (to facilitate approval of documents), Digital Rights Manager, or SOAP Integration Framework to extend functionality even further.

File formats

The system manages all kinds of assets, from text documents to images, movies, sound clips, animations, and, of course, QuarkXPress files. You have a powerful search function, which also uses keywords associated with the assets. You can track usage of the assets, manage revisions, and associate them with a specific workflow. The assets are available over LAN or globally over the Internet.

You can access the system with a specific client application, or from within QuarkXPress, Photoshop, or Microsoft Word.

Pricing

Quark Content Manager is intended for large corporations—and so is its price, which is around $200,000 (US) for the Content Manager. Usually you buy some modules and pay an annual maintenance fee, which entitles you to all the upgrades that are released during this period at no cost. For detailed information, please contact Quark directly.

North Plains TeleScope

TeleScope is a typical Digital Asset Management system designed for archiving and retrieval. It provides metadata storage, workflow management, a user rights system, and storage management. The system offers integration interfaces for other applications and supports rights management for content distribution. It is typically used to manage data in large companies and to make that data available to partners and licensees.

Table A1.17 *North Plains TeleScope: general information*

Manufacturer	North Plains Systems Corp.
Type of DAM	Digital Asset Management
Architecture	Client/server
Platform	Server: Windows NT; Solaris
	Client: Windows; Macintosh; Linux
Used by	Large corporations
Reference customers	AOL, Boeing, Pfizer
Website	www.northplains.com

Technical description

TeleScope is a client/server system, offering both Mac OS and Windows clients as well as a web interface for simple data access. The server has interfaces for external systems, allowing tight integration with existing solutions. With its customizable workflow system, TeleScope allows for complex workflows. For example, it can be integrated with Microsoft Office, Lotus Notes, or QuarkXPress.

File formats

TeleScope supports all of the standard formats used today in publishing, pre-press, broadcasting, post-production, and advertising. The system provides an API for extending the support to other file formats and processes.

Archiving/retrieval features

Unlimited metadata can be stored together with the assets and used for full text searches. TeleScope provides features for archive management.

Version control

TeleScope offers check-out/check-in and versioning functionality.

Pricing

TeleScope costs around $100,000–200,000 (US) for a workgroup solution.

eMotion Creative Partner

eMotion's Digital Asset Management system is an ASP solution (Application Server Provider), meaning you rent the system, which is installed on the provider's server. It allows companies to manage and share their digital assets across several locations with minimum effort. Using web-based clients there is no installation required to use the system.

Table A1.18   *eMotion Creative Partner: general information*

Manufacturer	eMotion
Type of DAM	Digital Asset Management
Architecture	Client/server
Platform	Web-based ASP solution, accessible with any browser
Used by	Large corporations
Reference customers	PeopleSoft, Thales, ABC Television
Website	www.emotion.com

Technical description

There are no technical requirements, no installation efforts, and virtually no maintenance costs for such an ASP solution. Of course, user rights and asset ingestion still has to be done, but you can start using the system right away.

The system offers advanced markup features with the additional application AssetWizard, which allows non-destructive annotations on assets stored in the database, zooming, color correction, and image rotation. AssetWizard runs on Windows NT, 98, 2000, XP and Macintosh OS 9 as well as OS X.

File formats
Most common file formats, like AVI, Flash (SWF), MPEG1, MPEG2, QuickTime (MOV, QT), GIF, AIFF, AU, MIDI, MP3, SND, WAV, DOC, PPT, XLS, PDF, INDD, AI, BMP, PCD, PICT, PSD, PNG, TIF, TGA, and SGI, are supported.

Archiving/retrieval features
Each asset can have 90 fields of metadata. There is a wizard for assigning keywords and a natural language search engine. Boolean search (AND/OR/NOT) can be used.

Since Creative Partner is an ASP solution hosted on a central server data, backup is taken care of by eMotion.

Version control
Creative Partner does not offer version control features.

Pricing
Services run at around $2000–5000 (US) per month for a typical eMotion workgroup installation.

Getty Images Media Management Services

Getty is the leading image stock library worldwide. It also offers an ASP solution for other companies for rent, for which it partners with Artesia.

Table A1.19 *Getty Images Media Management Services: general information*

Manufacturer	Getty Images
Type of DAM	Digital Asset Management
Architecture	Client/server
Platform	Web-based ASP solution
Used by	Large corporations
Reference customers	20th Century Fox, NBA
Website	http://creative.gettyimages.com/source/services/MediaManagement.aspx

Technical description
The Getty Images Media Management Services are a set of ASP services that allow companies to use Getty's asset management solutions in their company. Consisting of MediaManager,

MediaStore, and MediaPrint, the solution offers asset storage, retrieval, and printing services via web browsers.

The Media Management Services offer all the functionality that Getty itself is using to sell assets to its customers. It is concentrated more on making images available via an easy-to-use ASP interface than on providing advanced asset management functionality, such as versioning.

Pricing

For pricing information, please contact Getty Images directly.

Avid Alienbrain

Alienbrain is a client/server solution integrating Software Configuration Management with Digital Asset Management, with a strong focus on the production process.

Table A1.20   *Alienbrain: general information*

Manufacturer	Avid
Type of DAM	Production Asset Management
Architecture	Client/server
Platform	Windows; Mac OS 9/X; Linux
Used by	Content creators
Reference customers	Electronic Arts, SPI, id Software, Lionhead
Website	www.alienbrain.com

Technical description

Offering both advanced versioning functionality and metadata storage, Alienbrain offers features for Digital Asset Management that can be used during and after content creation. The database supports versioning, labeling, branching, and change sets, offering features that are used in complex software development. All features are available with the graphical client via a very user-friendly interface with thumbnail and previewing functionality, similar to many other DAM systems.

Metadata can be stored in unlimited amounts, with the search facility allowing the user to search any metadata field in the database. With built-in workflow and assignment functionality, an instant messenger system, and image annotations, the system offers advanced communication functions.

The clients are customizable and there are APIs in C++, Java, Windows Scripting, and COM that can be used to customize the user interface and automate repetitive tasks. The Alienbrain system is directly integrated into many common content creation tools, such as Photoshop, Alias Maya, Softimage XSI, 3D Studio Max, Microsoft Office, and others.

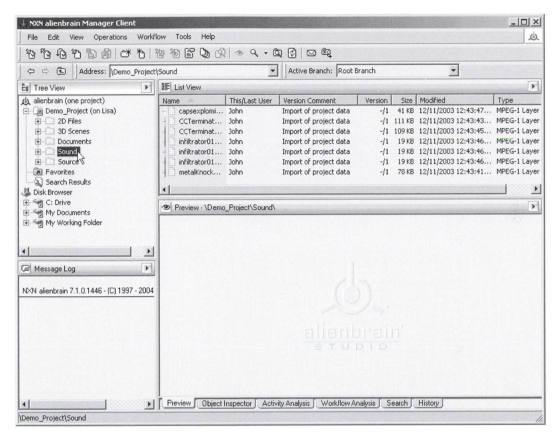

Figure A1.28 *The interface of Alienbrain*

File formats

The Alienbrain database can store any kind of file and offers viewing for most Bitmap formats—for example, PSD, Amiga IFF, GIF, JPEG, PCD, CIN, DPX, PICT, IFF, MNG, EXR, PSP, PXR, PNG, SCT, RGB, PIC, TIM, TM2, RAS, Sun IFF, TIFF, TGA, BMP, CUR, DIB, ICO, XBM, XPM, PCX, and many others.

Additionally, bitmap images can be stored as previews for any file type, so it is possible to have large previews for 3D files when the previews are embedded correctly.

Archiving/retrieval features

Alienbrain can be extended with an arbitrary amount of meta-information, which can be used to search for files. Customers can modify the type and amount of metadata offered to the user by the client and can also create scripts to automate metadata storage.

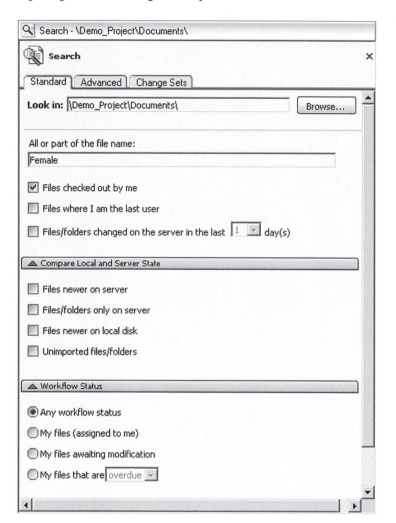

Figure A1.29   *The standard search options*

Version control

Alienbrain offers advanced versioning functions like those found in SCM tools, but additionally these functions are available for all file types. Versioning information is stored for file changes and structural changes such as rename and move inside the database. Metadata is versioned for each file version, allowing the system to track metadata changes. Changes in the assets themselves are reversible, allowing users to return to any previous point in the creative process.

Advanced versioning functions such as branching and change sets (collections of changes) are available. Entire database versions can be marked using labels, offering retrieval of complete database states from the past.

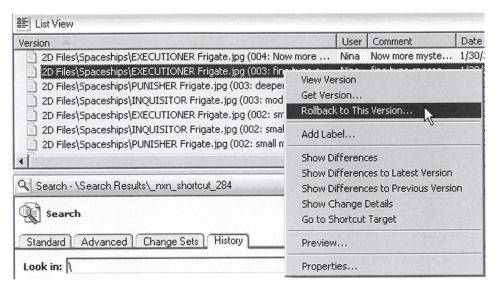

Figure A1.30 *Labeled file version in the Version Control History*

Pricing

Developer client: $690 (US). Designer client: $1250 (US). Manager client: $2190 (US). Linux and Mac OS: $1250 (US).

Licenses are per seat, with no additional costs for the server.

Picdar Media Mogul workflow suites

Media Mogul is a Digital Asset Management solution with specific features for the print market.

Table A1.21 *Media Mogul: general information*

Manufacturer	Picdar
Type of DAM	Digital Asset Management
Architecture	Client/server
Platform	Client: Windows 2000, XP; Macintosh OS 9/X
	Server: Windows NT, XP; Unix; Linux; Solaris
Used by	Content creators
Reference customers	The Economist, Jane's, Thomson Travel
Website	www.picdar.com

Technical description

Media Mogul supports storage and retrieval for any kind of digital media, with advanced search options. FastFlow, its workflow system, can automate many tasks in the DAM system, such as importing, modifying, and exporting to specific file formats.

The server runs on several Unix flavors, including Linux, and clients are available for Mac OS and Windows. With a web browser, the system is accessible from other operating systems as well. Access rights in the database can be set at both user and asset levels.

Media Mogul offers integrations with publishing programs such as QuarkXPress, InDesign, and Photoshop, and is able to manage the files these programs produce and their dependency information.

Media Mogul is also available as a hosted solution (ASP).

File formats

Media Mogul supports common file formats such as image formats, video and sound, web pages, PDF, Quark and Illustrator, Office documents, text files, and any other digital file.

Archiving/retrieval features

Media Mogul uses metadata to store information about the files in the database. Additionally, the system can store usage information, which makes assets searchable by usage in certain publications. The system offers free text search or complex searches with advanced criteria.

Version control

Media Mogul offers versioning on an asset level, which can be generated either automatically or manually.

Pricing

Since Media Mogul is not an out-of-the-box solution, prices vary for each implementation. Typically, license costs are in the range of $25,000 (US).

MediaBin

Interwoven MediaBin is a powerful extensible Digital Asset Management system with a strong emphasis on image data. It originally was the product of a company with the same name, which was acquired by Interwoven in 2003 to enhance their market position for rich media. MediaBin now integrates with Interwoven TeamSite (see the sections "Enterprise Content Management", "Document Management", and "Brand Asset Management").

Table A1.22   *MediaBin: general information*

Manufacturer	Interwoven, Inc.
Type of DAM	Digital Asset Management
Architecture	Multi-user client/server application
Platform	Server: Microsoft Windows 2000 Server SP3, 2003 Server
	Client: Microsoft Windows 98, NT, 2000, XP; Mac OS X $\geqslant$ 10.3
Used by	Marketing organizations/departments
Reference customers	Ford, John Deere, Reebok
Website	www.interwoven.com

Technical description

MediaBin stores all assets in a server-side repository, which is accessed either by a customizable web-based interface or by native Windows or Mac OS X clients. Authentication and authorization can be controlled through standard LDAP, Windows Active Directory, or Windows NT domains.

You can define hot folders whose contents are constantly monitored. When there are new files inside, they are ingested automatically and copied/moved to default locations depending on their type.

All access to the database is logged so that administrators can easily see who downloaded what and when.

Usually only one core image asset is stored, from which renditions are created as required. An Adobe Photoshop file, for example, could be queried as JPEG or EPS without the need to store multiple versions in the database. The same is possible with Illustrator files. A number of processing functions can be applied to images upon retrieval—for instance, scaling, crop, skew, and color conversion.

The software also offers basic version control functionality, such as versioning of assets, locking, restoring of previous versions (rollback), and metadata.

Embedded metadata is automatically extracted from many types of incoming assets—for example, EXIF data or Microsoft Office properties. Together with the asset attributes, such as size, resolution, etc. and user-defined metadata, a strong base for advanced searches is provided. Additionally, it is possible to conduct visual searches based on color, shapes, and textures.

There are several modules to extend the functionality of MediaBin. Among these are modules for the ingestion of documents like letters and faxes, or for the support of QuarkXPress files. Also available is an SDK to customize the application with C++, COM, .NET, or Java.

Supported file types

MediaBin can handle all types of files. It offers previews for most image formats, including Adobe Illustrator, Photoshop and EPS, vector EPS, TGA, TIFF, JPEG, GIF, PNG, BMP, Photo CD and StiNG, for Microsoft Office files, PDF, and streaming video previews for various video formats.

Pricing

Pricing starts at $100,000 (US).

Web Content Management

The Web Content Management market has seen immense growth through the 1990s and at the beginning of the twenty-first century. In the last few years, this growth has reached a plateau, however. Most companies already have a WCM solution and the Internet hype is definitely over. The number of manufacturers has diminished significantly, mainly due to mergers and acquisitions. The systems offer more and more functions, and the differentiation from Document Management and Enterprise Content Management has become close to impossible. In this section we will list products whose main strength is WCM. You should also have a look at the systems in the next category when looking for a WCM, because those programs generally offer WCM features as well.

RedDot Professional

RedDot has two main products: RedDot CMS and the Extended Content Management System XCMS. The latter extends the WCM solution to Enterprise Content Management. It includes functionality for document management, collaboration, and back-end integration.

Table A1.23   *RedDot Professional: general information*

Manufacturer	RedDot Solutions
Type of DAM	Web Content Management/Enterprise Content Management
Architecture	Client/server application
Platform	Server: Windows NT, 2000, 2003
	Client: any browser
Used by	Mid-size to larger corporations
Reference customers	AMD, FedEx, Mazda, The Bank of New York
Website	www.reddotsolutions.com

Technical description

RedDot CMS is also part of XCMS. We'll have a closer look at RedDot CMS first. Setting up and modifying the workflow is relatively painless compared to other big WCM systems. Usually no programming is needed for customization. The system is easy to learn. When you are logged in as an editor, every editable object in the browser has a red dot. If you click on it, you can edit it directly.

The RedDot CMS server runs on a Windows server. When the pages are ready to be published, they are transferred as static pages to any web server—they are not created dynamically. Content can be published on the Web and other channels by defining templates in which the content is set. It is also possible to have different navigation schemes—for example, for Web and wireless (WML).

The software is available in nine languages and double-byte characters are supported. It can maintain several versions of the same site for different languages.

RedDot CMS includes Asset Manager, a tool for managing all the photos and graphic files that are part of a website. It acts as a central repository for a corporate website, intranet and extranet. The system catalogs image dimensions, file names, and creates thumbnails.

The RedDot XCMS provides features for cooperation and works with a separate server called Content Collaboration Server (CCS). It offers library services, discussion boards for the staff, versioning for documents, workflow features, and integrates with Microsoft Office and Outlook. It is accessed with a browser or directly from Outlook. It can handle any file format but is intended mainly for documents, so its image or video handling capabilities are not too impressive. A drawback is that XCMS's repository is separate from CMS's repository, though it has been announced that this will change in a later release.

Workflow and version control

RedDot CMS has version control and locking features for its content, so team members overwriting each other's changes is not possible. You can define a specific workflow based on user rights, so that new or changed content has to be approved by an editor before it is published on the site. Automatic e-mail notification is also possible when something is ready for approval.

Publication dates for content and schedule can be set to appear on different parts of the site at different times. This is useful, for example, for news about a specific event; it could be placed on the homepage while the event is taking place and afterwards moved to the archive section of the site.

Pricing

A RedDot CMS system starts at around $30,000 (US) and XCMS is about double the price for a 50-seat license.

Zope

Zope is a very extensible and stable Web Application Server based on the Python programming language. Numerous plug-ins are available which extend Zope's functionality or introduce full applications for e-commerce, content and document management, or bug and issue tracking.

Due to it being Open Source and its strict adherence to open standards, Zope integrates into nearly everything.

Table A1.24 *Zope: general information*

Manufacturer	Zope Corporation/Open Source
Type of DAM	Web application server/Web Content Management framework
Architecture	Web server/web server extension
Platform	Server: Almost all Unix platforms; Windows NT-XP
	Client: Browser-based access on all platforms
Used for	Web or intranet applications of all sizes, such as portals
Reference customers	Viacom, SGI, Red Hat, NASA, US Navy
Website	www.zope.org

The software is useful for building web-based content and document management systems as well as any web application, especially together with the Zope Content Management Framework (CMF). In most cases, you might not be interested in Zope itself, but in the software built on top of Zope. Please see "Products based on Zope" for reference. The normal usage is to extend Zope with available free or commercial out-of-the box products, and/or to write custom applications based on Zope to meet requirements.

A number of applications are readily available—for example, entire Web Content Management systems such as Plone, a wiki, a web mail software, an issue tracking system, a credit card processing system, and many more.

Usually the installation effort is very little as Zope does not need extensive configuration upon setup.

Because Zope can handle large numbers of developers and users, it is a strong foundation for heavy collaborative applications such as distributed content and document management. But due to its through-the-web approach, it isn't very useful as a basis for DAM software because it can be pretty time-consuming to transmit large assets over the network each time they are accessed.

Technical description

Zope is powered by its own transactional object database, which can use either the local file system or a relational database as a back-end. This database is accessed by the Zope core, which provides functionality to execute applications. The core is accessed via the Zope server (ZServer), which offers HTTP, FTP, WebDAV, and XML-RPC serving capabilities, but can also be used in conjunction with other HTTP servers such as Apache or Microsoft IIS.

The software offers very basic version control functionality, such as locking and restoring of previous versions.

Zope can execute Python, Perl, and DTML (Document Template Markup Language, a Zope-specific, server-sided preprocessing language) applications, which makes it easy to find programmers able to extend Zope. The software itself is written mainly in Python, making it easy to modify or extend.

It offers another template language called ZPL (Zope Page Templates) that is worth mentioning. This language is less potent than DTML, but provides better separation of application logic, presentation logic and content, and is XML based, therefore making it possible to create templates that are valid XHTML. It is based on the XML standards TAL (Template Attribute Language) and METAL (Macro Expansion for TAL) and has gained a reputation outside of Zope, being adopted in other languages and with the potential to become an industry-wide standard.

Because management and administration are done through a web browser interface, it's easy to protect sessions with strong cryptography using SSL.

Products based on Zope

A good starting point for Zope applications is the applications list on the Zope homepage at www.zope.org/Products/all_products. Here are some selected applications:

- Plone (plone.org) is a ready-to-use content management system based on the Zope CMF, augmenting its behavior with content entry forms and validation.
- Icoya (www.icoya.de/index_html?set_language=en&cl=en) is a retail content management system based on Plone.
- Silva (www.infrae.com/products/silva) is a web browser-based publication system for creating publications for different media, including web and paper. Silva focuses on the authoring, versioning, and publishing of complex documents.
- Bizar Software (bizarsoftware.com.au) offers a fully featured e-commerce application built on Zope.

Pricing

Zope is Open Source software released under the ZPL (Zope Public License, www.zope.org/Resources/ZPL), a GPL-compatible Open Source license.

The original creator of Zope, Zope Corporation (zope.com), offers a number of services for Zope, including an Enterprise CMS.

Enterprise Content Management, Document Management, and Brand Asset Management

The term Enterprise Content Management is used for systems that offer features of Document Management, Brand Asset Management, and often some functions for Web Content Management. What they all have in common is that they are aimed at the enterprise-level market—in their scope and also in their prices.

For these solutions it is hard to give reliable figures for their price tags. Most vendors sell their systems together with maintenance contracts. These grant you free upgrades and support during this time. It is also hard to compare prices because you always have to calculate the effort of setting up the system, which can differ greatly from system to system. If you are interested in such a system, contact the manufacturer directly and ask them about charges for system choice consultation, installation, and maintenance, in addition to the price of the software.

TeamSite 6

Interwoven TeamSite is a scalable enterprise-sized content management system for websites, intranets, and extranets with version control functionality. It is supplemented by Interwoven's Digital Asset Management solution MediaBin (see the category "Digital Asset Management").

Table A1.25   *TeamSite 6: general information*

Manufacturer	Interwoven, Inc.
Type of DAM	Enterprise Content Management
Architecture	Multi-user client/server application
Platform	Server: Sun Solaris 2.7, 2.8; Microsoft Windows 2000 SP2
	Client: Microsoft Windows XP SP1, Windows 2000
Used by	Maintainers of large web and intranet portals
Reference customers	Toshiba, Cisco, Frank Russel, Tesco
Website	www.interwoven.com

Technical description

TeamSite uses a central server-side object repository, which is accessed using the Interwoven ContentServices SDK (CS SDK). CS SDK communicates via SOAP and WSDL, two widely used standard protocols. It can also use multiple repositories to scale across storage devices. TeamSite, in fact, relies on several servers: TeamSite Content Management Server, LiveSite Content Publishing Server, and Team XML Server.

The software supports multiple dependent or independent websites. Each site has a staging area and private virtual workspaces in context of the live site.

Version control functionality includes whole-site versioning, locking of assets, and restoring previous versions. You can visually compare different versions and use a merge tool for consolidating changes. For every single asset, its change history can be recorded as well as for defined sets of assets. Branching features allow the parallel development of a project by different teams.

On the client side, TeamSite offers a fully customizable interface that comes in two variations: Standard, which is designed for occasional contributors and non-technical users; and Professional, which provides powerful authoring, versioning, and workflow tools.

Other features include support for multi-byte content, strong XML support, asset-level access control, a robust search function, advanced metadata management, storage of asset relationships and visual annotations, sign-off, and publishing support.

For editors, working with TeamSite is easy. Administrators, however, sometimes have a tough job because many settings can only be achieved by changing configuration files manually.

Supported file types
TeamSite has no limitations concerning file types.

Pricing
Pricing for a departmental implementation of TeamSite, which is fully functional but limits the number of users and size of the web implementation, starts around $49,000 (US); the full enterprise version starts at $159,000 (US).

Stellent Content Server

Stellent calls the entity of all its applications "Universal Content Management". It consists of several products that should cover all the needs of any organization's asset management issues—from records and document management to web content management and financial processes.

Table A1.26 *Stellent Content Server: general information*

Manufacturer	Stellent Inc.
Type of DAM	Enterprise Content Management/DAM
Architecture	Client/server with web browser access
Platform	Server: Microsoft Windows; Sun Solaris; Linux; Hewlett-Packard HP-UX; IBM AIX
	Client: Any browser
Used by	Large corporations with many media assets
Reference customers	Agfa, GlaxoSmithKline, Merrill Lynch, Procter & Gamble, The Home Depot
Website	www.stellent.com

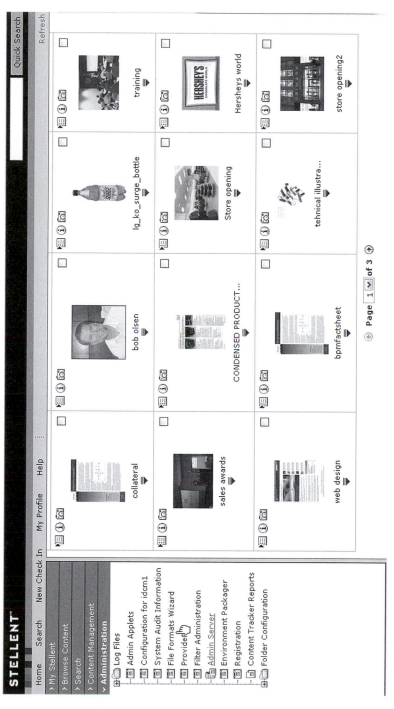

Figure A1.31 *Stellent's main window after a search. Images courtesy of Stellent, Inc.*

Technical description

The foundation of all of Stellent's products is its Content Server. It works closely together with other modules like the Content Publisher (which brings the content to the Web), Site Studio (where you create templates), or Dynamic Converter (which changes assets into the appropriate formats for web delivery). The Content Server is a central repository for any assets in an entire enterprise. We will focus on Content Server in this description. It can be accessed by any browser or by a WebDAV-capable application. It sets up on a database—for example, Microsoft SQL Server, Oracle, or IBM DB2.

You can design complex workflows with Microsoft Visio, which are then implemented by the Content Server (an additional module is required for this). Automatic e-mail notification when assets change or when new assets are added is possible.

When assets are ingested into the system, they are automatically indexed and keywords are assigned. When you look at an asset, you see metadata fields that are specific to the actual situation, meaning that the visible fields are selected by file type, location, your user rights, and the context in which you retrieved this asset. This makes orientation for the user easier, while it is still possible to have a great number of different fields.

Templates for Content Publisher can be created visually, without coding. You define which parts of your content should go where on the page and can control the result in a browser preview. You can also do it the traditional way and create your templates with Dreamweaver or a code editor.

There are revision control/versioning features for any asset. With the Content Publisher you can even roll back to any state of your site so you can see exactly what was online at any given date.

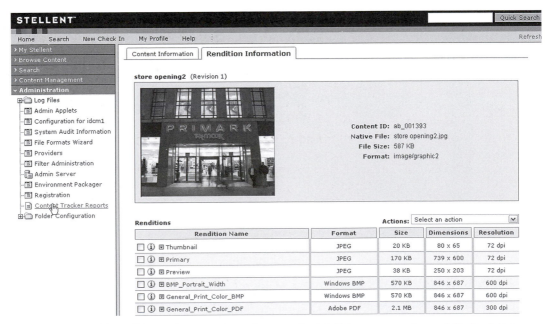

Figure A1.32 *All renditions of an asset can be seen in detail. Images courtesy of Stellent, Inc.*

Stellent Content Server supports most file formats, including Microsoft Office documents, CAD files, e-mails, HTML pages, Flash, Photoshop, image and audio files. It also accepts AVI, MOV, and MPEG video files, for which it creates thumbnails or streaming previews. You can reference specific scenes in a video and provide several renditions in different qualities/formats in one source. Similar features can be used for image files—for example, to provide a hi-res version for print as well as a thumbnail and a large image for web publication.

Pricing

Prices start with a five- to six-figure US dollar price tag for a typical installation for Digital Asset Management.

Documentum

Documentum is a scalable and extensible Enterprise Content Management and Document Management system with basic version control functionality.

Table A1.27 *Documentum: general information*

Manufacturer	EMC Corporation
Type of DAM	Enterprise Content Management
Architecture	Multi-user client/server application
Platform	Server: Windows NT 4.0 Server SP 6a and IIS 4, Microsoft Windows 2000 Server
	Client: Windows 95 SP2, 98, NT 4 SP 6a, 2000 Professional, XP
	Browser-only access is possible on any platform
Used by	Large companies
Reference customers	Lufthansa, Bechtel Corporation, Ford Motor Co, Ernst & Young
Website	www.documentum.com

Technical description

Documentum stores all assets in a central repository that can be accessed by multiple content servers, which may be at multiple locations. The content servers provide all functionality to the Documentum clients or applications—for example, an FTP publishing application.

Functionality includes automatic extraction of properties, generation of thumbnails and renditions, and transformation of image data—for example, cropping and rotating and XML library services. It's also possible to add custom functions. These functions can be triggered on such events as the import or retrieval of an asset.

Third-party applications can be integrated into Documentum using a number of standard APIs—for instance, WebDAV, FTP, ODBC, JDBC, and the web service standards UDDI and WSDL.

The software offers basic version control features, such as versioning, locking, and restoring previous versions.

For many file types, Documentum needs to store only one version in the repository and can generate renditions for these assets—for example, converting a Microsoft Word document into HTML or PDF. Where automatic generation of renditions isn't available or desired, an asset can have multiple renditions associated with it, which are stored in the repository.

Upon import or update, properties can be automatically extracted where possible. Assets linked from an asset can also be imported automatically; relationships will be stored in Documentum. A number of other relationships between objects can be established—for example, the relationship between a document and a note object representing annotations to the document. In addition to the pre-defined ones, users can define custom relationships.

Documentum offers a native Windows client and browser-based client, which makes it usable on any platform.

Supported file types
Documentum has no limitations concerning file types.

Pricing
Prices range from $200 to $600 (US) per seat. Alternatively, a per-CPU pricing model is available, which ranges from $7000 to $120,000 (US).

FileNet P8

FileNet originally offered only Document Management for financial and legal departments. Over the years, they added support for many other asset types and features that are intended for the management of assets of all departments, so today they claim to do Enterprise Content Management.

Table A1.28   *FileNet P8: general information*

Manufacturer	FileNet Corporation
Type of DAM	Document Management
Architecture	Client/server architecture
Platform	Windows 2000; Sun Solaris for the server
Used by	Financial and other departments of large corporations
Reference customers	Bank of America, BP, Pacific Mutual, US Department of State
Website	www.filenet.com

Technical description
FileNet is a suite of products that are tightly integrated: Content Manager, Web Content Manager, Image Manager, and Business Process Manager. You can buy only what you need and purchase further modules later. The Content Manager module is the basis for all applications. It categorizes content and makes it accessible for users and for other applications. It manages multiple versions of assets and traces relationships between them. Access rights ensure that everyone can only retrieve that which he or she is so authorized. Check-in/ check-out mechanisms ensure that you can't overwrite other people's changes. Versioning and renditions are available for structured and unstructured content. You can combine assets

to be managed as a single entity—for example, assets that complement each other or several versions of the same asset in different languages.

FileNet features several searching and browsing functions. You can search several different repositories at once and combine the results in one view. Wildcards, phonetic search, synonym expansion, and stemming of search terms are available.

The system can manage all types of assets from scanned letters to Office documents, HTML, PDF, e-mails, images of virtually any format and video—although if you are working a lot with images, you should also get Image Manager, which can handle large files much better. Its main focus is on scanned documents, however.

FileNet has an event-driven architecture. This means that, for example, an asset that is ingested into the system is automatically indexed and the person who is responsible is notified automatically. When he or she is finished working with it, the next person in the workflow can be notified.

Pricing

Please contact FileNet directly for pricing information.

Vignette V7 Services

Vignette offers a content management solution consisting of six modules—for content, portal, integration, collaboration, process, and analysis services. Each of these contains a number of separate products. It provides an open, standards-based platform to build enterprise web applications.

Table A1.29 *Vignette V7 Services: general information*

Manufacturer	Vignette Corporation
Type of DAM	Web Content Management
Architecture	Web application server
Platform	Server: Windows NT/2000; IBM AIX; Sun Solaris; Linux; HP-UX
	Webserver: Apache; IBM HTTPD; iPlanet; Microsoft IIS; Sun one
	Client: Web browser
Mainly used for	Large web and intranet portals
Reference customers	Hewlett-Packard, Sun Microsystems, Conseco
Website	www.vignette.com

A CMS would usually be built around the Vignette Content Services module, using the other modules as desired:

- Portal Services allow rapid deployment of web and intranet portals.
- Integration Services provide means to integrate disparately structured or unstructured content with only very little need for coding. Pre-defined integrations for a number of technologies and applications are available—for example, for SAP and Artesia.

- Collaboration Services support sophisticated online and offline communication among colleagues, partners, customers, and prospective customers.
- Process Services enable the creation and maintenance of workflows and business processes in Microsoft Visio, which can then be executed and monitored by the process workflow engine included in the platform.
- Analysis Services provide interactive analyzing and monitoring tools for content interactions—for example, website hits.

Technical description

The software is built around a virtual repository that manages assets in virtually any data format—for example, documents, program code, rich media, images, and even database objects. It allows defining custom metadata as well as metadata searches.

Vignette offers basic version control functionality, such as locking (check-in/check-out) and restoring of previous versions.

It's possible to create C, C++, TCL, JSP, and ASP scripts for Vignette, so that its functionality can easily be extended.

Vignette is accessed and administered using the Command Center, a role-based management web interface that can be accessed by a web browser. Because of this and the various server platforms on which it runs, Vignette is one of the most platform-independent content management systems.

Pricing

Please contact Vignette directly for pricing information.

Artesia Teams

Artesia Teams is aimed at large enterprises that have to manage images, video, and other media assets for broadcasting, print, web, and other channels.

Table A1.30   *Artesia Teams: general information*

Manufacturer	Artesia Technologies
Type of DAM	Enterprise Content Management
Architecture	Client/server model
Platform	Server: Windows 2003; Sun Solaris
	Client: Windows; Macintosh OS X; browser access also possible
Used by	Media/broadcasting companies; enterprises that have much media content
Reference customers	Random House, GM, Time Warner, Discovery Channel
Website	www.artesia.com

Technical description

Teams' repository is based on an Oracle database, which stores metadata and the path to the file.

It provides basic version control features, project report functions, and workflow integration. Teams integrates with QuarkXPress and has extensive video features. The program works tightly with Apple's Final Cut Pro or Virage VideoLogger. It can read more than 200 different file types; among these are all-important image, audio, and video file formats, as well as PowerPoint, Illustrator, and Photoshop files.

It provides an open API and support for industry standards such as Java, CORBA, and XML. Teams' client is based on Java. The database can also be accessed by a web browser from the Internet, which makes it available across virtually any platform.

Teams offers versioning, check-in/check-out, and locking to prevent several people working on the same asset at the same time. For each asset, it is recorded who used it for what in which project. This comes in handy to make sure a specific image was not already used by another project—or when you want to make sure you use an image exactly the way it was used before. It has strong workflow features to ensure any asset travels its own custom path for creation, approval, and publication.

You can browse or search for assets, and save the searches for later use and/or sharing with other users.

There are several ways to automate generation of metadata for an asset. It can also be retrieved automatically from an external data repository like an enterprise database (e.g. SAP or Siebel).

Pricing
With a price tag starting at $100,000 (US), Teams is clearly aimed at large companies.

Appendix 2: Glossary

For explanations of the different types of DAM and other "… Management", see Chapter 5, Section 5.2, page 101. Also refer to the Index.

ActiveX control   ActiveX is a model for writing programs so that other programs and the operating system can call them. With ActiveX controls, the functionality of Internet Explorer can be extended.

Apache   Open Source web server that runs on Windows, Macintosh OS X, and most flavors of Linux/Unix.

API (Application Programming Interface)   Programming interfaces that allow access to core functionality by Java, Perl, and Python.

Artifact   Undesired degradation of an image/video/sound, mostly due to too much compression.

Atomic transaction   Atomic transactions on the server are operations that are either done entirely or not at all. This guarantees a consistent set of files on the server. It prevents data loss and corrupt files if the system crashes or there are problems with the connection. Atomic transactions will also be visible to other users only if they are completed.

Batch processing   Performing the same change to several files at once—for example, changing their size and file formats.

Boolean operators   AND, OR, NOR, and other operators used to connect terms logically. Important for searching because using these greatly improves the quality of search results—for example, find all images that I created last year AND that have the keyword "animals".

Branch   A branch can be considered a copy of a project. This can be useful when, for example, you want to maintain more than one version of your baseline (for another platform or in another language, etc.). The copy can be changed without changing the original and vice versa. Usually this term (and this technique in general) is used for programming code.

Branch merging   Incorporation of a branch back into the baseline or another branch of your project—for example, if you used a feature branch to implement a major new functionality and want to include it in the final product.

Cache   Intermediate or temporary storage. Usually files are cached to improve performance.

Capture To convert audio or video into a digital file.

Change set, change list A group of one or more files that is logically associated with a change to the software system (e.g. a bug or feature request). Once all file modifications have been done, the change set (not the individual files) is submitted to the server. This makes it easy to roll back entire changes without having to search manually for the files that implemented that change.

Check in, submit When you check an item into a DAM system, any modifications you made are updated on the server copy and a new revision is made.

Check out To copy a file or folder from the server to your local machine and reserve it for local editing. Depending on the settings, this may "lock" the server copy for your exclusive control.

Clip A sequence of digital frames in a movie. Generally stored using one file per frame in a common disk folder. A clip will often correspond to a take of a compositing layer in a shot.

Cloak To mark a file or folder in your project so that when you perform an action to copy files from the server to the local machine, these marked files and folders are not copied to the local machine.

CMYK Stands for Cyan, Magenta, Yellow, blacK in the CMYK color model. Used for images intended for print.

Color management Technique to ensure that images are displayed in the correct colors on different devices.

Color model Common system to describe the colors in an image. There are certain color models for different purposes like display on screen, printing, and so on (for example, RGB, HLS, CMYK).

Command line Simple terminal window to type in text commands, like the old DOS shell.

Compositing Combining two or more layers into one, like adding titles or subtitles to a video.

Compression Reducing the size of files by applying certain algorithms that describe the file's contents. There are lossless compressions (like TIFF or WAV) that don't alter the contents and lossy compressions (like JPEG or MP3) that reduce the volume of information by dropping information that is not or is hardly realized by human perception.

Context menu A context menu is a popup menu that displays the commands relevant to a certain selection in the user interface. Typically, a context menu is displayed when right-clicking something in the user interface, depending on the type of operating system.

Controlled vocabulary A collection of words and terms that can be used as keywords for the description of an asset's contents. Using it makes sure all persons assigning keywords use the same terms.

DCOM (Distributed Component Object Model) A communication standard that offers application services over the network.

Dependency   Connections between assets that need each other to be of use—for example, a page layout is dependent on the images and fonts used, which usually are not part of the file.

Disk farm, storage pool   Summary term for the central storage allocated to a production. It usually has several volumes or partitions, including the frame pool and model pool.

DNS (Domain Name Server)   An Internet service that translates domain names into IP addresses.

DPI (Dots Per Inch)   Measurement for the number of pixels that make up an image. Most CRT displays have 72 dpi; laser printers are usually between 300 and 600 dpi.

Encode   Converting digital audio or video to digital files.

Event   An occurrence on the server or the client that may trigger an action, such as script execution.

Exclusive check-out   See *Locking*.

EXIF (Exchangeable Image File)   Information that records data in digital camera photos of the JPEG standard—like camera model, date, time, shutter speed, exposure, etc.

File server   A computer that stores files for access by other computers.

File system   The software that manages files on a hard disk, usually part of the operating system. Examples are HFS, NTFS, and UFS.

Filter   Manipulation tool for audio, video, or images to alter their sound/impression. Used for sharpening/blurring or to add a special impression.

Flattened file   When artists work with a program like Adobe Photoshop, they use several layers to compose each image. This way it is possible to modify the image later without too much work—for example, to exchange the photo of a person or to correct text that is part of the image file. It is a good idea to keep these layered documents, not just the final image file (which is called "flattened" because all layers are reduced to one).

Frame   A single picture of a video. Video usually consists of 25 or 30 frames per second (fps).

Frame pool, image farm   Storage in the disk farm allocated for the rendered and scanned/digitized film frames.

Graphical User Interface (GUI), user interface   An interface (in this case, a screen or view) that has pictures as well as words, including items such as windows, icons, and pull-down menus.

HLS   Stands for Hue, Lightness, Saturation—the three describing components of the HLS color model.

HSB   Stands for Hue, Saturation, Brightness. Each color is described by these three values in the HSB color model.

IPTC   International Press Telecommunications Council. This organization agreed upon a standard for the description of photos used for the press (like photographer, time, location, motive). These descriptions can be embedded in JPEG files.

Jukebox Automatic system that changes disks or tapes to be played in a reader. Used for large libraries.

Keyword A word that describes the contents of an asset. Usually several keywords are used to make sure the asset can be retrieved.

Labeling Normally, when items are copied to the server, a regular comment or other sort of note is sufficient to describe the work done on the files for your (and your project members') later reference. However, when you reach important milestones in a developing project or want to denote file versions for a specific use, you may want to set a label on an entire project, folder, or file for easier tracking.

LAN (Local Area Network) A network that connects computers that are close to each other, usually in the same building.

Layer Layers are used in image composition programs like Adobe Photoshop to organize the different items that make up an image. They can contain text, shapes, photos, or effects. When all layers are reduced to one, the image is considered flattened.

Local client The computer in a client/server architecture that requests files or services from the server. The client also means the software that makes the connection possible.

Locking, exclusive check-out If you check out a file exclusively, no one else in the project is allowed to check that file out until you check release the lock and copy it back to the server.

Log off To exit or disconnect from a network or remote system.

Log on To access a network or remote system. Logging on usually requires a password.

Merge conflict After a multiple check-out, changes from concurrent users may have to be merged before the file can be copied back to the server. If the changes are in different parts of the file and are therefore not in conflict, the merge may be done automatically. If there are conflicts, the user has to resolve the conflicts visually.

Merging The process of combining the content or structure of files or folders, either within the same branch or between two branches.

Mesh A 3D model defined by vertices, faces, and edges. It typically consists of triangles.

Metadata Data about data. This includes attributes such as date stamps, last user, file contents, etc.

MIME Multipurpose Internet Mail Extensions. A standard that allows the easy exchange of images, video, and audio over the Internet.

Model pool, model farm Storage in the disk farm allocated for human-generated production data, including models, textures, scene files, etc.

Nearline storage Saving files on a medium that is accessible automatically but to which access can be slow. Files that are seldom retrieved are moved to nearline storage to save storage space on costly high-speed storage media. Often, jukeboxes are used for this; cheaper disk arrays are now becoming more and more common.

Network Attached Storage (NAS)   Unlike server-resident storage that resides internally or attaches externally to a file server, Network Attached Storage (NAS) is a class of storage products defined by its direct connectivity to an existing network infrastructure, such as Ethernet, or to an SAN. Network Attached Storage systems provide large volumes of disk space via a "black box" appliance that attaches to the local area network.

Offline storage   Saving files on media that are not accessible over the network. The most common offline storage media are CD/DVD-ROMs and data tape.

Online storage   Saving files on media that are directly accessible—usually this means on your own hard disk or server.

Orphan file, zombie file   Files that are part of a project but that are no longer used—usually no one knows what they are, but even if someone does, he or she doesn't dare erase them.

Palette   Colors of some image formats like GIF are taken out of a restricted selection, which is called a palette. In the case of GIF, it contains up to 255 different colors. Windows of a software application that are always on top of all other windows are also called palettes.

Pins   Also called labels, which are placed on individual folders or files rather than an entire project.

Pixel, picture element   The smallest element a monitor or printer can produce to display an image. It is used as a measurement of the information that is within an image file.

Plug-in   An add-in software module that adds functionality to a software package.

Preview   Small, usually low-quality, view of a video or image. Saves you from opening the file.

RAID   Redundant Array of Independent Disks. Two or more hard disks that are controlled together to improve performance or data security.

Render   A 3D model or scene is rendered to create final or preliminary visuals out of the abstract description of the models and their movements.

Render farm   Summary term for centrally available CPU resources for rendering and compositing.

Renditions   Different copies of the same file that are in different formats, sizes, or resolutions. For example, there may be a Photoshop file from which a hi-res TIFF, a small JPEG, and a tiny GIF version are created—all renditions of the same file.

Repository   A directory on the hard drive used for storage.

Resolution   The amount of information stored in an image or video file, usually measured in dpi. In video, resolution usually describes the measurement of a video image in pixels.

Revision   A revised version of a file or group of files.

RGB   Stands for Red, Green, Blue. These three values describe the colors in images that use the color model RGB. Used for images that are to be displayed on screen.

Rollback   To retrieve an older version of a file and make it the current version. This function is helpful when you want to undo unwanted changes made to a file.

Sandbox   See *Workspace*.

Scene   A setting of a movie in which a certain part of the action takes place, one distinct place in a certain time. Usually composed of several shots.

Script   Sequence of commands written in a script language like JavaScript, Apple Script, or Visual Basic for Applications. Scripts are often used to automate processes.

Sequence   An auxiliary logical unit of film, generally a number of shots that are grouped into a meaningful set based on the storyline of the film. Related industry term: *Scene*, a setting in which a certain part of the action takes place, one distinct place at a certain time.

Share   A link between two locations, or a drive, directory, folder, etc., that can be accessed by machines other than the one it lives on. A shared drive is the location on the server machine that houses a project. All team members should be able to access this drive.

Shot   One camera cut or one camera "shot", the smallest part of a movie. Generally a contiguous sequence of images between two transitions (cuts). A 90-minute film will contain between 1000 and 1500 shots.

Sign off   To approve a stage or portion of a project's development as complete. Usually a project leader reviews an asset to see if it needs further modification.

Source code   Program code of an application in human-readable form. It is usually saved in plain text files.

Storage Area Network (SAN)   Provides large volumes of disk space through a file server that manages an array of high-speed disk drives, which are typically connected to the file server via fiber channel or SCSI. The file server is responsible for the file system, so there are many different implementations.

Synchronize   To make identical or to act simultaneously. Usually this refers to the synchronization of a server copy and a local copy of a file.

Take   Version of a clip, either raw or composited.

Tape robot   Mechanical device that automatically retrieves magnetic tapes like DAT media from a library and inserts it into a drive. Used for extremely large libraries, mostly in broadcasting.

TCP/IP (Transmission Control Protocol/Internet Protocol)   The suite of communications protocols used to connect hosts on the Internet.

Texture   Image that is mapped to a 3D model to define its surface.

Thumbnail   A miniature display of an image or page. Thumbnails allow fast browsing through multiple images.

Time code   Index for video. Measures the time that passed from the start of the video or tape.

Version history   Usually a list with version number, user, and comment for each version of a file that is saved.

Versioning   Keeping several or all versions of an asset.

WebDAV   Set of extensions to the HTTP protocol, which allows users to collaboratively edit and manage files on remote web servers. It is a standardized, easy, and widely used method for remote collaboration.

Workspace   The area in which an individual user manages their data. It is a general concept comprised of all data (and directories) that a user is working with. Each user has their own unique workspace in which all projects and data related to the projects are contained.

WORM (Write Once, Read Many)   Storage medium on which you can write data only once. It is used when legal requirements or security concerns make it necessary to keep records that can't be changed. Most common are optical WORM discs, which come in a broad variety of different standards. CD-R and DVD-R are usually not considered to be WORM media because you can write on them in several sessions.

XMP (eXtensible Metadata Platform)   Adobe's proprietary format to include metadata into documents.

Appendix 3: References

The Digital Asset Management landscape is evolving fast, and the market is so diverse that it's hard to keep up to date with what's out there. Here are a few resources to help you stay on top of your game.

Steve McConnell (1996) *Rapid Development. Taming Wild Software Schedules*. Microsoft Press, 647 pages, $35 (US).

This is a classic for every project manager who leads a programming effort of any kind. The tips come from McConnell's extensive experience and are always accompanied by a clear explanation and an amusing example.

Anyone managing complex projects should read this book. Even if you have no programming experience you'll benefit from it. Most advice is equally valid for web development or animation projects exceeding a certain size.

Ben Carter (2004) *The Game Asset Pipeline*. Charles River Media, 302 pages, $40 (US).

A great title for anyone who wants to become more professional in their game development. It is an easy read for project managers and programmers alike. The author explains how a professional workflow should look, which steps are industry best practice, and what the common mistakes are. The book also features a section on Digital Asset Management for game production.

Marc Saltzman (2004) *Game Creation and Careers. Insider Secrets from Industry Experts*. New Riders, 707 pages, $50 (US).

The journalist Marc Saltzman interviewed more than 150 pros from the game industry for this book. These findings are sorted into organized chapters with commentaries, tips, anecdotes, and forecasts of leading experts on a broad range of topics.

Topics include writing the game design document, finding and cooperating with a publisher, tips for programming, developing the perfect interface, proper testing, and marketing.

Although sometimes it can become a bit repetitive and lengthy to read the interviews in succession, this book offers invaluable insight for anyone producing computer games. And you don't have to read it all at once!

Marcia Kuperberg (2002) *A Guide to Computer Animation for TV, Games, Multimedia and Web.* Focal Press, 249 pages, $24 (US).

This book tells you everything you could want to know about computer animation. The book is well designed—not only is it structured in a logical way, but it also has color illustrations on virtually every page and it is fun to read.

It is perfect for any novice project manager in animation. Its only drawback is that 3D computer design pros will find too many technical things they already know scattered all through the chapters. Anyone else who is not so well acquainted with the 3D tools in use and the underlying basics will appreciate this approach, though. It makes the learning seem like little effort.

Catherine Winder and Zahra Dowlatabadi (2001) *Producing Animation.* Focal Press, 315 pages, $25 (US).

The two authors are seasoned veterans in the animation industry. In this book they share their knowledge on how to manage the entire process of producing animation—from the first idea to final delivery. They even give details on how much animation costs and how long it takes. Of course, they give only a rough guide for calculation—anything else could not be accurate.

Every role and production step is described in detail. The authors don't cover many technical aspects—so this book can be used for traditional animation using pen and paper to hi-tech 3D computer animation with motion tracking and any other hi-tech features.

Kelly Goto and Emily Cotler (2002) *Web ReDesign. Workflow that Works.* New Riders, 253 pages, $45 (US).

Though not suggested by the title, this book is for anyone creating a website. It reveals best practices to make sure your project is finished on time, within budget, and with the desired quality. There are many tips for working with customers that are also worth the expense of the book. Several checklists and simple document templates help you to set up and manage your own web project perfectly.

Tom Brinck, Darren Gergle, and Scott D. Wood (2002) *Usability for the Web. Designing Web Sites that Work.* Morgan Kaufmann, 481 pages, $35 (US).

This is a must for anyone who wants to create a website that really works. It is common sense by now that usability is key for the success of nearly every major site, and that usability doesn't mean making boring pages and killing any interesting design. Here you learn how to integrate usability techniques into your workflow without causing major delays or costs—the book even shows you how you can save time and money by applying the appropriate technique at the right time.

Russel Nakano (2002) *Web Content Management. A Collaborative Approach.* Addison-Wesley, 238 pages, $40 (US).

This book is a great introduction to the fundamental principles of Web Content Management. It doesn't describe setting up or choosing a WCM system or offer feature lists, but instead it describes which workflow is best for different situations. It shows you how to get the most out of WCM—whether you are just planning to introduce such a system or you have already used one for years.

David Austerberry (2004) *Digital Asset Management. How to Realize the Value of Video and Image Libraries.* Focal Press, 352 pages, $50 (US).
Anyone working in video production or broadcasting will benefit from this book. It explains in detail which workflows are best in this industry, which systems are used (hardware and software), and how best to manage anything from a short video clip to huge tape libraries. It really dives deep into technical details and important topics like correct indexing of video data or keyword generation for movie content.

http://sitemaker.umich.edu/dams
University of Michigan DAM Initiative. Its aim is to test a DAM system for usage of researchers and administrative staff all over the university. It offers several valuable links to reports and findings on their experience with Digital Asset Management.

www.ec2.edu/dccenter/dam/
University of Southern California Digital Commerce Center. Another good source for further information on Digital Asset Management and related topics.

www.metagroup.com/metaspectrum
The META Group analyzes the market for Enterprise Content Management, Web Content Management, and the like. There are several so-called METAspectrum reports covering these topics.

www.gistics.com
Gistics is a market research firm that focuses on Digital Asset Management. It publishes a yearly report on the DAM market which costs several hundred dollars. Great if you can afford a copy, but if you don't work in the marketing or IT department of a big corporation, the free executive summaries are probably enough for your information needs anyway.

www.uemedia.net/CPC/index.shtml
Several forums from United Entertainment Media for film and TV producers, writers, animation artists, and directors.

www.current.org/tech/tech0209metadata.html
Information on using metadata in public broadcasting. Has great FAQs, which can be interesting to anyone trying to get a grip on metadata.

www.highend3d.com
Portal site for 3D artists with a vast number of references.

www.siggraph.org
Siggraph, annual international conference on computer graphics and interactive techniques.

www.g-sam.org

Global Society for Asset Management. It offers industry news, an event calendar, and links to further information.

www.ipa.org/tech/dam.php3

IPA—the Association of Graphic Solution Providers. It has an interesting list of resources for Digital Asset Management which is not updated too often, but is valuable nonetheless.

Journal of Digital Asset Management

The only journal to date that focuses on this topic. It covers mainly aspects that are interesting for people working in large corporations. The needs of game producers, web agencies, and 3D animators are just touched on. The Editor is Michael Moon, founder of Gistics and frequent speaker at international conferences on Digital Asset Management and related fields.

More information can be found at www.damjournal.com.

Index

2D artwork, 7–9, 38, 42, 55, 127–9
3D artwork, 4, 8–19, 34–5, 41–2, 55, 60–9, 83,
  88–9, 104–6, 127–9, 144–5, 162–70
  concepts, 41–2, 65–7, 88, 127–9
  DAM benefits, 41–2, 127–9

Abstraction challenges, CG animation, 35
ACDSee, 146–50, 191–5
Administrators:
  database responsibilities, 119–21
  education, 123–4
Adobe:
  Illustrator, 8, 40, 41, 49, 51, 64–9
  Photoshop, see Photoshop
Advertising agencies, 17–19, 41, 87, 108–10,
  171, 180
Aiff files, 64
AIX, 206, 226
Aladdin Flashback, 21, 88, 210–12
Alias Maya, see Maya
Alienbrain, 21–5, 73, 79, 82, 89, 99, 113–15,
  129, 139–40, 144–5, 162–5, 168–70,
  216–19
Allume Systems Inc., 211
Analog film/tapes, 4
Animation, 2–9, 13–14, 17–19, 33–5, 46–54,
  60–4, 76–7, 83, 87–9, 105, 113–15, 134–45,
  161–70, 171
Apache, 201, 231
Appendices, 6, 102, 105, 171–233
Apple:
  iTunes, 101
  Script, 103, 128
  see also Macintosh
Application Service Providers (ASPs), 105,
  214–15

Applications:
  multi-user applications, 21, 88–115, 198, 201,
    204, 206, 207, 220, 225, 229
  product overview, 6, 87–115, 171–233
  single-user applications, 21, 87–8, 96–7, 172,
    176, 185, 188, 192, 211
  see also Individual products; Software…
Approval processes, artwork, 130–1
Architecture issues:
  current situation, 54–5
  technical requirements, 120–1, 131–3
  web development, 40, 46–54, 56–9, 67–9, 117–21
Archiving/retrieval features, 5, 10–12, 16–17,
  19–20, 30–3, 45, 60–4, 72–5, 78–85, 88–133,
  146–50, 156–60, 172–94
  concepts, 60–1, 72–5, 78, 88
  media types, 78
  product overview, 90–1, 172–5, 182–3, 187,
    191, 194–5
Artesia Teams, 21–2, 76, 89, 93–4, 215, 232–3
Artists, 7–19, 37–8, 46–54, 55, 56–9, 70–1, 118–21,
  130–3, 135–40, 146–50
  approval processes, 130–1
  programmers, 71
ASPs see Application Service Providers
Assessment needs, current situation, 43–59
Asset management:
  central controls, 16–17, 78–85, 106–7
  concepts, 1–6, 7–42, 43–59, 134–70
  current situation, 43–59
  DAM implementation, 6, 43–59, 70–1, 89,
    116–33, 154–60
  desired improvements, 55–9, 64–86, 102–15,
    116–33
  needs, 19–20, 55–9, 60–86, 102–15, 116–33
  problems, 1–6, 7–16, 53–9, 133

Asset management (*contd*)
    standard tools, 16
    use cases, 22–4
    workflow types, 60–4, 71–7
    see also Digital…; Systems
Assets:
    concepts, 1–6, 44–59, 64–9
    creation, 1, 44–5, 72
    current situation, 43–59
    definitions, 2–3
    labels, 80–5, 106
    management problems, 1–6, 7–16, 53, 133
    needs, 19–20, 55–9, 60–86, 102–15, 116–33
    see also Files
Attitude Studio, 161–5
Audio, 2, 3–6, 10, 13–14, 28–9, 55, 64–9, 98, 104,
        106–7, 148–50
Automation:
    automotive designs, 18
    conversions, 79–85, 127–8
    repetitive tasks, 127–8, 131–3
    workflow integration, 126–33
Avi files, 64
Avid:
    Alienbrain, 21–5, 73, 79, 82, 89, 99, 113–15,
        129, 139–40, 144–5, 162–5, 168–70, 216–19
    Media Composer, 144

Backups, 13–14, 17–19, 27, 56–9, 78–85, 88,
        91–115, 119–20, 132–3
BAM *see* Brand Asset Management
Beta testing, 20, 39, 41, 48–53, 58–9, 83
    see also Tests
Binary data, ProdAM, 99–100
BitKeeper, 197, 207–8
Bitmaps, 8–16
BizDesign Inc., 195
Black & White (game), 6, 15, 135–40
Bmp files, 13, 20, 42
Brainstorming sessions, 8
Branching practices, programmers, 83, 106, 130
Brand Asset Management (BAM), 5, 21, 22–3,
        90, 93–4, 95, 225
    concepts, 90, 93–4, 95
    product overview, 225
Braun, Tom, 165
Broadcasting, 18–19, 98
BrowseIt, 144–5
Browsing, catalogs, 73–4
Budgets, 26, 45, 46–7, 143–5

Bullfrog Productions, 134
Business processes:
    assessment needs, 44–59, 67–9
    case studies, 46–54, 67–9
Businesses:
    critical success factors, 45, 53
    objectives, 60–4
Buzzwords, 6, 101–2, 234–40

C++ , 103, 129, 216, 232
C, 232
CAD, 28, 229
Calendars, 16
Camera data, 14, 108–10, 126
Canto Cumulus, 21–5, 88, 92, 93, 108–10, 148–50,
        175, 180–4
Carmack, John, 15
Case studies, 2, 7–10, 15–16
    business processes, 46–54, 67–9
    GreatGames Inc., 54–5, 57–9, 131–3
    implementation, 131–3
    project management, 15–16, 110–15
    ProperPictures, 7–10, 76–7, 84, 113–15
    ProperProduction, 46–54, 67–9, 110–13
Catalog Content Management (CCM), 102
Catalogs, 5, 21–5, 73–5, 79–80, 90–3, 106–13,
        146–50, 171–97
    automatic generation, 79–80
    browsing, 73–4
    printed catalogs, 74–5, 79–80, 93, 106–7
    ProdAM contrasts, 24
CBT *see* Computer-Based Training
CCM *see* Catalog Content Management
CD/DVD-ROM, asset publication, 44–53, 74
Central controls, needs, 16–17, 78–85, 106–7
Cerious Software, 188–91
CG animation *see* Computer-generated
        animation
Cgi files, 14, 68–9, 118, 195, 196
Change:
    asset needs, 67–9, 83–5
    communications, 14, 44, 47, 50–3, 56–9, 83–5,
        96–7
    flexibility benefits, 27, 125
    requests, 44, 47, 50–3, 56–9, 67–9, 83–5
    sets, 83, 96–7
Check-in/check-out features, file locks, 80–5,
        106
The ChubbChubbs (film), 140
Cinema 4D animation, 165–70

ClearCase, 21–5, 197, 206
Client/server applications, 5–6, 44, 120–1, 131–3, 166–70, 175–84, 197–233
CMS *see* Content Management System
CollabNet, 201
Collaboration work, workflow types, 60–4, 72–7, 88–9, 94, 98, 106
Combinations, systems, 103–4
Communications:
  change, 14, 44, 47, 50–3, 56–9, 83–5, 96–7
  messaging uses, 84, 106
  production processes, 12, 13–14, 25, 35, 37–8, 44–59, 83–5, 88, 137–40
  teams, 12, 13–14, 25, 35, 37–8, 44–59, 61–4, 83–5, 88–9, 123–6, 137–40
Completed assets, use cases, 22–4
Complexity issues, DAM systems, 90–102
Compressed files, 65–9
Computer platforms, 5–6, 44, 54–5, 120–1, 131–3, 166–70, 175–84, 197–233
  current situation, 54–5
  requirements, 120–1, 131–3
  see also Linux; Macintosh; Unix; Windows
Computer-Based Training (CBT), 17–18
Computer-generated animation (CG), 11–12, 16, 17–19, 33–5, 88, 140–5, 161–5
  concepts, 11–12, 33–5, 88
  DAM benefits, 33–5
  data structures, 11–12
  historical background, 33–5
  key challenges, 35
  production processes, 33–5, 88
Conceptual documents, 7, 135–40
Conferences, 4
Configurations, 22–3, 24, 83, 146, 195–210
Consistency expectations, DAM, 19
Content creation:
  DAM support features, 22–4, 73, 106–7
  web development, 40–1, 46–54, 56–9, 67–9, 117–21
Content Management System (CMS), 62, 70, 80, 110, 112, 148–50, 158
Conversions:
  automatic conversions, 79–85, 127–8
  costs, 32, 79, 127–8
Cooperation benefits, customers, 59, 74
Copywriters, 61–3, 146–50
CORBA, 233
Cost/benefit analysis, DAM gains, 57–9

Costs:
  conversion costs, 32, 79
  production processes, 26, 32, 45, 46–54, 89, 143–5
Creative brief, web development, 39–41, 46–54, 56–9, 67–9, 117–21
Creative people, 7–9, 35–42, 117–21, 130–3, 135–70
Critical success factors, businesses, 45, 53
CRM *see* Customer Relationship Management
Css style sheets, 4, 40, 47–53, 68–9
Cumulus, 21–5, 88, 92, 93, 108–10, 148–50, 175, 180–4
Current situation, 43–59, 103
Custom tools, 85, 106
Customer Relationship Management (CRM), 101
Customers, 32, 41, 46–54, 56–9, 74, 110–13, 117–21, 125–6
  cooperation benefits, 59, 74
  feedback, 41, 47–53, 125–6
  loyalties, 32
  web development, 41, 46–54, 56–9, 110–13, 117–21
CVS, 97, 146, 197–201, 202

DAM *see* Digital Asset Management
Data:
  mining, 101
  structures, 10–12, 112–3, 117–21
  tape, 78
  see also Files
Databases:
  ProdAM contrasts, 24
  responsibilities, 119–20
Dates, naming conventions, 46
DB2, 190, 228
Deadlines, 15–16, 19, 26
Delays, production processes, 15–16, 19, 26
Deletion problems, directories, 12, 19, 117
Departmental benefits, DAM, 28–9, 105–13, 128
Dependencies, file types, 14, 130
Design agencies, 2, 39–41, 46–54, 56–9, 67–9, 110–13, 117–21, 171
Design documents, 36–7, 44
Desired improvements, asset management, 55–9, 64–86, 102–15, 116–33
Development processes, 7–16, 33–42, 44–59, 135–70
Differentiation issues, DAM, 23–5, 87–115

Digital Asset Management (DAM):
    3D design industry, 41–2, 127–9
    access permissions, 10–12, 20, 23, 28, 75–7,
        107, 117, 120
    application scenarios, 107–13
    archiving/retrieval features, 5, 10–12, 16–17,
        19–20, 30–3, 45, 60–4, 72–5, 78–85, 88–133,
        146–50, 156–60, 172–95
    ASP solutions, 105, 214–15
    Attitude Studio, 162–5
    benefits, 1–2, 7–42, 43–59, 71–86, 105–13, 170
    central controls, 16–17, 78–85, 106–7
    CG animation industry, 33–5, 88
    complexity issues, 90–102
    concepts, 3–6, 7–42, 43–59, 60–86, 87–115,
        138–40
    conversion savings, 32, 127–8
    cost/benefit analysis, 57–9
    definitions, 3, 20–5, 90–1, 98
    departmental benefits, 28–9, 105–13, 128
    differentiation issues, 23–5, 87–115
    evolution, 1
    expectations, 19–20, 71–7, 117
    features' needs, 19–20, 50–9, 60–86, 102–15,
        116–33
    flexibility benefits, 27, 125
    Framfab, 153–60
    games industry, 35–8, 85, 131–3
    general benefits, 25–9
    glossary, 6, 234–40
    historical background, 3
    individual benefits, 27–8, 105–13
    industries, 33–42
    intellectual property rights, 28–9, 75–7
    Lionhead Studios, 6, 15, 36, 134–40
    mail savings, 32
    needs, 17–20, 55–9, 60–86, 102–15, 116–33
    organizational benefits, 25–9, 105–13
    over-engineering dangers, 105
    ownership issues, 116–17
    parallel work, 27, 64–9, 83
    performance needs, 85, 107
    pitfalls, 116–33
    Pixelspell Animation Studios, 167–70
    ProdAM, 5, 21, 23–42, 87, 88, 90, 99–101,
        113–15
    product overview, 6, 87–115, 210–25
    productivity benefits, 25–33, 84
    quality benefits, 26–7, 30–3, 47–53, 56–9,
        105–13
    references, 6, 241–4

    reliability benefits, 26, 85–6
    rental options, 105
    ROI, 26, 29–33, 156
    rollback/history features, 27, 80–5, 140
    scalability benefits, 26, 85, 121
    scenarios, 107–13
    Scholz & Volkmer, 104, 146–53
    selection criteria, 86, 87–115, 131
    software integration, 75, 126–33
    Sony Pictures Imageworks, 144–5
    storage savings, 32, 79, 100
    tests, 37, 38, 39, 41, 46–54, 55, 56–9, 67–9,
        107–13, 121–3, 131–3, 135–70
    transparency issues, 15–16, 28
    types, 3–6, 21–5, 87–115
    usability needs, 86, 107–13
    user identification, 54
    user needs, 70–86, 102–15, 116–33
    vendors, 107
    versioning features, 8–9, 13–14, 19–20, 23–9,
        67–9, 78–85, 96–7, 139–70
    web-development industry, 39
    workflow types, 60–4, 71–7
    workflow/versioning features, 8–9, 13–14,
        19–20, 23–9, 30–3, 37–42, 52–4, 60–86, 96–7,
        139–70
    see also Implementation
Digital assets:
    concept, 2–6
    definitions, 2–3
    metadata, 2–3, 22–3, 72, 78–85, 88, 91–3, 98,
        126–33, 156, 162–5
    rights, 2–3, 28–9, 75–7, 91
Digital chunks, creation, 17–19
Digital content production, types, 17–19
Digital designs, creation, 17–19
Digital ingredients, creation, 17–19
Digital Media Management Systems (DMMS),
    102
Digital products, creation, 17–19
Digital Rights Management (DRM), 5, 75–7, 90,
    101
Directories, 8–16, 112–13, 146–50, 170
    access permissions, 10–12, 20, 23, 28, 75–7,
        107, 117, 120
    deletion problems, 12, 19, 117
    old versions, 13–14, 17–20, 27, 80–5
    problems, 8–16, 170
    see also Files
Disasters, files, 12, 17, 19
DM *see* Document Management

Doc files, 64–9, 96
Document Management (DM), 5, 21, 22–3, 89, 90, 93, 94, 95, 101, 220–33
  concepts, 21, 22–3, 90, 93, 94, 95
  product overview, 22, 89, 90, 94, 220–33
Documentum, 22, 89, 94, 229–30
Doom (game), 15
Dreamweaver, 47–53, 80, 146
DRM *see* Digital Rights Management
Duke Nuke'm Forever (game), 15–16
Dv files, 64
DVDs, asset publication, 44–5, 74
Dxf files, 64–9

E-commerce:
  DAM solutions, 89–90
  workflow types, 60–4
E-learning, 102
E-mails, 1, 4, 7, 16, 22, 44, 46–53, 58–9, 84, 106, 130, 137–8, 166–70, 229, 231
ECM *see* Enterprise Content Management
Education, system administrators, 123–4
Egos, teams, 70–1
EIPs *see* Enterprise Information Portals
EMC Corporation, 229–30
eMotion Creative Partner, 214–15
Employees *see* Human resources
Enterprise Content Management (ECM), 5, 22, 95–6, 101, 171, 220–33
  concepts, 95–6
  product overview, 95–6, 220–33
Enterprise Information Portals (EIPs), 101
Enterprise solutions, 5, 21–2, 76, 89–90, 95–6, 101, 171, 210, 221–33
Eps files, 64–9, 106
Excel, 46–53, 92, 106, 109, 112, 143, 152
Existing systems, extensions, 103
Experience levels, teams, 70–1
Explorer, 24
Extensions, existing systems, 103
Extensis Portfolio, 108, 175–80
External contractors, 54–5, 59
Extranets, 5, 225–6

Fashion designs, 18
Faster work, DAM benefits, 27, 29–33
Faxes, 1, 4, 22–3
Features:
  compiled list, 78–85
  needs, 19–20, 50–9, 60–86, 102–15, 116–33
  SCM, 22–3, 97–8, 110–13, 114, 197

software systems, 1–2, 75, 87–115, 116–33, 143–5, 197–201
Feedback, 41, 47–53, 125–6
File servers, 120–1
File systems, 3, 7–16, 21–5, 64–9, 87, 90–1, 112–13, 139–40, 146–50, 167, 172–233
File/network share-based solutions, 209
FileMaker, 104, 167
FileNet P8, 230–1
Files, 3, 7–16, 19–20, 27, 32, 60–86, 116–33, 139–40, 146–50, 167
  access permissions, 10–12, 20, 23, 28, 75–7, 107, 117, 120
  archiving/retrieval features, 5, 10–12, 16–17, 19–20, 30–3, 45, 60–4, 72–5, 78–85, 88–133, 146–50, 156–60, 172–220
  backups, 13–14, 17–19, 27, 56–9, 78–85, 88, 91–115, 119–20, 132–3
  compressed files, 65–9
  conversions, 32, 79–85, 127–8
  DAM expectations, 19–20, 71–7, 117
  dependencies, 14, 130
  forecasts, 67–9
  formats, 4, 13–14, 64–9, 106–7
  linked files, 65–9, 83
  locks, 80–5, 106
  naming conventions, 3, 8–9, 16–17, 46, 112–13, 139–40, 144–5
  needs, 19–20, 55–9, 60–86, 116–33
  numbers, 51–3, 67–9
  old versions, 13, 17–20, 27, 80–5
  overwriting dangers, 12, 17, 19, 56–9, 80–5, 117
  problems, 7–16, 133
  re-use facilities, 20, 61, 69
  resolution needs, 64–9, 79
  rollback/history features, 27, 80–5, 140
  sample rates, 65–9
  storage savings, 32, 79, 100
  types, 4, 13–14, 64–9, 106–7, 130
  see also Asset…; Directories; *Individual file-types*
FinalCutPro, 162
Finder, 24
Firewalls, 5
Fla files, 4, 48–53, 68–9
Flash, 4, 14, 46–53, 68–9, 152, 229
Flexibility benefits, DAM, 27, 125
Flowcharts, 1, 4
Focus requirements, DAM systems, 86
Forecasts, files, 67–9

Java, 14, 83, 103, 112, 118, 200, 216, 233
Johnson, Eliel, 153
Jones, Manson, 142
Jpeg files, 4, 13, 32, 47–53, 64–9
JSP, 118

Kaena (film), 33
Kaki the cockroach, *La Cucaracha* (film), 165–70
Kerberos, 199
Keystrokes, programmers, 71
Keyword searches, 74
Knowledge Management (KM), 101, 171
Kraus, Thorsten, 145

La Cucaracha (film), 165–70
Labels, assets, 80–5, 106
LANs *see* Local area networks
Launch, web development, 41, 46–54, 56–9, 67–9, 117–21
Learning Management (LM), 102
Legal notes, 22
Letters, 22–3
Level designers, games, 38, 55
Library systems, 5, 21–5, 87, 90–3, 106–13, 126–7, 146–50, 171–95
    see also Image…
Lighting data, 14
Linked files, 65–9, 83
Linux, 55, 91, 131, 146, 148, 180, 195, 198, 201, 204, 206, 207, 213, 216, 219, 226, 231
Lionhead Studios, 6, 15, 36, 134–40
LM *see* Learning Management
Local area networks (LANs), 5, 54–5, 85
Local sandboxes, users, 80
Locks, files, 80–5, 106
Log files, web development, 41, 47–53
Lotus Notes, 213–14
Loyalties, customers, 32

Macintosh, 21, 46, 55, 87, 91, 108, 131, 146, 168, 172, 176, 180, 185, 195, 198, 200–3, 212, 213–16, 219–20, 232
    OS 9, 172, 176, 212, 213–14, 216, 219
    OS X, 21, 55, 113, 131, 146, 148, 172, 176, 180, 185, 195, 198, 200, 201, 207, 215, 220, 232
McLaughlin, Paul, 135
Macromedia:
    Dreamweaver, 47–53, 80, 146
    Flash, 4, 14, 46–53, 152, 229

Magazines, 61–3, 176, 185–8
Magneto-optical discs, 78
Mail savings, DAM benefits, 32
Maintenance needs, 41, 47–53, 56–9, 119–21
MAM *see* Media Asset Management
Manage completed assets, use cases, 22–4
Management by walking around, 137
    see also Project managers
Management problems, assets, 1–6, 7–16, 53, 133
Marketing departments, DAM benefits, 29
Max files, 64–9
Maxon Bodypaint, 144
Maya, 38, 42, 144, 162
Mb files, 64–9
Media Asset Management (MAM), 102
Media Mogul, 219–20
Media publishers, 3–6, 17–19, 98, 175–6, 185–8
MediaBin, 91, 158, 220–1
Meetings:
    minutes, 4
    status meetings, 76–7
    users, 125–6
Mercedes-Benz, 148–50, 151–2
Messaging uses, communications, 84, 106
Metadata, digital assets, 2–3, 22–3, 72, 78–85, 88, 91–3, 98, 126–33, 156, 162–5
Microsoft:
    Excel, 46–53, 92, 106, 109, 112, 143, 152
    Explorer, 24
    IIS, 235
    Office, 168–70, 211–14, 229, 231
    PowerPoint, 4, 106, 109, 146–50, 232–3
    Project, 46–53
    Visio, 40, 51
    Visual SourceSafe, 139–40, 209–10
    Word, 46–53, 87, 92, 96, 112, 152
    see also Windows
Mind maps, 7
Minutes of meetings, 4
Mission, 138
Mixed Tape website, 148–50, 151–2
Miyamoto, Shigeru, 15
Mobile phones, 1
Modified systems, 103–4
Molyneux, Peter, 15, 134–5
MotionBuilder, 162
Motivation issues, teams, 26, 137, 170
The Movies (game), 36
MP3 files, 2, 64–9, 148–50
Mpeg files, 64

Mpp files, 68–9
MS SQL Server, 190, 228
Multi-channel publishing, 20
Multi-user applications, 21, 88–115, 198–209, 220–1, 225–33
Multiple versions, 20

Naming conventions:
    dates, 46
    files, 3, 8–9, 16–17, 46, 112–13, 139–40, 144–5
Needs, DAM systems, 1–2, 17–20, 55–9, 60–86, 102–15, 116–33
Network architecture, 120–1, 131–3
    see also Computer platforms
News production, 3, 18–19, 61–3, 98, 175, 185–8
Nintendo, 15
North Plains TeleScope, 89, 213–14
Notepad, 87
Numbers, files, 51–3, 67–9

Objectives, business, 60–4
OCR *see* Optical character recognition
Office, 168–70, 211–14, 229, 233
Old versions, files, 13, 17–20, 27, 80–5
OmniGraffle, 40, 51, 112
Open Source, 3, 131, 146, 198–201, 203, 226
Optical character recognition (OCR), 23, 72
Optimization prospects, DAM implementation, 126–33
Oracle, 190, 228, 233
Organizational benefits, DAM, 25–9, 105–13
Outline files, 68–9
Over-engineering dangers, DAM solutions, 105
Overview, 1–6, 87–115, 171–233
Overwriting dangers, files, 12, 17, 19, 56–9, 80–5, 117
Ownership issues, DAM systems, 116–17

Page layouts, 14
Parallel work, DAM benefits, 27, 64–9, 83
PDAs, 1, 20, 95
PDF files, 39, 46–53, 64, 68–9, 106, 152
Pearl scripts, 49
Perforce, 22, 98, 113, 140, 197, 203–6
Performance needs, DAM systems, 85, 107
Permissions, file access, 10–12, 20, 23, 28, 75–7, 107, 117, 120
Phonetic searches, 74
Photographs, 17–19, 60–4, 108–10, 126–33, 171–5, 180–95

Photoshop, 4, 13, 24, 32, 40–1, 46–53, 64–9, 112, 127, 146–50, 168–70, 229, 232–3
PHP, 47–53, 112, 118, 148, 152
Picdar Media Mogul, 89, 219–20
Pitfalls, DAM implementation, 116–33
Pixar Animation Studios, 33
Pixelspell Animation Studios, 165–70
Planning, 7–9, 15–16, 37–8, 39–41, 43–59, 60–86, 116–33, 135–70
    concepts, 15–16, 37–8, 39–41, 46–54, 56–9, 60–86, 116–33
    DAM implementation, 43–59, 116–33
    games, 37–8, 131–3
    problems, 15–16, 53, 133
    questions, 116–17
    web development, 39–41, 46–54, 56–9, 67–9, 117–21
Platforms *see* Computer platforms
Playstation, 13
Png files, 64–9
Portfolio Extensis, 108, 175–80
Portfolio Server, 88, 175–80
PowerPoint, 4, 106, 109, 146–50, 232–3
Preliminary versions, 14–15, 44, 56–9, 80–5, 156–60
Printed catalogs, 74–5, 79–80, 93, 106–7
Problems, production processes, 7–16, 53–9, 133
Process-oriented workgroups, concepts, 88–9
Production Asset Management (ProdAM):
    benefits, 25–42, 99–101
    binary data, 99–100
    catalog contrasts, 24
    concepts, 5, 21, 23–42, 87, 88, 90, 99–101, 113–15
    database contrasts, 24
    differentiation issues, 23–5, 99–101
    SCM contrasts, 24, 99–100, 113
    WCM contrasts, 24
    see also Digital…
Production departments, DAM benefits, 28
Production planning, 9, 76–7, 116–33
Production processes, 2–6, 7–42, 44–59, 87–115, 117–21, 130–3, 134–70
    3D design industry, 41–2, 127–9
    CG production, 33–5, 88
    communications, 12, 13–14, 25, 35, 37–8, 44–59, 83–5, 88, 137–40
    concepts, 2–6, 7–42, 44–59, 107–13, 134–40, 153–60, 162–70
    costs, 26, 32, 45, 46–54, 89, 113, 143–5

current situation, 43–59, 103
delays, 15–16, 19, 26
design documents, 36–7, 44
digital content production, 17–19
games, 37–8, 54–5, 131–3
needs, 17–20, 55–9, 60–86, 102–15, 116–33
preliminary versions, 14–15, 44, 56–9, 80–5, 156–60
problems, 7–16, 53–9, 133
ProdAM, 5, 21, 23–5, 99–101, 113–15
reviews, 9, 38, 56, 130–1, 133, 139–40, 143–5
steps, 9, 24, 34–5, 37–8, 39–42, 44, 76–7, 135–40, 143–5, 146–50, 153–60, 162–5
value creation/destruction assessment, 45, 86
web development, 39–41, 46–54, 56–9, 67–9, 110–13, 117–21
Productivity:
    DAM benefits, 25–33, 84
    measures, 25, 29–33
Products:
    current situation, 43–59
    overview, 6, 87–115, 171–233
    see also Asset…
Programmers, 28–9, 36–8, 46–59, 70–1, 83, 97–101, 110–13, 117–21, 131–3, 146–50, 197–210
    artists, 71
    branching practices, 83, 106, 130
    games, 36–8, 54–5, 58–9, 131–3
    keystrokes, 71
    user needs, 70–1, 117–21
    web development, 39–41, 46–54, 56–9, 67–9, 110–13, 117–21
Project, Microsoft, 46–53
Project definition, production step, 9, 77
Project managers, 1–2, 7–42, 44–59, 76–7, 106–7, 110–15, 116–33, 135–70
    business processes, 44–5, 67–9
    concepts, 1–2, 7–42, 53, 56–9, 76–7, 106–7, 110–15, 116–33, 137–40, 142–5, 146–50, 153–60, 162–70
    database responsibilities, 119–21
    games, 37–8, 54–5, 131–3
    management by walking around, 137
    problems, 7–16, 53, 56–9, 133
    teams, 16, 44, 46–54, 88, 116–33, 137–40, 166–70
    transparency issues, 15–16, 28
    web development, 39–41, 46–54, 56–9, 67–9, 110–13, 117–21

ProperPictures, case studies, 7–10, 76–7, 84, 113–15
ProperProduction, case studies, 46–54, 67–9, 110–13
Prototypes, 14–15, 40, 44, 56–9, 80–5, 156–60
Psd files, 64–9
    see also Photoshop
Public image, 32
Publication work, workflow types, 60–4, 74–5

Quake (game), 15
Quality issues:
    DAM benefits, 26–7, 30–3, 47–53, 56–9, 64–9, 77, 105–13
    measures, 26–7
    production step, 9, 47–53, 77
    web development, 39–41, 46–54, 56–9, 67–9
Quark Content Manager 3, 212–13
QuarkXPress files, 108–10, 182–4, 212–13, 232–3
Qxd files, 64–9

Rational ClearCase, *see* ClearCase
Raw files, 64–9
RCS, 21, 88, 97
Re-use facilities, files, 20, 61, 69
Records Management (RM), 102
RedDot Professional, 95, 110, 222–3
References, 6, 10, 241–4
Reliability benefits, DAM, 26, 85–6
Rental options, DAM, 105
Repetitive tasks, automation, 127–8, 131–3
Reports, 1
Requirements *see* Needs
Resolution needs, image files, 64–9, 79
Responsibilities:
    databases, 119–20
    users, 116–17, 119–20
Retrieval features, 5, 10–12, 16–17, 19–20, 30–3, 45, 60–4, 72–5, 88–133, 146–50, 156–60, 172–95
Return On Investment (ROI), 26, 29–33, 156
Reviews, 9, 38, 56, 77, 130–1, 133, 139–40, 143–5
Revision control, 21, 88, 96–7
Richards, Sam, 142
Rights, digital assets, 2–3, 28–9, 75–7, 91
RM *see* Records Management
ROI *see* Return On Investment
Rollback/history features, 27, 80–5, 140
Rtf files, 64–9

Sales departments, DAM benefits, 28–9
Samba, 131
Sample rates, files, 65–9
Scalability benefits, DAM, 26, 85, 121
Scenarios, DAM application, 107–13
Schmidt, Sabine, 145
Scholz & Volkmer, 6, 104, 145–53
SCM *see* Software Configuration Management
Scripts, 4, 13–14, 47–53, 83, 103, 106, 128
Search engines, 41
Searching facilities:
    concepts, 72–5, 78–85, 88–115
    needs, 72–5, 78–9, 88–115
    types, 73–4
    see also Retrieval features
Secure data transmission, 168
Segal, Bernie, 153
Selection criteria:
    DAM systems, 86, 87–115, 131
    teams, 16, 46
Server scripts (CGI), 14, 68–9, 118, 196
Servers, 5–6, 41, 44, 46–54, 120–1, 131–3, 166–70,
        175–84, 197–233
    access permissions, 10–12, 20, 23, 28, 75–7,
        107, 117, 120
    client/server applications, 5–6, 44, 46–54,
        120–1, 131–3, 166–70, 176–84, 197–233
    problems, 8–16
Simplification benefits, workflow, 74–5
Singh, Jasjyot, 153
Single-user applications, 21, 87–8, 96–7, 171–80,
        185–95, 210–12
Sitemaps, 4, 46–54
SMB, 210
Software Configuration Management (SCM),
        22–3, 24, 87, 97–8, 110–13, 113, 146, 197–210
    concepts, 22–3, 24, 97–8, 110–13
    features, 22–3, 97–8, 110–13, 197–9
    ProdAM contrasts, 24, 99–100, 113
    product overview, 98, 110–13, 197–210
Software systems:
    DAM integration, 75, 126–33
    features, 1–2, 75, 87–115, 116–33, 143–5, 197–8
    product overview, 6, 87–115, 171–233
    requirements, 1–2, 75
    see also Applications; *Individual products*
Sony Pictures Imageworks, 6, 140–5
Sony Playstation, 13
Source Code Management *see* Software
    Configuration Management

Specific requirements catalogs, 1–2
Spider-Man (film), 140–2
Spreadsheets, 16, 46–53
SQL databases, 148, 178, 180, 189–91, 228
Status meetings, 76–7
Stellent Content Server, 226–9
Storage savings, DAM benefits, 32, 79, 100
Storyboards, 15, 118–21
Stuart Little (film), 140–2
Style sheets, 4, 14, 40, 47–53, 68–9
Subversion, 97, 112, 197, 201–3
Success stories, 6, 25, 53, 134–70
    Attitude Studio, 161–5
    Framfab, 153–60
    Lionhead Studios, 6, 134–40
    Pixelspell Animation Studios, 165–70
    Scholz & Volkmer, 6, 104, 145–53
    Sony Pictures Imageworks, 6, 140–5
Sun Solaris, 180, 206, 212, 213, 219, 225–6,
        230–2
"Super-users", training, 123, 125
Support features, content creation, 22–4, 73,
        106–7
Svg files, 68–9
Swf files, 4, 46–53, 68–9
Switzky, Rachel, 153
Sxc files, 68–9
Sxw files, 64–9
System administrators:
    database responsibilities, 119–21
    education, 123–4
Systems:
    combinations, 103–4
    current situation, 43–59, 103
    features' needs, 19–20, 50–9, 60–86, 102–15,
        116–33
    modified systems, 103–4
    product overview, 6, 87–115, 171–233
    see also Applications; Digital Asset
        Management

Tape libraries, 78
TCP/IP, 182
Teams, 1–2, 7–42, 44–59, 61–4, 70–86, 88–9,
        117–33, 135–70, 215, 232–3
    CG production teams, 34, 88
    communications, 12, 13–14, 25, 35, 37–8,
        44–59, 61–4, 83–5, 88–9, 123–6, 137–40
    concepts, 1–2, 7–42, 46–59, 70–86, 88–9,
        117–33, 135–40, 146–50, 165–70

current situation, 46–59
DAM, 54
egos, 70–1
experience levels, 70–1
extra manpower, 8–9, 10, 12, 15, 135–6
faster work, 27, 29–33
file access, 10–12, 20, 23, 28, 75–7, 107, 117, 120
human errors, 140
implementation preparations, 123–6, 131–3
members, 10, 34, 117, 131, 137
motivation issues, 26, 137, 170
platforms, 54–5
problems, 7–16, 53–4, 133
project managers, 16, 44, 46–54, 88, 116–33, 137–40, 166–70
selection criteria, 16, 46
training issues, 13–14, 26, 123–6, 132–3, 154–60
user needs, 70–86, 117–21
virtual teams, 165–70
workflow types, 61–4
see also Human resources
TeamSite, 22, 158, 225–6
Technical requirements, 120–1, 131–3
see also Computer platforms
Telephone calls, 4, 44, 46–53
Templates, HTML pages, 80, 112
Tests, 37, 38, 39, 41, 46–54, 55, 56–9, 67–9, 107–13, 121–3, 131–3, 135–70
Text documents, 4, 14, 16, 22–4, 64–9, 87, 99–100, 104
Thumbnails, 73, 76, 79, 91–3, 98, 100, 109, 139–40
ThumbsPlus, 87–8, 91–3, 188–91
Tiff files, 4, 42, 64–9
Tim files, 13
Timing issues, DAM implementation, 121
Toy Story (film), 33
Tracking features, 16–17, 19–20, 22–3, 26, 72–3, 84–5, 96–7, 118–21, 130–3
TrackIt system, Imageworks, 143–5
Training issues, 13–14, 26, 123–6, 132–3, 154–60
Transparency issues, project managers, 15–16, 28
Txt files, 64–9

UML tools, 146
Unix, 21, 128, 195, 198, 200, 201, 203, 204, 207, 219, 220, 223
Usability testing:
DAM systems, 86, 107–13, 121–3
web development, 39–41, 47–53, 110–13

Users:
cases, 22–4
egos, 70–1
identification, 54, 107
implementation preparations, 123–6, 131–3
lists, 120
local sandboxes, 80
meetings, 125–6
needs, 70–86, 102–15, 116–33
responsibilities, 116–17, 119–20
training issues, 13–14, 26, 123–6, 132–3, 154–60

Value creation/destruction assessment, 45, 86
Vendors, DAM questions, 107
Versioning features, 8–9, 13–14, 19–20, 23–9, 67–9, 78–85, 96–7, 139–70
concepts, 8–9, 13–14, 19–20, 23–9, 67–9, 78, 96–7
product overview, 171–223
revision control, 21, 88, 96–7
Videos, 1, 3–6, 14, 21, 24, 39, 44–5, 64–9, 98, 104, 106–7, 161–5, 232–3
Vignette, 22, 95, 231–2
Villarreal, Bill, 142
Virtual teams, 165–70
Visio, 40, 51
Vision, 38, 138, 154
Visual Basic, 103
Visual searches, 74
Visual SourceSafe (VSS), 139–40, 197, 209–10
VnP system, Imageworks, 143–5
VPN, 5
VSS *see* Visual SourceSafe

Watermarks, 76–7
Wav files, 64
WCM *see* Web Content Management
Web, 2, 3–6, 11–12, 16–24, 39–41, 46–69, 87, 105, 110–13, 117–21, 145–53, 165–70, 171, 184, 185, 188, 192, 196–7
architecture issues, 40, 46–54, 56–9, 67–9
concepts, 11–12, 39–41, 46–54, 56–9, 67–9, 110–13, 117–21
creative brief, 39–41, 46–54, 56–9, 67–9
DAM benefits, 39–41
data structures, 11–12, 112–13, 117–21
design, 2, 3–6, 11–19, 39–41, 46–59, 67–9, 105, 110–13, 117–21, 145–53, 171, 188, 191, 195–7
file numbers, 51–3, 67–9
launch, 41, 46–54, 56–9, 67–9
log files, 41, 47–53

Web (*contd*)
   maintenance, 41, 47–53, 56–9, 119–21
   planning, 39–41, 46–54, 56–9, 67–9, 117–21
   production processes, 39–41, 46–54, 56–9,
      67–9, 110–13
   programmers, 39–41, 46–54, 56–9, 67–9
   project managers, 39–41, 46–54, 56–9, 67–9,
      110–13
   quality assurance, 39–41, 46–54, 56–9, 67–9
   testing, 39–41, 46–54, 56–9, 67–9, 110–13
   see also Internet
Web Content Management (WCM), 5, 22–4, 90,
      94–5, 101, 221–5
   concepts, 22–4, 94–5, 101
   ProdAM contrasts, 24
   product overview, 95, 221–5
WebDAV, 203, 227, 230
Weston, Kirsty, 153
Windows, 21, 55, 87, 91, 101, 120–1, 131, 146,
      158, 168, 171–233
   3.1, 210
   95, 188, 195, 209, 211, 229
   98, 172, 176, 188, 192, 195, 198, 201, 204, 207,
      209, 211, 212, 220, 229
   2000, 172, 176, 180, 185, 188, 192, 195, 198, 201,
      204, 206, 207, 209, 212, 219, 220, 222, 225,
      229, 230, 231
   2003, 180, 206, 209, 220, 222, 232
   ME, 172, 176, 188, 192, 195, 198, 201, 204, 207,
      209
   NT, 21, 91, 185, 188, 195, 198, 206, 207, 209,
      212, 213, 219, 220, 222, 223, 229, 231
   Scripting Host, 128

SMB, 209–10
XP, 55, 131, 172, 176, 180, 185, 188, 192, 195,
      198, 201, 206, 207, 209, 212, 219, 220, 223,
      225, 229
Wireless, 20
Word, 46–53, 87, 92, 96, 112, 152
Wordpad, 87
Workflow:
   definitions, 130
   design, 1, 71–7, 126–33
   integration prospects, 126–33
   simplification benefits, 74–5
   types, 60–4, 71–7
Workflow/versioning features, 8–9, 13–14, 19–20,
      23–9, 30–3, 37–42, 52–4, 60–86, 96–7, 139–70
   concepts, 8–9, 13–14, 19–20, 23–9, 30–3, 37–8,
      52–4, 60–86, 96–7
   needs, 71–7, 78–85, 102–15
   product overview, 171–223
Workgroups, concepts, 21, 88–9
Working versions, asset needs, 67–9
Workshops, 4

Xcf files, 68–9
XHTML, 106, 224
Xilam, 33
Xls files, 64–9
XML, 68–9, 106, 224, 225, 229, 233

Zelda (game), 15
Zender, Ralf, 165
Zip disks, 46–53
Zope, 110, 223–5

DATE DUE

TK 5105.888 .J32 2005
Implementing digital a
asset management system

DEMCO